Dachshund
in the
Federal Courts

edited by
JOSHUA WARREN

DEDICATION

In memory of
Nikki
beloved dachshund rescued from a bagel store

TABLE OF CONTENTS

ACKNOWLEDGMENT

This book would not be possible without the continuing support of my wife, my family and all our wonderful dogs.

CHRONOLOGICAL
TABLE OF AUTHORITY

page 22
Rogers v. Okin,
No. 86-1777,
UNITED STATES COURT OF APPEALS
FOR THE FIRST CIRCUIT,
821 F.2d 22, June 12, 1987

This is the fee tail of a very long dachshund of civil rights litigation involving mental patients at a state...

page 37
Clifford v. M/V Islander,
No. 89-1196,
UNITED STATES COURT OF APPEALS
FOR THE FIRST CIRCUIT,
882 F.2d 12, August 8, 1989

We think that the key precedent is another long dachshund of a case,

page 43
United States v. Connor,
No. 90-1025,
UNITED STATES COURT OF APPEALS
FOR THE FIRST CIRCUIT,
926 F.2d 81, February 21, 1991

This appeal requires that we revisit a long dachshund of an indictment...

page 68
Royal Indem. Co. v. Werner,
No. 92-1595EM,
UNITED STATES COURT OF APPEALS
FOR THE EIGHTH CIRCUIT,
979 F.2d 1299, November 12, 1992

owned a dachshund and a cockapoo.

page 172
Stover v. Eagle Prods.,
Case No. 93-4047-SAC,
UNITED STATES DISTRICT COURT
FOR THE DISTRICT OF KANSAS,
896 F. Supp. 1085, August 17, 1995

the breeding stock was built to a population of approximately three hundred, including fourteen toy breeds, bishons, Chihuahuas, Japanese Chins, dachshunds, Maltese, papillions, Pekingese, pomeranians, toy poodles, pugs, Shih Tzus, shelties

page 198
Blakley v. United States,
NO. MO-94-CA-224-F,
UNITED STATES DISTRICT COURT
FOR THE WESTERN DISTRICT OF TEXAS, MIDLAND-ODESSA DIVISION,
96-2 U.S. Tax Cas. (CCH) P50,693, September 12, 1996

Vienna Bronze Dachshund

page 240
Imperial Toy Corp. v. Goffa Int'l Corp.,
97 CV 7072,
UNITED STATES DISTRICT COURT
FOR THE EASTERN DISTRICT OF NEW YORK,
988 F. Supp. 617, December 18, 1997

only the whale, penguin, turtle, lion, dolphin, toucan, lobster, frog, dachshund and goldfish are at issue in this case. ... The Dachshund Imperial's dachshund looks nothing like a real dachshund, because the body is not elongated and the feet are oversized.

page 282
Engle v. Liberty Mut. Fire Ins. Co.,
Civ. No. 04-00256 SOM/BMK ,
UNITED STATES DISTRICT COURT
FOR THE DISTRICT OF HAWAII,
402 F. Supp. 2d 1157, July 11, 2005

one could refer to "dogs, including collies, cocker spaniels, and dachshunds."
"Including," by Plaintiffs' reading, means "having as members,"

page 259
Ripple Junction Design Co. v. Olaes Enters.,
Case No. 1:05-CV-43 ,
UNITED STATES DISTRICT COURT
FOR THE SOUTHERN DISTRICT OF OHIO,
WESTERN DIVISION,
2005 Copy. L. Rep. (CCH) P29,079 September 8, 2005

selling t-shirts that sometimes bear an image of a Dachshund and with the sayings
"My Wiener is Happy,"

page 85
Garcia v. Rivera,
07 Civ. 2535 (PAC) (AJP),
UNITED STATES DISTRICT COURT
FOR THE SOUTHERN DISTRICT OF NEW YORK,
August 16, 2007

... he attacked a twelve year old, eighteen pound dachshund, and
"kicked the dog while wearing boots ...

page 117
Word v. Christian County,
CIVIL ACTION NO. 5:07-CV163-R,
UNITED STATES DISTRICT COURT
FOR THE WESTERN DISTRICT OF KENTUCKY,
October 5, 2007

Katrina, pure bred miniature daschund...

page 268

Embroidery Library, Inc. v. Sublime Stitching, LLC,
Civil No. 09-2766 (JNE/AJB),
UNITED STATES DISTRICT COURT
FOR THE DISTRICT OF MINNESOTA,
January 20, 2010

*Sublime Stitching's copyright in its "Spaced Out," "Monkey Love,"
"Darling Dachshunds," "Vital Organs," "Sexy Librarians and Secretaries,"
and "Winterland" embroidery pattern ...*

page 121

McLean v. Broadfoot,
4:10CV00019,
UNITED STATES DISTRICT COURT
FOR THE WESTERN DISTRICT OF VIRGINIA,
DANVILLE DIVISION, May 13, 2011

*the Plaintiff was approached by a dachshund that had a history of attacking
people in the community... in light of the dog's aggressive behavior,
he shot the dachshund.*

page 148

City of Riviera Beach v. Unnamed Gray,
No. 10-10695,
UNITED STATES COURT OF APPEALS
FOR THE ELEVENTH CIRCUIT,
649 F.3d 1259, August 19, 2011,
US Supreme Court certiorari granted by, Lozman v. City of Riviera
Beach, 132 S. Ct. 1543, Reversed by Lozman v. City of Riviera Beach,
(Jan. 15, 2013)

Lozman had failed to muzzle his ten-pound daschund

page 169
Smith v. Astrue,
1:10-cv-01527 GSA,
UNITED STATES DISTRICT COURT
FOR THE EASTERN DISTRICT OF CALIFORNIA,
November 4, 2011

cares for and feeds three dogs: a Labrador and two Dachshunds.

page 186
Degiorgio v. Fitzpatrick,
Case No. 08-CV-6551 (KMK) (LMS),
UNITED STATES DISTRICT COURT
FOR THE SOUTHERN DISTRICT OF NEW YORK,
March 12, 2013

a Chihuahua; actually, the dog was a Dachshund,

EDITOR'S NOTE

The following are nearly full federal court opinions with minimal editing. As best as possible, footnotes retain their numbering but original page numbers have been removed. In each case the phrase "dachshund" has been **bolded** and made larger for easier visibility. An index of select terms of interest is also provided at the end of this book.

FOREWARD

The idea of studying law by searching for a single term would usually be considered poor legal research. Dachshund is a word but this raw search view of law will not yield any kind of complete picture of law related to daschunds. The law deals with abstract concepts of responsibilities and liabilities, causation and consideration. Learning the law for a type of object requires more than merely the history of legal interactions regarding that object.

Nevertheless because of computer search technology it is now relatively easy to search for words and read the cases. This is both entertaining and informative for those with interest in law and dachshunds. These real case decisions should be read primarily for entertainment but also to increase the readers' vocabulary of legal procedure for general understanding of American jurisprudence.

INTRODUCTION TO STRUCTURE
of the U.S. FEDERAL COURTS

U.S. SUPREME COURT

U.S. COURT OF APPEALS
12 Circuit Courts of Appeals
1 U.S. Court of Appeals for the Federal Circuit

U.S. DISTRICT COURTS
94 Judicial Districts
U.S Bankruptcy Courts

U.S. COURT OF INTERNATIONAL TRADE
U.S. COURT OF FEDERAL CLAIMS

OTHER FEDERAL COURTS
Military Courts (Trial and Appellate)
Court of Veteran's Appeals
U.S. Tax Court
Federal administrative agencies and boards

for much more information about the structure and jurisdiction of the US Courts see their website at UScourts.gov
http://www.uscourts.gov/EducationalResources/FederalCourtBasics.aspx

INTRODUCTION TO READING
COURT OPINIONS FOR FUN
(and learning)

THE ONLY RULE is PATIENCE

If you are reading this then, you already know how to read. Go somewhere with appropriate lighting and a comfortable chair and read patiently. Mark unusual words and move on, and later use a legal dictionary and internet search engines to amplify your understanding. With patience you will learn to read more.

As you begin to read a case, notice the year and notice what branch of the federal court is writing the opinion. Identify the parties, what they are seeking, what prior legal actions have occurred. Or just jump right to any paragraph you want and start reading.

This book is designed to read cases. There is no over-reaching legal thesis and the cases are not individually summarized. These real cases are simply arranged with hopes of sparking interest in reading law. The goal is merely to enjoy the reading.

Reading law will improve your ability to read law.

As you read you may consider yourself as a law clerk and try to summarize the arguments and holdings of each opinion. This is good practice and any attempt to write (and re-write) a case summary will promote your thinking. But if you prefer, just sit under a tree and enjoy the writings of the U.S. Federal Courts.

These are all serious legal texts each with a serious legal purpose but they are also appreciable as the high art of American legal civilization. This collection is gathered with the hope of finding entertainment in these works of jurisprudential art.

INTRODUCTION TO DACHSHUND IN THE FEDERAL COURTS

This book includes the judicial opinions from twenty cases in the U.S. Federal Courts.

Most of these cases use the spelling "dachshund" but two cases spell it as "daschund" (these cases are in Florida and Kentucky). Perhaps there are other alternative spellings that are not included in this book.

Three opinions are from the First Circuit of the U.S. Court of Appeals. All three of these cases involve Judge Selya and refer to "long dachshund of a case" as an unexplained metaphor.

Other opinions include reference to actual dogs, to statues shaped like dogs, and other intellectual property modeled after the breed.

DACHSHUND
IN THE
FEDERAL COURTS

1

"Long dachshund of a case"

In 1987 Judge Coffin opened his opinion in *Rogers v. Okin* referring to the case as "the fee tail of a very long dachshund of civil rights litigation"

Also on the appellate panel for Rogers was Judge Selya.

Two years later in *Clifford v. M/V Islander*, Judge Seyla used the following citation: *United States v. Michael Schiavone & Sons Inc.*, 304 F. Supp. 773 (D.Mass. 1969), *aff'd in part and vacated in part*, 430 F.2d 231 (1st Cir. 1970), *opinion after remand*, 325 F. Supp. 48 (D.Mass.), *modified*, 450 F.2d 875 (1st Cir. 1971). Describing *Schiavone & Sons* as "key precedent" and "another long dachshund of a case".

And then almost two years after that, Judge Selya repeated the phrase to refer to the case of *US v Connor*.

In this section:

Rogers v. Okin,	821 F.2d 22 (1st Cir., 1987)
Clifford v. M/V Islander,	882 F.2d 12 (1st Cir., 1989)
United States v. Connor,	926 F.2d 81 (1st Cir., 1991)

Rubie Rogers, et al.,
Plaintiffs, Appellees,
v.
Robert Okin, et al.,
Defendants, Appellants

No. 86-1777
UNITED STATES COURT OF APPEALS
FOR THE FIRST CIRCUIT
821 F.2d 22
June 12, 1987

Suzanne E. Durrell, Assistant Attorney General, with whom Francis X. Bellotti, Attorney General, was on brief for Appellants.

Marshall Simonds and Richard W. Cole with whom Stahlin and Bergstresser, Inc. was on brief for Appellees.

Coffin, Bownes and Selya, Circuit Judges.

Coffin, Circuit Judge.

This is the fee tail of a very long **dachshund** of civil rights litigation involving mental patients at a state hospital, which began in 1975 and in due course involved all three levels of federal courts as well as the Supreme Judicial Court of Massachusetts. [1] The merits having at last been resolved, the present issue is what fees and costs, if any at all, should be paid counsel for plaintiffs under the authority of 42 U.S.C. § 1988.

1 *Mills v. Rogers,* 457 U.S. 291, 73 L. Ed. 2d 16, 102 S. Ct. 2442 (1982); *Mills v. Rogers,* 454 U.S. 1136, 71 L. Ed. 2d 288, 102 S. Ct. 990 (1982); *Mills v. Rogers,* 454 U.S. 936, 70 L. Ed. 2d 245, 102 S. Ct. 471 (1981); *Okin v. Rogers,* 451 U.S. 906, 101 S. Ct. 1972, 68 L. Ed. 2d 293 (1981); *Rogers v. Okin,* 738 F.2d 1 (1st Cir. 1984); *Rogers v. Okin,* 634 F.2d 650 (1st Cir. 1980); *Rogers v. Okin,* 478 F. Supp. 1342 (D. Mass. 1979); *Rogers v. Commissioner, Department of Mental Health,* 390 Mass. 489, 458 N.E.2d 308 (1983); *In re Guardianship of Roe, III,* 383 Mass. 415, 421 N.E.2d 40 (1981).

The underlying lawsuit was brought by seven patients against the Massachusetts Commissioner of Mental Health, directors of separate mental health units of Boston State Hospital, and various psychiatrists and psychologists, seeking declaratory and injunctive relief against the forcible administration of anti-psychotic drugs to and the involuntary seclusion of both voluntarily and involuntarily committed mental patients in non-emergencies. Compensatory and punitive damages were also sought. A class was certified -- all patients who have been or will be secluded or medicated without their consent at the two units of the hospital.

The stages of the litigation began with a temporary restraining order preventing then existing non-emergency seclusion and medication practices. It continued with settlement efforts, summary judgment motions, an interlocutory appeal, and a 74-day trial followed by a district court decision granting injunctive relief but denying damage claims. An appeal only from relief as to medication led to an appellate decision affirming in most respects the district court's decision. There was then a grant of certiorari by the Supreme Court followed by a remand to us and our eventual certification of some nine questions to the Supreme Judicial Court of Massachusetts concerning the applicability of a recent decision involving the right of a non-institutionalized mental patient to refuse anti-psychotic drugs. Subsequently that court provided a set of rules governing the administering of anti-psychotic drugs, a decision which we recognized created federally protected liberty interests and also provided adequate state law process making unnecessary the continuation of a federal court injunction. The district court's order dissolving the injunction was entered in June, 1984, some nine years after the filing of the complaint.

The present proceedings, relating to plaintiffs' request for attorney's fees and costs, have encompassed multiple depositions, interrogatories, one non-evidentiary hearing, a three-day trial, dozens of exhibits, and some 260 pages of proposed findings of fact. The district court made the following six findings: (1) plaintiffs were the "prevailing party" within the meaning of 42 U.S.C. § 1988, their claims concerning forced medication and seclusion being "essentially vindicated" and the rejected damages claims sharing a common core of facts and related legal theories with the claims for injunctive relief;

(2) the time spent by plaintiffs' attorneys in the trial, appellate, and fee phases was reasonable and involved no unnecessary duplication; (3) time records since mid-1977 were detailed and contemporaneous and, prior to this time, the reconstructed estimates of undocumented time were sufficiently reliable; (4) in the case of one of plaintiffs' attorneys, preclusion from other employment is a relevant factor; (5) the customary community hourly rate testimony of plaintiffs' expert, Barshak, was adopted and that of defendants' expert rejected, the court further accepting present legal rates as an "appropriate means to compensate counsel for the delay in fee payment"; and (6) other factors -- the results obtained, skill of counsel, unattractiveness and contingent nature of the litigation -- do not require an upward adjustment in the lodestar. The court accordingly made a total award of fees and costs in the amount of $1,467,242.43. 638 F. Supp. 934.

There are three issues that merit discussion: (I) whether the district court's finding that plaintiffs were "prevailing parties" is supportable under the teaching of *Hensley v. Eckerhart*, 461 U.S. 424, 76 L. Ed. 2d 40, 103 S. Ct. 1933 (1983); (II) whether the Commonwealth enjoys an Eleventh Amendment sovereign immunity precluding adoption of current legal hourly rates to compensate for delay in payment of the fee award under the teaching of *Library of Congress v. Shaw*, 478 U.S. 310, 106 S. Ct. 2957, 92 L. Ed. 2d 250 (1986); (III) whether the district court's lodestar findings as to time spent and hourly rates are supportable.

I. Prevailing Parties

In assessing whether the district court exercised its discretion appropriately, we look first to *Hensley v. Eckerhart*, 461 U.S. 424, 434-435, 76 L. Ed. 2d 40, 103 S. Ct. 1933 (1983):

> Many civil rights cases will present only a single claim. In other cases the plaintiff's claims for relief will involve a common core of facts or will be based on related legal theories. Much of counsel's time will be devoted generally to the litigation as a whole, making it difficult to divide the hours expended on a claim-by-claim basis. Such a lawsuit cannot be viewed as a series of discrete claims. Instead the district court should focus on the significance of the overall relief obtained by the plaintiff in relation to the hours reasonably expended on the litigation.

Particularly pertinent to this case are the following comments by the Court:

> We agree with the District Court's rejection of "a mathematical approach comparing the total number of issues in the case with those actually prevailed upon." Such a ratio provides little aid in determining what is a reasonable fee in light of all the relevant factors. Nor is it necessarily significant that a prevailing plaintiff did not receive all the relief requested. For example, a plaintiff who failed to recover damages but obtained injunctive relief, or vice versa, may recover a fee award based on all hours reasonably expended if the relief obtained justified that expenditure of attorney time.

461 U.S. at 435-36 n.11 (citation omitted).

In this case plaintiffs' counsel coded all their time and deleted some 363 hours spent on damage issues wholly unrelated to claims for injunctive relief. Research of the law dealing with the good faith immunity defense to the federal damage claims was an example. Although defendants express amazement that out of more than 10,000 hours, so little a portion could so be spent, we have no basis for faulting the district court's finding in effect that most of the evidence relevant to damage claims was also necessary to justify injunctive relief. The district court's conclusion remarkably paralleled those of the district court that were upheld in *Riverside v. Rivera*, 477 U.S. 561, 106 S. Ct. 2686, 91 L. Ed. 2d 466 (1986). [2]

> 2 All claims made by plaintiffs were based on a common core of facts. The claims on which plaintiffs did not prevail were closely related to the claims on which they did prevail. The time devoted to claims in which plaintiffs did not prevail cannot reasonably be separated from time devoted to claims on which plaintiffs did prevail.
>
> *Riverside*, 106 S. Ct. at 2693 (citation omitted).

That plaintiffs achieved success on the significant injunctive issues, medication and seclusion, "which achieve[d] some of the benefit the parties sought," *Nadeau v. Helgemoe*, 581 F.2d 275, 279 (1st Cir. 1978), seems clear to us. Defendants have adopted the kind of "mathematical approach" criticized in the above-quoted footnote from *Hensley* by including their own twelve-page accounting of the extent of plaintiffs' success on all of the discernible issues.

Defendants, for example, claim victory on no fewer than 224 federal and state damage issues. Their attack is reminiscent of the unsuccessful effort in *Riverside v. Rivera*, 106 S. Ct. at 2686, to overturn the award of the district court. In that case, as now Chief Justice Rehnquist noted in dissent, out of 256 separate claims against 32 defendants, plaintiffs finally won modest damages against only six defendants, claims for injunctive and declaratory relief having been dropped. *Riverside*, 106 S. Ct. at 2702 (Rehnquist, J., dissenting).

The Commonwealth further depreciates the results achieved by claiming that any real relief must be attributed to the Supreme Judicial Court's decision based on state law and a pre-existing state statute merely interpreted by the district court. Yet it concedes, as it must, not only that partial relief was achieved as to both the medication and seclusion claims for injunctive relief (Appellants' Brief at 25-26) but that there has been "an impact in the real world in terms of policies and practices regarding forcible medication of involuntary patients in state care facilities." (*Id.* at 33.)

We are not strangers to this case. For the Commonwealth to argue that the results of plaintiffs' lawsuit -- their success in both the district court and before us, the significant rulings of the Supreme Judicial Court (which we have recognized as describing a federally protectible liberty interest), and the policy statements issued by the Department of Mental Health, with their impact on mental health facilities and Family and Probate Court procedures now in place in Massachusetts -- do not qualify them as very substantially "prevailing parties" seems to us more the result of long entrenched partisan advocacy than of dispassionate analysis. The district court's ruling was well within its discretion.

II. Sovereign Immunity

The district court, very sensibly we think, adopted plaintiffs' expert's suggestion that in an attenuated case like this, where more than a decade of inflation has continually eroded the value of the dollar, current (1986) hourly rates should be awarded to compensate for the delay in payment of attorneys' fees.

Only a few days after the district court issued its fee award, however, the Supreme Court issued its opinion in *Library of Congress v. Shaw*,

478 U.S. 310, 106 S. Ct. 2957, 92 L. Ed. 2d 250 (1986). In that case, the district court, in calculating an attorney's fee for a plaintiff who had prevailed in a lengthy litigation under Title VII of the Civil Rights Act of 1964 against the Library of Congress, increased the lodestar fee by 30 percent to compensate counsel for the delay. Justice Blackmun, writing for the Court, noted the history of the rule recognizing the immunity of the federal sovereign, absent its consent, from claims of interest. He then addressed the Title VII fee statute at issue, 42 U.S.C. § 2000e-5(k), which not only gave a prevailing party a "reasonable attorney's fee" as part of the costs, but also provided, "and the United States shall be liable for costs the same as a private person." The Court then held that none of the key phrases or words -- "the same as a private person," "reasonable attorney's fee," or "costs" -- constituted a waiver of sovereign immunity. Finally, the Court dealt with an alternative argument, that the no-interest rule did not prohibit the award of compensation for delay, saying:

> We are not persuaded. Interest and a delay factor share an identical function. They are designed to compensate for the belated receipt of money. The no-interest rule has been applied to prevent parties from holding the United States liable on claims grounded on the belated receipt of funds even when characterized as compensation for delay.

106 S. Ct. at 2965.

Plaintiffs make three arguments against the applicability to this case of *Library of Congress*. The first is that defendants failed to raise the Eleventh Amendment issue in the district court, even by a motion for reconsideration. This, however, is a jurisdictional defense and may be raised at any time. *Edelman v. Jordan*, 415 U.S. 651, 677-678, 39 L. Ed. 2d 662, 94 S. Ct. 1347 (1974).

A second argument is that the Commonwealth waived its immunity when, in a brief to the district court, it argued that if, as it had urged, historic hourly rates were applied, "an upward adjustment [of 8 percent] for delay in payment would be appropriate . . . . based on what other courts have done." [3] This undertaking was of course not expressly a willingness to accept current rates. Nor can its generalized acceptance, based on the then current practice of courts within the circuit, of awarding prejudgment interest against a state, fairly be said to be stated "by the most express language or by such overwhelming

27

implications from the text as [will] leave no room for any other reasonable construction." *Edelman v. Jordan*, 415 U.S. 651, 673, 39 L. Ed. 2d 662, 94 S. Ct. 1347 (1974). In short, if the Commonwealth reasonably concluded that there was nothing to waive, how can it be said *clearly* to have waived it?

> 3 Defendants' proposed finding of fact No. 25 cited *Brown v. Gillette*, 536 F. Supp. 113 (D. Mass. 1982); *Gabriele v. Southworth*, 712 F.2d 1505 (1st Cir. 1983); *Heritage Homes of Attleboro, Inc. v. Seekonk Water District*, 548 F. Supp. 167 (D. Mass. 1982).

On the merits, plaintiffs urge that 42 U.S.C. § 1988 was enacted pursuant to Congress's enforcement power under section 5 of the Fourteenth Amendment and that therefore the Eleventh Amendment immunity from prejudgment interest on fee awards has been abrogated. We recognize that Congress could achieve this result. As the Court made clear in *Hutto v. Finney*, 437 U.S. 678, 696, 57 L. Ed. 2d 522, 98 S. Ct. 2565 (1973), "Congress [may] amend its definition of taxable costs and have the amended class of costs apply to the States . . . without expressly stating that it intends to abrogate the States' Eleventh Amendment immunity." Our problem in the instant case is that Congress has not yet made any statement suggesting that a § 1988 attorney's fee award should include prejudgment interest. Indeed, as recently as 1986 the Court in *Library of Congress* reiterated that "Prejudgment interest . . . is considered as damages, not a component of 'costs' . . . . A statute allowing costs, and within that category, attorney's fees, does not provide the clear affirmative intent of Congress to waive the sovereign's immunity." 106 S. Ct. at 2965. This observation was made despite the fact that the fee statute in question (42 U.S.C. § 2000e-5(k)) provided that "the United States shall be liable for costs the same as a private party."

Not only does the language of the statute fail to provide support for plaintiffs' argument, but the legislative history also is completely silent on the subject of prejudgment interest. Although the Senate Report describes the objective of what was to become 42 U.S.C. § 1988 as giving "citizens . . . the opportunity to recover what it costs them to vindicate [their civil rights] in court," S. Rep. No. 1011, 94th Cong., 2d Sess., *reprinted in* 1976 Code Cong. & Ad. News 5908, 5910, it makes only one oblique reference to the problem giving rise to prejudgment interest. And that reference is to a different solution. The reference is the following: "In appropriate circumstances, counsel fees under S. 2278 may be awarded pendente lite. *See Bradley v. School Board of the City of Richmond*, 416 U.S. 696, 40 L. Ed. 2d 476, 94 S. Ct. 2006 (1974) (footnote omitted). Such awards are especially appropriate where a party has prevailed on an important matter in the course of litigation, even when he ultimately does not prevail on all issues." *Id.* at 5912. In *Bradley* the Court, dealing with a complicated school desegregation case where many orders could be expected to issue over its course, said: "To delay a fee award until the entire litigation is concluded would work substantial hardship on plaintiffs and their counsel . . . . A district court must have discretion to award fees and costs incident to the final disposition of interim matters." 416 U.S. at 723. This specific mention of the possibility of interim fee awards to cushion the burden on plaintiffs seems to us to cut against any implication that the alternative approach of prejudgment interest was contemplated.

We recognize that a comparison of *Hutto v. Finney*, 437 U.S. at 696-99, and *Library of Congress*, 106 S. Ct. at 2963, suggests that the degree of congressional clarity required to abrogate the states' Eleventh Amendment immunity under § 1988 is less than that required to waive the federal government's sovereign immunity under Title VII. The apparent reason for the different standards of statutory interpretation is that while the Fourteenth Amendment limitation on the states' immunity is present in a § 1988 action, no similar constitutional limitation on sovereign immunity is present in a Title VII action against the federal government.

Yet where, as here, neither the statutory language nor the legislative history gives any basis for an inference that Congress actually intended to remove the states' Eleventh Amendment immunity from substantial sums of prejudgment interest on attorneys' fee awards -- or indeed that Congress even considered the question of prejudgment interest on such awards -- we think that there is enough vitality in that Amendment to resist the inference. We are not happy about this result from a policy standpoint; indeed, particularly where private and unfunded counsel are expected to be enlisted to assist the private attorney general plaintiff, one can hardly overestimate the chilling effect of an interminable wait for payment in sharply shrunken dollars. The situation cries out for congressional remedy.

One ingenious remedy sought by plaintiffs, in the event that we upheld the Eleventh Amendment defense to current hourly rates, is to remand to the district court "to determine if present hourly rates should be applied, based on factors other than delay in payment, or to determine whether an upward adjustment of the lodestar figure is necessary to fully and fairly compensate the plaintiffs." (Appellees' Brief at 24.) We do not feel this route is viable. The district court specifically recognized "that upward adjustments of a lodestar figure for quality of representation and results obtained 'are to be few and far between.' *Wildman v. Lerner Stores Corp.*, 771 F.2d 605, 610 (1st Cir. 1985); *see also Blum v. Stenson*, 465 U.S. 886, 79 L. Ed. 2d 891, 104 S. Ct. 1541 (1984); *Garrity v. Sununu*, 752 F.2d 727, 739 (1st Cir. 1984)." To these authorities we add *Pennsylvania v. Delaware Valley Citizens' Council*, 478 U.S. 546, 106 S. Ct. 3088, 3098, 92 L. Ed. 2d 439 (1986), with its warning:

> In short, the lodestar figure includes most, if not all, of the relevant factors comprising a "reasonable" attorney's fee, and it is unnecessary to enhance the fee for superior performance . . . .

We add that although the Supreme Court heard reargument on whether fees "may be multiplied or otherwise enhanced to reflect the risk that plaintiffs might not have prevailed," 106 S. Ct. 3331 (1986), we do not view, in light of the early and continuing success attained by plaintiffs in this case, such a risk here as to make this a "rare" or "exceptional" case. *Blum v. Stenson*, 465 U.S. 886, 898-901, 79 L. Ed. 2d 891, 104 S. Ct. 1541 (1984); *Hall v. Ochs*, 817 F.2d 920 (1st Cir. 1987).

The result of this reasoning is that we must replace the current (1986) hourly rates established by plaintiffs' credited expert Barshak with the historic rates he specified for the years 1975 through 1985 for the attorneys who represented the plaintiffs at trial, on appeal, and in the fee proceeding. As we shall later explain in more detail, this recalculation represents a total reduction of about 40 percent, from the district court's figure of approximately $1,470,000 to approximately $895,000.

III. Lodestar Findings: Time and Rates

Having come this far, we now face a battery of specific criticisms of the district court's decision as to time spent and appropriate rates. This fee litigation has resulted in what the Court in *Hensley* warned against: "a second major litigation." 461 U.S. at 437. Although the Commonwealth has assured us that it has only taken seriously our advice in *Brewster v. Dukakis*, 786 F.2d 16, 19 (1st Cir. 1986), to "mount[] challenges to specific claims," it has gone far beyond "target[ing] significant and vulnerable areas for testing." *Id.* The result is that we find ourselves confronting 200 pages of briefs, seven cartons of records, a transcript of a three-day trial, and dozens of exhibits.

There has been no effort to prioritize. The issue advanced by the Commonwealth that we deem the most meritorious, the Eleventh Amendment issue, was allowed only five pages in its 98-page main brief. In contrast, although plaintiffs' counsel quickly conceded error in the inclusion of a $26 charge for lunch, this item was alluded to in both brief and oral argument to demonstrate plaintiffs' counsels' irresponsibility. Apart from the "prevailing parties" issue, the Commonwealth aimed at some ten targets. We discuss them seriatim.

1. We are urged to disallow 50 percent of time allegedly spent between 1975 and mid-1977 (when we announced in *King v. Greenblatt*, 560 F.2d 1024 (1st Cir. 1977), that contemporaneous time records should be kept) before detailed records were kept. The district court considered the evidence as to how plaintiffs' attorneys had reconstructed their time and found it reliable. The time allegedly spent by plaintiffs' lead attorney in these first three years (1,370 hours in 1975, 870 in 1976, and 1,164 in 1977 -- the heaviest years for him by far) do not seem shocking. Indeed, such a time investment was very similar to that testified to by the Commonwealth's lead counsel during the same period.

2. We are asked to make a 50 percent downward adjustment to reflect losing issues. Our prior discussion of the "prevailing parties" issue covers this point.

3. Rates should be set at figures testified to by defendants' consulting non-lawyer expert. The problem here is that the court specifically accepted the historic rates testified to by plaintiffs' lawyer expert.

The remaining criticisms are alike in that while most are very precise, a judgment of their accuracy requires us to accept defendants' witnesses' testimony and very often defendants' assumptions and unverified worksheets -- contrary to the findings of the district court. We list them seriatim and then comment.

4. Deduct between 12 and 16 percent of the time of all of plaintiffs' counsel for duplicative efforts.

5. Deduct some 125 hours in 1977-1979 as being "non-compensable."

6. Deduct some 1663 hours between 1975 and 1979 as being "excessive."

7. Deduct some 446 hours between 1979 and 1984 as being "excessive."

8. Deduct 50 percent of costs to reflect expenses on losing issues.

9. Deduct for non-legal work and for non-core legal work.

10. Deduct for making exorbitant fee request.

Underlying Nos. 1, 2 and 4-9 is the theme that, contrary to the teaching of *Hensley v. Eckerhart*, 461 U.S. at 437, plaintiffs did not "exercise 'billing judgment' with respect to hours worked." In addition to the deletion we have noted of some 363 hours spent on discrete work related only to damages, plaintiffs also refrained from requesting compensation for time spent before the Supreme Judicial Court in connection with the *Roe* proceeding and for considerable time spent with their individual patient clients. It seems to us that the following statement by the Court in *Riverside v. Rivera* is applicable to the present case:

> Petitioners maintain that respondents failed to exercise "billing judgment" in this case, since they sought compensation for all time spent litigating this case. We think this argument misreads the mandate of *Hensley*. *Hensley* requires a fee applicant to exercise "billing judgment" not because he should necessarily be compensated for less than the actual number of hours spent

> litigating a case, but because the hours he does seek compensation
> for must be *reasonable*. "Counsel for the prevailing party should
> make a good-faith effort to exclude from a fee request hours that
> are excessive, redundant, or otherwise unnecessary . . . ." *Id.*, at 434.
> In this case the District Court found that the number of hours
> expended by respondents' counsel was *reasonable*. Thus, counsel did,
> in fact, exercise the "billing judgment" recommended in *Hensley*.

Riverside, 106 S. Ct. at 2692 n.4.

Indeed, we find it instructive to compare both the findings and asserted errors of judgment in *Riverside* with those of the present case. The eight findings of the district court in *Riverside*, as set out in Justice Powell's concurring opinion, are of the same general tenor as the six findings we have summarized. Indeed, they may be less detailed. *Riverside*, 106 S. Ct. at 2699 (Powell, J., concurring). The criticisms, voiced by then Justice Rehnquist in his dissent, parallel many of defendants' here: action of the court in awarding "to the penny, the entire 'lodestar' claimed," approval of 209 hours of "prelitigation time"; 197 hours of time spent in conversations between plaintiffs' two attorneys; 143 hours in preparation of a pre-trial order; 45.50 hours of "stand-by time" for an attorney awaiting a jury verdict. *Riverside*, 106 S. Ct. at 2702-03 (Rehnquist, J., dissenting). Even Justice Rehnquist, however, might have been less critical in the case at bar for this, in contrast to *Riverside*, is the kind of case he would find meritorious under *Hensley*'s description -- "complex civil rights litigation involving numerous challenges to institutional practices or conditions" justifying a large award. *Riverside*, 106 S. Ct. at 2705 (Rehnquist, J., dissenting).

A further problem with such an indiscriminate targeting of manifold alleged errors is that the cumulative result places a palpable strain on our credulity. We have attempted to price defendants' criticisms, by accepting their figures, extrapolating them, and applying hourly rates to time that should allegedly be deducted. Our calculations are admittedly not exact, for defendants have not specified the rates to be applied to hours which they urge be deducted, nor have we been given information as to whether the deductions urged overlap or are cumulative. So what we have calculated may well be a "worst case scenario." But we think it illuminative of defendants' problem of lack of focus. If the defendants' historical hourly rates are accepted, plaintiffs' total attorneys' fees and costs for the twelve-year period would be slightly over $11,000. If the plaintiffs' historical hourly rates were to be applied, the total deductions would exceed the $895,000 figure of total time claimed at historical hourly rates by some $25,000.

We do not mean to imply that the district court scrutiny was as helpful as it could have been or that there was no basis for effective criticism. What we do say is that the realities of fee award reviews compel those who would object to such awards on appeal on the basis of time spent to select priority targets and marshal the facts as effectively as possible. To a far greater extent than is true of discrete legal issues, the battle is likely to be determined in the trial court.

Having said all this critically, we address more favorably the Commonwealth's criticism of fees attributed to the fee litigation itself -- some 1,110 hours, or over one tenth of all time claimed. The time is claimed not only by Cole and Burdick, the Greater Boston Legal Services counsel, but their outside counsel, Bergstresser, and ultimately two specially retained fee counsel, Simonds and Simons. [4] Considerable time was spent by the first two in reconstructing their records between 1975 and mid-1977, as well as in briefing outside counsel, and in attending hearings and depositions. In contrast to the billing judgment plaintiffs demonstrated by eliminating time spent on the damage claims from their fee request, plaintiffs apparently did not eliminate any duplicative hours spent on fee litigation. We have a deep conviction that, contrary to the finding of the district court, the fee requests included some duplicative and non-compensable effort, stemming from the ambiguity created when counsel become clients. *Cf. White v. City of Richmond*, 559 F. Supp. 127, 131 (N.D. Cal. 1982). Defendants have suggested that 195.22 hours be disallowed from the time claimed by Cole, Burdick and Bergstresser. We approximate this by exacting a 20 percent reduction of the time claimed by each at 1985 rates. The compensation is:

Attorney	Hours	1985 Rates	Total	20% Reduction
Cole	565.95	125	70,743.75	14,148.75
Burdick	61.95	125	7,743.75	1,548.75
Bergstresser	306.05	145	44,377.25	8,875.45
			Total Reduction	$24,572.95

4 Although in this unusual case the engagement of specially retained fee counsel seems appropriate, such a practice is inherently wasteful in many respects and should not be encouraged by the district courts in the absence of good cause.

IV. Computation and Conclusion

We have asked ourselves whether we should remand the case to the district court to perform the actual computations. We conclude that this would be of service neither to that court nor the parties. Accordingly, we have undertaken this function, as we did in *Hart v. Bourque*, 798 F.2d 519 (1st Cir. 1986), and in *Grendel's Den, Inc. v. Larkin*, 749 F.2d 945 (1st Cir. 1984).

In accordance with the foregoing we have rejected the then current hourly rates used by the district court, and have applied the historical rates testified to by plaintiffs' expert, Attorney Barshak, to the time claimed in Exhibits 44, 46, 48, and 49 submitted at the hearing on fees. Where he has given one figure for the beginning year of a period and another for the ending year of that period (e.g., 1980-1985), we have extrapolated. And we have done some rounding. As we have already noted, we find the total "lodestar" fees (time spent multiplied by historical hourly rates) plus costs to be $895,076.32. From this we deduct, for excessive charges for the fee litigation, $24,572.95. The net total award is therefore $870,503.37.

Following the order used by the district court, we report the following:

1. For Greater Boston Legal Services,	$673,925.07
a. $450,000 for all the work of Richard Cole less $14,148.75 reduction for fee litigation.	$435,851.25
b. $225,000 for all the work of Robert Burdick less $1,548.75 reduction for fee litigation.	$223,451.25
c. Costs in the amount of $14,622.57 (total costs of $28,527.24 minus $13,904.67 in costs paid to date).	$14,622.57
2. For Stahlin and Bergstresser,	$172,709.23
a. $170,000 for all the work of Clyde D.	

Bergstreser less $8,875.45 reduction for fee litigation.	$161,124.55
b. $6,695 for the work of members of Bergstresser and Stahlin.	$6,695.00
c. Costs in the amount of $4,889.68 (Total costs of $5,485.01 minus $595.33 in costs paid to date).	$4,889.68
3. For Goodwin, Procter and Hoar,	$23,869.07
a. $16,765.00 for the work of Marshall Simonds (95.80 hours at the rate of $175.00 per hour).	$16,765.00
b. $5,286.75 for the work of Kenneth Simons (79.50 hours at the rate of $66.50 per hour).	$5,286.75
c. Costs in the amount of $1,817.32.	$1,817.32
Total fees and costs allowed:	$870,503.37

The judgment is vacated and the matter remanded to the district court for an appropriate order consistent with this opinion.

BARRY CLIFFORD,
Plaintiff, Appellant,

v.

M/V ISLANDER
AND WOODS HOLE,
MARTHA'S VINEYARD AND
NANTUCKET STEAMSHIP AUTHORITY,
Defendants, Appellees

No. 89-1196
UNITED STATES COURT OF APPEALS
FOR THE FIRST CIRCUIT
882 F.2d 12
August 8, 1989

Allan H. Tufankjian on brief for Appellant.

Frank H. Handy, Jr. and Kneeland, Kydd & Handy on brief for
Appellees.

Bownes, Torruella and Selya, Circuit Judges.

SELYA, Circuit Judge.

We revisit for a third and hopefully last time the subaqueous exploits
of plaintiff-appellant Barry Clifford, a highly-skilled diver who, under
difficult and dangerous conditions, effected emergency repairs to the
ferry M/V ISLANDER after she was holed in March 1980.
Following these heroics, Clifford sought compensation from the
ISLANDER's owner, defendant-appellee Steamship Authority.
Litigation proved necessary.

I

The district court found that the Steamship Authority was liable to
plaintiff under an oral maritime contract and awarded him $ 150,000
based on a quantum meruit calculation. *Clifford v. M/V Islander*, 565
F. Supp. 922 (D.Mass. 1983) (*Clifford I*). We affirmed the liability
determination but ruled that the trial judge had insufficiently
explained the basis for the damage computation. *Clifford v. M/V*

Islander, 751 F.2d 1 (1st Cir. 1984) (*Clifford II*). We therefore remanded "for further findings concerning what damages should be awarded under the contract." *Id.* at 8. Without taking additional evidence, the district court fleshed out its findings and again entered judgment for $ 150,000. *Clifford v. M/V Islander*, No. 80-2160-N (D. Mass. Oct. 2, 1987) (unpublished) (*Clifford III*). At the same time, the court denied plaintiff's request for prejudgment interest. *Id.* We affirmed. *Clifford v. M/V Islander*, 846 F.2d 111 (1st Cir. 1988) (per curiam) (*Clifford IV*).

Plaintiff then applied for, and received, an execution from the district court clerk. On its face, the execution indicated that the date of entry of the original (*Clifford I*) judgment, July 14, 1983, marked the starting point for computation of postjudgment interest. Defendants moved for clarification. The district court amended the execution, ruling that the entry date of the later (*Clifford III*) judgment, October 2, 1987, controlled. Although its rationale was somewhat inexplicit, the court apparently concluded that denial of prejudgment interest, *see Clifford IV*, 846 F.2d at 113-14; *Clifford III, supra,* foreclosed an award of interest, however labelled, for any interval before October 2, 1987.

Plaintiff appeals, arguing that postjudgment interest should be computed from the time of the initial (*Clifford I*) damage award. We think plaintiff has correctly assayed the fluxes and refluxes of the interest equation.

II

This suit was brought under the federal courts' maritime jurisdiction, 28 U.S.C. § 1333; accordingly, the matter of postjudgment interest is governed generally by federal law and specifically by 28 U.S.C. § 1961. *See Gele v. Wilson*, 616 F.2d 146, 148 (5th Cir. 1980); *Moore-McCormack Lines v. Amirault*, 202 F.2d 893, 895 (1st Cir. 1953). Insofar as pertinent here, section 1961(a) provides that postjudgment "interest shall be calculated from the date of the entry of the judgment." This deceptively straightforward language has led federal judges to a plethora of conflicting conclusions. In cases where a judgment for money damages was entered, then later vacated, then eventually supplanted by a second dollar judgment (in whatever amount), the circuits are in great disarray as to when the postjudgment interest meter clicks into the "ON" position. *Compare, e.g., Bailey v. Chattem, Inc.*, 838 F.2d 149, 153-55 (6th Cir.) (equitable considerations normally require that postjudgment interest accrue on the amount common to both judgments from entry date of the first judgment), *cert. denied*, 486 U.S. 1059, 108 S. Ct. 2831, 100 L. Ed. 2d 931 (1988); *Twin City Sportservice, Inc. v. Charles O. Finley & Co.*, 676 F.2d 1291, 1310-12 (9th Cir.) (provisions of 28 U.S.C. § 1961 are mandatory and dictate that postjudgment interest must run from entry date of initial judgment), *cert. denied*, 459 U.S. 1009, 74 L. Ed. 2d 400, 103 S. Ct. 364 (1982); *Ashland Oil, Inc. v. Phillips Petroleum Co.*, 607 F.2d 335, 336 (10th Cir. 1979) (per curiam) (section 1961 requires that, for purposes of postjudgment interest, entry date of second judgment controls; vacated judgment should be treated as nullity), *cert. denied*, 446 U.S. 936, 64 L. Ed. 2d 788, 100 S. Ct. 2153 (1980). [1]

1 The myriad variations upon these themes were recently catalogued, circuit by circuit, by Justice White. *See Chattem Inc. v. Bailey*, 486 U.S. 1059, 108 S. Ct. 2831, 2832, 100 L. Ed. 2d 931 (1988) (White, J., dissenting from denial of certiorari). We need not repastinate this ground, for the Court has lately agreed to review a case which squarely presents the question and which will presumably afford much-needed guidance to the splintered courts of appeals. *See Bonjorno v. Kaiser Aluminum & Chemical Corp.*, 865 F.2d 566 (3d Cir.), *cert. granted*, 491 U.S. 903, 109 S. Ct. 3184, 105 L. Ed. 2d 693, 57 U.S.L.W. 3821 (U.S. 1989).

Notwithstanding the division on the issue throughout the circuits, the district court was bound to follow the prior decisions of this court - and this panel is equally bound. *See Jusino v. Zayas*, 875 F.2d 986 (1st Cir. 1989); *Lacy v. Gardino*, 791 F.2d 980, 985 (1st Cir.), *cert. denied*, 479 U.S. 888, 93 L. Ed. 2d 259, 107 S. Ct. 284 (1986). We think that the key precedent is another long **dachshund** of a case, *United States v. Michael Schiavone & Sons Inc.*, 304 F. Supp. 773 (D.Mass. 1969), *aff'd in part and vacated in part*, 430 F.2d 231 (1st Cir. 1970), *opinion after remand*, 325 F. Supp. 48 (D.Mass.), *modified*, 450 F.2d 875 (1st Cir. 1971). Because we view *Schiavone* as controlling, we examine it in some detail.

In *Schiavone*, the government charged a shipper with having euchred an illegal rebate from a railroad, and sought treble damages as a civil penalty. Following a trial, the district court entered judgment in plaintiff's favor for treble damages (totalling $ 663,339). 304 F. Supp. at 781. We upheld the liability finding, but vacated the judgment and

"remanded to the district court for reassessment of the illegal rebate."
430 F.2d at 236. The district court then refigured the kickback,
gauged it to be under $ 28,000, multiplied by three, and entered a
revised judgment. 325 F. Supp. at 50. On appeal, we modified the
award, authorizing treble damages of $ 113,578.86. 450 F.2d at 876-
77. We also determined that postjudgment interest should accrue
from the date of the original judgment:

> Regardless of whether the judgment itself contains a specific award
> of interest, once final judgment has been entered in a civil suit in a
> federal court the prevailing party becomes a judgment creditor and
> is entitled to post-judgment interest under the mandatory terms of
> 28 U.S.C. § 1961. . . . It is settled law that subsequent action by this
> court in reducing a judgment does not prevent interest from
> attaching upon the reduced amount from the date of the original
> judgment. . . .

Id. (citations omitted). *See also Marshall v. Perez-Arzuaga*, 866 F.2d 521,
523-24 (1st Cir. 1989) (holding that "entry of the judgment" as used
in section 1961(a) means the initial entry of judgment on the jury
verdict, not the entry of the court's later denial of a motion for
judgment n.o.v.).

Schiavone remains the law of this circuit [2] and governs the question on
appeal. Once a final judgment has been entered as to liability and
damages, vacation of the damage award on appeal and issuance of an
order requiring further proceedings to quantify recoverable damages
will not prevent accrual of postjudgment interest at the federal
statutory rate on the amount common to the earlier and later
judgments from the date the original judgment was entered. *Accord
Bailey*, 838 F.2d at 153-55; *Twin City Sportservice*, 676 F.2d at 1311. [3]

---

2 Our decision in *Explosives Corp. v. Garlam Enterprises Corp.*, 817 F.2d 894
(1st Cir.), *cert. denied*, 484 U.S. 925, 108 S. Ct. 286, 98 L. Ed. 2d 247 (1987),
did not undermine *Schiavone*. In *Garlam*, we concluded that it would be
inappropriate to allow postjudgment interest to run before a final,
appealable judgment had been entered in the district court. *Id.* at 903-04.
After all, "if the judgment was not final for liability purposes, it could not
be final on damages." *Id.* at 904. That, of course, is far different from cases
like *Schiavone* and the case at bar (where the initial judgment, albeit vacated

on appeal, was final when entered). *See also Marshall*, 866 F.2d at 522-23 (distinguishing *Garlam*).

3 A different situation may obtain where, rather than vacating the first judgment and requiring further proceedings below to ascertain the damage amount, the court of appeals modifies an award (or reverses a judgment which failed to grant certain damages) and directs the entry of a particular monetary judgment. Under such circumstances, Fed.R.App.P. 37 applies and the appellate court's mandate "shall contain instructions with respect to allowance of interest." *Id.* In formulating such instructions, general equitable considerations are often taken into account. *See, e.g., Affiliated Capital Corp. v. City of Houston*, 793 F.2d 706 (5th Cir. 1986) (en banc). Here, we vacated the initial judgment and remanded for further proceedings without directing entry of a specific dollar judgment. *See Clifford II*, 751 F.2d at 8-9. Rule 37 is, therefore, not implicated.

III

We note, too, that this result is not only demanded by precedent and statute, but is consistent with the equities of the situation. Plaintiff's services were rendered in 1980. By 1983, it was firmly established that defendants owed Clifford the fair value of those services. [4] All that remained in dispute then and thereafter was the pointed question: how much? The amount was originally set at $ 150,000 by the district court, and -- two appeals and an intervening remand later -- was again set at the same figure.

4 Indeed, the Steamship Authority conceded in the district court that it had an obligation to pay plaintiff "the reasonable value" of the services which it so gladly accepted. *Clifford I*, 565 F. Supp. at 928.

"In the world of commerce, time equates with money." *United States v. Ven-Fuel Inc.*, 758 F.2d 741, 764 (1st Cir. 1985). If equity were thought to control, the most relevant inquiry would seem to be which party should, in fairness, bear the financial onus arising from plaintiff's loss of use of the funds owed to him. It seems much more evenhanded to assign this cost to the Steamship Authority rather than to plaintiff, at least from and after the time defendants' liability for payment was conclusively established. *See Marshall*, 866 F.2d at 524; *Nissho-Iwai Co. v. Occidental Crude Sales, Inc.*, 848 F.2d 613, 624

(5th Cir. 1988); *see also* Comment, *Interest on Judgments in the Federal Courts*, 64 Yale L.J. 1019, 1048 (1955).

IV

We need go no further. Under *Schiavone*, plaintiff was entitled to postjudgment interest from the date of the initial (*Clifford I*) judgment. For that reason, we summarily reverse the district court's order anent postjudgment interest and remand for entry of a revised judgment bearing such interest from June 14, 1983 forward. 1st Cir.Loc.R. 27.1.

Reversed and remanded.

UNITED STATES OF AMERICA,
Appellee,
v.
FRANCIS CONNOR, JR.,
Defendant, Appellant

No. 90-1025
UNITED STATES COURT OF APPEALS
FOR THE FIRST CIRCUIT
926 F.2d 81
February 21, 1991

Barbara A. H. Smith, with whom Quinlan & Smith was on brief for Appellant.

Don O. Burley, Attorney, Office of Consumer Litigation, United States Department of Justice, with whom Stuart M. Gerson, Assistant Attorney General, Wayne A. Budd, United States Attorney, and John R. Fleder, Director, Office of Consumer Litigation, were on brief for Appellee.

Campbell and Selya, Circuit Judges, and Pollak, * Senior District Judge.

> * Of the Eastern District of Pennsylvania, sitting by designation.

SELYA, Circuit Judge.

This appeal requires that we revisit a long **dachshund** of an indictment brought, *inter alia*, under 18 U.S.C. § 513, 15 U.S.C. §§ 1984, 1990c, in which six persons, including Richard M. Penta and the present appellant, Francis A. Connor, Jr., were cited for a pack of charges related to the (alleged) alteration of odometer settings on used motor vehicles. [1] Penta pled guilty during trial, reserving certain appellate rights. A panel of this court rejected his ensuing appeal. *See United States v. Penta*, 898 F.2d 815 (1st Cir.), *cert. denied*, 498 U.S. 896, 111 S. Ct. 246, 112 L. Ed. 2d 205 (1990). Connor doggedly went the distance; the jury found him guilty on eighty counts. Following imposition of sentence, he filed this appeal. We affirm.

1 Connor was also charged with conspiracy, 18 U.S.C. § 371, and aiding and abetting, 18 U.S.C. § 2.

I

Initially, Connor's appellate counsel, new to the case, raised both substantive and procedural claims for our perscrutation. Then, the Supreme Court handed down its opinion in *Moskal v. United States*, 498 U.S. 103, 112 L. Ed. 2d 449, 111 S. Ct. 461 (1990). To all intents and purposes, *Moskal* sounded the death knell for appellant's merits-based argument. *See id.* 111 S. Ct. at 463 (holding that a motor vehicle title duly issued by a state, but containing an apocryphal mileage figure, can be considered "falsely made" within the contemplation of an analogous criminal statute). At oral argument, defense counsel properly conceded that *Moskal* was dispositive of appellant's substantive claim. Hence, only the procedural issue remains.

II

The Speedy Trial Act, 18 U.S.C. §§ 3161-3174, requires a defendant to be brought to trial within seventy days of either indictment or first appearing before a judicial officer. *Id.* at § 3161(c)(1). The Act permits certain exclusions from the computation. *Id.* at § 3161(h). Connor claims that two periods of delay were improperly excluded in his case. Had both periods been counted, he tells us, the includable days would have totalled more than seventy (eighty, to be exact). The Act would thereby have been violated, necessitating dismissal of the charges against him.

A.

The first period of delay involves the exclusion of time spent in implementing an intra-district transfer which moved the trial site from Springfield, Massachusetts to Boston, Massachusetts. This shift retarded the proceedings for twelve days. In *Penta*, we considered the identical transfer and ruled unequivocally that time consumed in effectuating *intra-district* transfers was not excludable under 18 U.S.C. § 3161(h)(1)(G) (permitting exclusion of time required for transfer

44

from "another district") or otherwise. *Penta*, 898 F.2d at 818-19. In the current appeal, the government has made no new arguments suggestive of a different result. Principles of *stare decisis* require, therefore, that we adhere to our earlier ruling. *See United States v. Reveron-Martinez*, 836 F.2d 684, 687 & n.2 (1st Cir. 1988) (generally, identical claims should be resolved in the same way for identically situated defendants); *United States v. 177.51 Acres of Land*, 716 F.2d 78, 81 (1st Cir. 1983) (similar; applying doctrine to legal issue previously resolved in eminent domain proceedings involving neighboring parcel). The twelve day interval should have been counted for Speedy Trial Act purposes.

B.

The fact that appellant wins the first dogfight does not signify that he wins the war. Counting the twelve days is not enough to overextend the temporal skein. Appellant must show that the second contested period of delay was improperly excluded as well; elsewise, the seventy day limit was unsullied.

This facet of Connor's claim involves a span of eighteen days, from June 7 to June 26, 1989. The underlying facts are simple. The government requested a two month postponement to procure the attendance of two essential witnesses who were incarcerated. On June 7, 1989, the trial judge denied the initial request but granted a much-abbreviated continuance, eighteen days, due to the asserted unavailability of the witnesses. The judge simultaneously excluded the eighteen day period for Speedy Trial Act purposes. Appellant contends that the exclusion was impermissible because convicts are not "unavailable" witnesses in the statutory sense. Whether or not the contention has the slightest merit - and we do not suggest that it does - it is not properly before us.

In the first place, we are not on virgin ground. Penta challenged the excludability of the same period. We rebuffed the onslaught, holding that the eighteen days were properly eliminated from the speedy trial computation. *Penta*, 898 F.2d at 819. The government asserts that what is sauce for its gander, *see supra* Part II(A), is equally sauce for appellant's goose, and that we should reject the appellant's exhortation out of hand on the basis of *stare decisis*.

We recognize that *stare decisis* is not a rigid, inflexible rule. Rather, the doctrine, which has its roots not in safeguarding the finality of judgments but in principles of stability and equality of treatment, "leaves some room for judgment as to its preclusive power." *E.E.O.C. v. Trabucco*, 791 F.2d 1, 2 (1st Cir. 1986). On the intra-district transfer issue, *stare decisis* was appropriately invoked against the government because the government offered all its arguments in *Penta* and lost. Connor, however, seeks in this appeal to advance a theory which, for aught that appears from the *Penta* opinion, was not previously aired. Such a distinction might very well leave room to apply *stare decisis* less woodenly, especially in a criminal case. *Cf. United States v. 177.51 Acres of Land*, 716 F.2d at 81 (*stare decisis* applies when, in the later case, "no new analysis" or "new arguments" are forthcoming).

Thus, even though the government's *stare decisis* argument is a powerful one, we prefer to rest our decision on another ground, forgoing any explicit determination on the *stare decisis* point. The record reveals a procedural obstacle which prevents us from reaching the meat of defendant's argument, come what may. We explain briefly.

While we agree with Connor that the appropriate response to a Speedy Trial Act infraction is dismissal of the indictment, the remedy is not self-executing:

> Failure of the defendant to move for dismissal prior to trial. . . shall constitute a waiver of the right to dismissal under this section.

18 U.S.C. § 3162(a)(2). Thus, in the precincts patrolled by the Speedy Trial Act, a motion for dismissal is effective only for periods of time which antedate the filing of the motion. Subsequent periods of delay, whether includable or excludable, are inconsequential. We agree with the Ninth Circuit that:

> In ruling on a motion to dismiss an indictment for failure to comply with the Speedy Trial Act, *a court need only consider [the] alleged delay which occurs prior to and including the date on which the motion is made*. The right to challenge any subsequent delay is waived absent the bringing of a new motion to dismiss.

United States v. Wirsing, 867 F.2d 1227, 1230 (9th Cir. 1989) (emphasis supplied); *see also United States v. Mayes*, 917 F.2d 457, 460 (10th Cir. 1990) (where defendant filed a motion to dismiss under the Speedy Trial Act, but failed to renew it, any subsequent delay was "irrelevant" to the court's inquiry); *United States v. Berberian*, 851 F.2d 236, 239-40 (9th Cir. 1988) (defendant waived the right to challenge delay that occurred subsequent to the filing of his motion to dismiss), *cert. denied*, 489 U.S. 1096, 103 L. Ed. 2d 934, 109 S. Ct. 1567 (1989).

Connor cannot scale this barrier. He filed his only motion for dismissal under the Speedy Trial Act on May 24, 1989. That was two full weeks prior to the inception of the interlude that he now seeks to challenge. His motion was denied by the court on June 7 (on the same day as, but shortly before, the eighteen day continuance was bestowed). The appellant did not renew his dismissal motion when the court granted the extra days to the prosecution. He did not serve a new motion to dismiss at any time thereafter. The point was, therefore, waived. It is far too late for Connor to argue on appeal, for the first time, that the speedy trial clock should have kept ticking during the eighteen day interval.

III

We need go no further. For the reasons stated, the judgment of conviction must be *Affirmed*.

2
Real Dachshund Dogs

They get kicked, they attack, they need muzzles, they need care, pure-bred, and similar to but notably distinct from chihuaha.

Murray v. United States,	154 Ct. Cl. 185 (1961)
Royal Indem. Co. v. Werner,	979 F.2d 1299 (8th Cir., 1992)
Stover v. Eagle Prods.,	896 F. Supp. 1085, (Kan. 1995)
Garcia v. Rivera,	07 Civ. 2535 (PAC) (AJP), (S.D.N.Y. 2007)
Word v. Christian County,	5:07-CV163-R, (W.D. Kent., 2007)
McLean v. Broadfoot,	4:10CV00019, (W.D. VA, Danville Div., 2011)

City of Riviera Beach v. Unnamed Gray, 649 F.3d 1259 (11th Cir., 2011),

> *US Supreme Court certiorari granted by, Lozman v. City of Riviera Beach, 132 S. Ct. 1543,
> Reversed by Lozman v. City of Riviera Beach, (Jan. 15, 2013)*

Smith v. Astrue,	1:10-cv-01527 GSA, (E.D. CA, 20011)
Degiorgio v. Fitzpatrick,	08-CV-6551 (KMK) (LMS), (S.D.N.Y. 2013)

JESSE FREDERICK MURRAY
v.
THE UNITED STATES

No. 237-57
UNITED STATES COURT OF CLAIMS
154 Ct. Cl. 185
June 7, 1961

Robinson O. Everett, for the plaintiff.

John R. Franklin, with whom was *Assistant Attorney General William H. Orrick, Jr.*, for the defendant.

Durfee, *Judge*, delivered the opinion of the court. Reed, *Justice (Ret.)*, sitting by designation; Laramore, *Judge*; Madden, *Judge*; and Jones, *Chief Judge*, concur.

On May 2, 1954, the Secretary of the Air Force directed that the plaintiff, then a master sergeant, be administratively discharged with a general discharge under honorable conditions under the provisions of Air Force Regulation 35-66 dated May 31, 1954, which pertained to homosexual conduct or tendencies. He was accordingly discharged on May 9, 1956. In this action he questions the validity of his discharge and seeks to recover damages in the form of various items of pay and allowances.

Before commencing this action, plaintiff sought without success to have his discharge changed to an honorable discharge and all reference to AFR 35-66 deleted by an Air Force Discharge Review Board. He attempted to obtain the same relief from an Air Force Board for the Correction of Military Records but the Correction Board refused to grant the relief requested.

The first issue raised by the defendant questions the authority of this court to review and determine the legality of the Secretary's action in issuing a general discharge instead of an honorable one. The defendant's position is that the Government may terminate the enlistment of an airman at any time and that such matters are not properly subject to judicial review. In the administrative proceedings leading up to this case, plaintiff did not challenge the right of the Secretary to terminate his enlistment but he did challenge the Secretary's authority to issue the type of discharge herein involved.

In *Harmon v. Brucker*, 355 U.S. 579 (1958) the Secretary of the Army had issued discharges under conditions other than honorable to the plaintiffs in that case. In so doing, he took into account certain pre-induction activities rather than basing his action exclusively upon the records of their military service. The petition in the District Court requested a ruling that the Secretary's action was void as in excess of his powers and an order directing him to issue honorable discharge certificates. The District Court held that it was without authority to review the determination of the Secretary of the Army and the Court of Appeals affirmed. Of these decisions, the Supreme Court said, at page 582:

> The District Court had not only jurisdiction to determine its jurisdiction but also power to construe the statutes involved to determine whether the respondent did exceed his powers. If he did so, his actions would not constitute exercises of his administrative discretion, and, in such circumstances as those before us, judicial relief from this illegality would be available.

In considering an Air Force discharge under other than honorable conditions, this court said in *Clackum v. United States*, 148 Ct. Cl. 404, 408:

> It is late in the day to argue that everything that the executives of the armed forces do in connection with the discharge of soldiers is beyond the reach of judicial scrutiny. (Citing *Harmon v. Brucker, supra*.)

We shall therefore proceed within our jurisdictional authority to examine the legality of the action of the Secretary of the Air Force in issuing a general discharge under honorable conditions rather than an honorable discharge to the petitioner. In addition to challenging the court's jurisdiction over this matter, the Government has attempted to blunt the plaintiff's argument by minimizing the difference between the two types of discharges. It asserts that in a general discharge under honorable conditions mere reference by number only to AFR 35-66 (which pertains exclusively to homosexuality) does not carry with it any stigma or penalty such as resulted in *Clackum* v. *United States, supra*, where the petitioner was issued an undesirable discharge. This is an unmerited conclusion; the Air Force itself says that a general discharge "may be a disadvantage to an airman seeking civilian employment. A general discharge received by a female airman precludes her reenlistment." AFR 39-10, dated October 27, 1953. The defendant has said in its brief that, in any event, the discharge was a reasonable and necessary precaution from the standpoint of the Air Force. Having rid itself of plaintiff, it goes on, the Air Force would hardly have wanted to make it possible for him to later reenlist somewhere else.

We need go no further in concluding that the discharge issued plaintiff is not the legal equivalent of the honorable discharge which he sought in the administrative review of his case. The refusal of the Air Force to issue plaintiff an honorable discharge in place of the general discharge does create a controversy of which we may take judicial cognizance.

The other issues raised by the parties deserve fairly extensive review because of the rather unusual exercise in hindsight by the Air Force in this case.

Apparently the plaintiff was a good soldier except for the incidents of homosexuality which formed the basis for his final discharge. He had received citations and good conduct medals, had been selected as "airman-of-the-month" and was a member of an Air Force character guidance council while in Korea during his third enlistment period. Air Force psychiatrists who had examined him in 1952 and in 1956 found that he had no existing homosexual tendencies and advised that he be retained in the service. Incidents of homosexual conduct by the plaintiff which had occurred during prior enlistments had been investigated and reported and he had thereafter been honorably discharged from those enlistments. Plaintiff's testimony before the board of officers convened in 1956 to consider his separation under AFR 35-66 that he had refrained from homosexual conduct since 1953 stands unrebutted.

The plaintiff served through three enlistment periods from each of which he received an honorable discharge. He reenlisted in Korea in October 1954 and was subsequently transferred to Shaw Air Force Base, South Carolina. At that post he requested that he be given a national security clearance which resulted in a background investigation being initiated. In the course of the investigation the previously admitted acts of homosexuality again came to light and plaintiff was notified that a board proceeding under AFR 35-66 would be initiated against him. A board of officers was convened for this purpose before which plaintiff and others testified. The findings of the board which were made on March 29, 1956, after the close of proof and oral argument said:

> Master Sergeant Jesse F. Murray AF 14 073 711, did engage in passive homosexual activities when 17 years old and later twice during 1949 and twice in 1953.

The 1949 and 1953 incidents occurred during his second and third enlistments. There was no evidence or finding of any acts of homosexuality after plaintiff's fourth and final enlistment. The board recommended that he be discharged under AFR 35-66 with a general discharge.

The first of plaintiff's several objections to the procedure of the board of officers is that it acted beyond its authority in receiving evidence of homosexual conduct during previous enlistments terminated by honorable discharge. He relies for support for his position on *Harmon* v. *Brucker, supra*, wherein the court said, in referring to the reliance of the Secretary of the Army on pre-induction activities in issuing the less than honorable discharges:

> We think the word "records", as used in the statute, means *records of military service*, and that the statute, properly construed, means that the type of discharge to be issued is to be determined solely by the soldier's military record in the Army. [1]

The Court held that the consideration of pre-induction activities as a basis for less than honorable discharge could not be sustained in law and remanded the case to the District Court.

1 The statute referred to by the Court was Title 38 U.S.C. § 693(h) (1952 Ed.) which created boards authorized to review actions of the service Secretaries. Under the statute, the findings of these boards "shall be based upon all available records of the service department relating to the person requesting such review * * *".

Everyone discharged from the military service must be furnished with a discharge certificate, with authority to issue them delegated to the appropriate Secretary. [2]

2 Title 10 U.S.C. § 652(a) (1952 Ed.).

In the *Harmon* case, the Army's construction of the statutory grant of power was found by the Court in paragraphy 2(b) of Army Regulation 615-375, where it is stated that "[the] purpose of a discharge certificate is to record the separation of an individual from the military service and to specify the character of service rendered *during the period covered by the discharge*." (Emphasis supplied.) Air Force Regulation 39-10, dated October 27, 1953, which pertained to the general provisions covering certain discharges and which was in effect at the time of plaintiff's discharge, provides that an honorable discharge certificate will be furnished when an airman has satisfied certain criteria "*during his current period of service*." (Emphasis supplied.) These criteria include approved character and efficiency ratings and freedom from conviction of a serious offense by court-martial during the current enlistment. [3] We think that by analogy to the *Harmon* case, the type of discharge to be issued in this case is to be determined solely by plaintiff's military record during his current enlistment.

3 AFR 39-10 incorporates the provisions of AFR 35-66, if applicable, by reference. However, paragraph 6 of the latter regulation specifically permits the granting of an honorable discharge in cases like the present one, even if proceedings are conducted under AFR 35-66.

The record is clear that during plaintiff's "current period of service," from his final enlistment on August 21, 1954, until his final discharge on May 9, 1956, his service measured up to the standards required for honorable discharge as set forth in the regulation. In addition to his regular duties, he served as a member of an Air Force character guidance council in Korea, and was also selected as "airman-of-the-month" and was awarded a one week paid vacation in Hong Kong. Special publicity was accorded to plaintiff's reenlistment by an article and picture in the Fifth Air Force newspaper circulated in the Pacific area.

Plaintiff was therefore, on his record of current service, entitled to an honorable discharge. Having chosen to institute proceedings for his untimely discharge, the Air Force is bound by its own regulations. *Service* v. *Dulles*, 354 U.S. 363 (1957); *Watson* v. *United States*, 142 Ct. Cl. 749 (1958).

Since action under AFR 39-10 confines the scrutiny of an airman's qualification for honorable discharge in this type of situation to his current enlistment, plaintiff's separation under AFR 35-66 with a less than honorable discharge based solely on evidence and findings of misconduct during prior enlistments, was in violation of Air Force regulations. Since we hold as we do respecting the validity of plaintiff's final discharge it is unnecessary to discuss other allegations of irregularity of proceedings raised by him.

Plaintiff is entitled to recover pay and allowances from the date of his discharge, May 9, 1956, until August 20, 1960, the date on which his final six year enlistment would ordinarily have expired. He has also claimed that in addition to, or in lieu of, active duty pay he should receive disability retired pay because of a service incurred disability. There is no evidence that plaintiff ever raised this issue before filing his petition in this court, nor do we have any competent evidence of disability or right to compensation based thereon. All that plaintiff ever requested the various Air Force boards to do was to change his general discharge to an honorable one and to delete all references to AFR 35-66. That portion of his petition relating to disability retired pay is, therefore, dismissed. In addition to the back pay and allowances referred to above, the plaintiff is entitled to recover $ 391.54, accrued credits improperly withheld by the defendant at the time of his discharge as a purported recoupment of part of his final reenlistment bonus. And, for the same reasons, the defendant's counterclaim asserted for the allegedly unearned portion of the reenlistment bonus is dismissed. Based on the foregoing findings and conclusions, judgment will be entered for the plaintiff with the amount of recovery to be determined pursuant to Rule 38(c).

It is so ordered.

FINDINGS OF FACT

The court, having considered the evidence, the report of Trial Commissioner Roald A. Hogenson, and the briefs and argument of counsel, makes findings of fact as follows:

1. Plaintiff is a citizen of the United States and resident of Durham, North Carolina. The date of his birth was August 17, 1909.

2. Plaintiff served as an enlisted man in the United States Army from April 29, 1942, to October 28, 1945, when he was honorably discharged as a staff sergeant and reentered civilian life. During the period from July 27, 1947, to November 21, 1948, he was enrolled in an inactive status in the United States Air Force Reserve. He thereafter served an enlistment in the Air Force as a staff sergeant from November 22, 1948, to January 26, 1950, when he was honorably discharged. Reenlisting in the Air Force on January 27, 1950, plaintiff served in the successive grades of staff sergeant, technical sergeant and master sergeant until August 20, 1954, when he was again honorably discharged. Reenlisting again in the Air Force on August 21, 1954, he served as a master sergeant until May 9, 1956, when he received a general discharge pursuant to Air Force Regulation 35-66, the validity of which discharge is challenged by plaintiff in this case. Throughout his military career, plaintiff was officially rated as excellent or superior in both character and efficiency.

Plaintiff's last enlistment on August 21, 1954, as provided in the enlistment form, was for six years "under the conditions prescribed by law, unless sooner discharged by proper authority," and his normal separation date would have been August 20, 1960.

3. Under date of December 28, 1951, two applicants for enlistment in the Air Force, Bobby D. Hedgepeth and Rex B. Howard, and one enlisted man in the Air Force, Remus E. Adams, executed sworn statements before Air Force Major John D. Moxley, plaintiff's

commanding officer, to the effect that plaintiff had made statements to them concerning homosexual conduct. Hedgepeth and Howard stated that on December 27, 1951, plaintiff had suggested to them that they submit to fellatio to be performed by a man at Raleigh, North Carolina. Adams stated that he had worked with plaintiff in the service for 15 months, that plaintiff had always talked about fellatio, and in his presence had asked prospective recruits how long it had been since they had had fellatio performed upon them. Adams was a master sergeant assigned to the Recruiting Station at Raleigh, North Carolina, where plaintiff was assigned. Adams further stated that Hedgepeth and Howard had informed him of the statements made to them by plaintiff on December 27, 1951, and that he had immediately reported the complaints of applicants Hedgepeth and Howard to Captain Johnson, Recruiting Officer of the Raleigh Recruiting Station.

4. As a result of these complaints, plaintiff was on December 28, 1951, with his consent hospitalized for psychiatric observation at the U.S. Army Hospital, Fort Bragg, North Carolina. Under date of January 18, 1952, Dr. Melvin Shulman, 1st lieutenant, M.C., a psychiatrist, made the following report of psychiatric examination:

> 1. This is to certify that Jessie F. Murray, Master Sergeant, AF 14 073 711, Army and Air Force Recruiting Office, Raleigh, North Carolina, has been a patient on the psychiatric service of the USAH, Fort Bragg, North Carolina since 28 December 1951 and has been observed since this date by the undersigned. Available at the time of his hospitalization were sworn statements by Bobby D. Hedgepeth, Rex B. Howard and Master Sergeant Remus E. Adams to the effect that Master Sergeant Murray was observed to have invited Mr. Hedgepeth and Mr. Howard to participate in fellatio.

> 2. This man was born on 17 August 1909, the oldest of 6 children. His birth and development were normal and there is no history of early neuropathic traits. He completed high school and took 2 years of college work at Duke University but was forced to leave because of the economic situation at home. He apparently lived a normal life during these years. He then worked for the WPA and civil service as a clerk. He enlisted in the Air Corps in April 1942 and was discharged honorably in October 1945 after having worked the bulk of that time as a teletype operator and clerk in a control room. After discharge he worked for the Veteran's Administration in Durham, North Carolina until he reenlisted in the Air Corps on 23

November 1948. Since that time he has worked at the Recruiting Office in Raleigh, North Carolina. He has received two promotions in the last 13 months. At present he is keeping steady company with a girl friend whom he hopes to marry this spring. His first heterosexual experience was at the age of 18. He describes a relatively active and normal heterosexual life since that time. He masturbated at an early age, but denies this activity since adolescence. This patient denies that he was ever attracted to members of his own sex before 6 or 7 months ago during a particularly strained period after having been jilted by an old girl friend whom he had planned to marry. At this time (6 months ago) the patient had fellatio performed upon himself by several different men, a total of 5 or 6 times. The patient was relatively intoxicated during each of these episodes. He denies that he would participate in such activities when completely sober. He denies any activities other than these few episodes mentioned. In reference to the sworn statements mentioned in paragraph one, the patient insists that he was merely offering the fellatio to Mr. Hedgepeth and Mr. Howard not with the intention of performing the activity himself but of getting someone else to perform the activity if Mr. Hedgepeth and Mr. Howard were interested. The patient denies ever having performed fellatio himself; he insists the only homosexual activity he has ever participated in were the aforementioned episodes of fellatio performed upon him. He denies the excessive use of alcohol and claims he has been drunk only on infrequent occasions. He denies the use of any drugs.

3. During his stay in the hospital, the patient was at all times clear, coherent, relevant, in contact and oriented. There was no evidence of any disturbance of thinking or feeling. There was no sign of any mental derangement or psychosis. He has at all times been pleasant and cooperative and helpful with the psychiatric staff. There has been no evidence noticeable that the patient willfully concealed or distorted the facts of his case.

4. Diagnosis: No psychiatric illness.

5. It is believed Sergeant Murray is not a homosexual.

6. There is no evidence of any mental disease, defect or derangement that interferes with this man's ability to distinguish between right and wrong or his ability to adhere to the right. He is sane and responsible and is mentally competent to assist counsel and cooperate in his own defense.

7. The medical recommendation is that this man be retained in military service.

8. There are no medical contraindications to administrative disposition.

5. Following the report of psychiatric examination, plaintiff returned to duty at the Raleigh Recruiting Station where he discovered that the nature of the complaints against him had become generally known among both the military and civilian personnel. At his request, his commanding officer effected his transfer in early 1952 to Dobbins Air Force Base, near Atlanta, Georgia.

6. In late 1953 it became common knowledge at Dobbins Air Force Base that master sergeants were being selected in order of their Air Force service classifications for shipment to Korean assignments. Because it appeared to him that he had been passed over, plaintiff inquired of the base adjutant what difficulties existed, and was told that it had been noted on his personnel record that he was not eligible for shipment pending a decision by the commanding officer of Dobbins Air Force Base. Plaintiff asked the adjutant if the delay in action on his reassignment was due to the previous complaints against him concerning homosexuality, and the reply was in the affirmative. The adjutant stated that he believed the problem would be resolved favorably, and shortly thereafter plaintiff was assigned for shipment to Korea.

7. Plaintiff left Dobbins Air Force Base in November and arrived in Korea in December 1953 and was assigned to the Air Installations Squadron, Seoul City, Fifth Air Force, until mid-February 1954, when he was assigned detached service with the Armed Forces Assistance to Korea program. Throughout his entire military service, plaintiff was assigned to administrative and personnel duties.

Under date of March 31, 1954, plaintiff in Korea voluntarily made a written statement to an agent of the Air Force Office of Special Investigations at the request of the agent, concerning passive participation in two acts of fellatio while he was stationed at Dobbins Air Force Base. He advised that a certain proprietor of a floral shop at Atlanta, Georgia, had performed the acts upon him on two different occasions. He also stated that on the second occasion, he took with him an airman, whose name he could not remember, and that he believed that the proprietor performed fellatio upon the airman.

Under date of April 15, 1954, plaintiff again voluntarily made a written statement at the request of the same OSI agent in Korea. This statement was made in considerable detail, and covered facts concerning his military service as well as family and personal history. Plaintiff stated that while stationed at the Raleigh Recruiting Station he had been the passive participant in acts of fellatio on 4 or 5 occasions. He asserted that the complaints made against him at Raleigh resulted from his refusal to permit enlistment of ineligible applicants sponsored by Sergeant Adams, one of the complainants. He stated that in response to inquiry of the two prospective recruits, the other complainants, he had told them they could resort to prostitutes for a certain charge at a certain hotel in Raleigh, or go to the basement of another hotel and find a homosexual without expense. He then related the circumstances of the affidavits presented against him, his hospitalization for and clearance by psychiatric examination, and subsequent transfer to Dobbins Air Force Base. He stated that while shopping for flowers for a sick girl friend at a certain floral shop in Atlanta, Georgia, in February 1953, the male proprietor invited him to return that evening to see his

champion **dachshund** dog. When plaintiff returned the proprietor gave him a drink of liquor, made sexual advances, and performed fellatio upon him. Plaintiff further stated that on two subsequent occasions when he had been drinking liquor, he went alone to the floral shop, and the proprietor performed fellatio upon him. He then related how he later took a young airman with him to the same shop at the request of the airman, and how they both resorted to having fellatio performed upon them by the proprietor. He stated that he had never been the active participant in such acts. He expressed great remorse for these mistakes, a determination to refrain from such acts, and a plea that he be permitted to remain in the Air Force.

8. As previously related in these findings, plaintiff was honorably discharged in Korea from his enlistment on August 21, 1954, and was immediately permitted to reenlist for six years. Under Air Force procedures and practices in effect at all times pertinent in this case,

an airman was not to be transferred or reenlisted if either a board action or an investigation was pending concerning homosexual activity on his part. Defendant has conceded that no such board proceedings nor administrative action was pending against plaintiff at the time of his reenlistment on August 21, 1954.

After his reenlistment in Korea, plaintiff remained on duty there until November 1954, when by operation of the so-called point system, he became eligible for and was transferred to the United States and to duty assignment at Shaw Air Force Base in South Carolina. Subsequent to his last reenlistment, plaintiff served in addition to his regular duties as a member of an Air Force character guidance council in Korea, and was also selected as the airman of the month by a board of officers and awarded a one-week paid vacation in Hong Kong. Special publicity was accorded to plaintiff's reenlistment on August 21, 1954, by an article and picture in the Fifth Air Force newspaper circulated in the Pacific area.

After plaintiff's return to the United States and assignment to Shaw Air Force Base, he made a request for national security clearance.

9. Thereafter an investigation of plaintiff was conducted by the 6th District Office of Special Investigations at the request of the Provost Marshal, Ninth Air Force, Shaw Air Force Base, South Carolina, to determine "if homosexual tendencies still existed." As a result of the investigation, plaintiff was advised on November 29, 1955, by his commanding officer at Shaw Air Force Base that it was intended that action would be requested against plaintiff pursuant to Air Force Regulation 35-66. In accordance with that regulation, plaintiff was tendered the option of applying for a discharge or appearing before a board of officers. Plaintiff elected to appear before a board. On December 1, 1955, a recommendation was duly made by plaintiff's commanding officer to the commanding general of Shaw Air Force Base to appoint a board of officers to determine whether plaintiff should be discharged pursuant to AFR 35-66, and such appointment was duly made by orders dated December 9, 1955. Commencement of proceedings of the board was delayed until March 28, 1956, because of hospitalization of plaintiff for a spinal operation at Maxwell Air Force Base, Alabama.

10. The duly appointed board of officers held its proceedings on March 28 and 29, 1956, at Shaw Air Force Base, South Carolina. The board consisted of five majors and a first lieutenant, the latter of whom was the legal member. Plaintiff was present in person and represented by counsel. The board received in evidence the affidavits of Hedgepeth, Howard, and Adams, previously mentioned in finding 3 herein, plaintiff's counsel stating that there were no objections thereto.

The board recorder then offered into evidence a photostatic copy of a written statement, dated September 25, 1953, purportedly in the handwriting of and signed by one Larry R. Hart, in which the assertions were made that the affiant was an airman, that some unnamed master sergeant, known to the affiant as "Jake", at Dobbins Air Force Base had taken Hart to a certain floral shop in Atlanta, Georgia, where another man committed fellatio upon Hart in the presence of the master sergeant. Plaintiff was neither named nor described in this document. The name of the floral shop was the same as that mentioned in the statements later given by plaintiff in Korea. The statement also contained admissions by Hart of passive participation in other acts of homosexuality with other persons. This document was obviously incomplete, as the pages were numbered from 1 to 6, except that there was no page numbered 3, and there was a lack of continuity between pages 2 and 4. Plaintiff's counsel objected to this statement of Hart because it was not an original document, that there was no authentication of the document, that there was no proof of the signature subscribed to the document, and that the document was obviously incomplete and hearsay. Plaintiff's counsel further stated that he had waived the appearance of Hedgepeth, Howard and Adams in connection with the previous statements admitted in evidence, subject to rebuttal testimony, but would not waive the appearance of Hart. Over these objections, the board admitted the Hart affidavit into evidence, subject to a showing that there was some connection between the statements therein and plaintiff. This affidavit was then read to the board, but thereafter the board ordered it stricken from the record, and the board members were instructed to disregard it.

The board recorder also offered into evidence the two statements made by plaintiff in Korea to the OSI agent, previously mentioned in finding 7, and the board received them in evidence over the objections of plaintiff's counsel that these statements of plaintiff amounted to confessions and were inadmissible because no evidence in corroboration had been presented to the board.

The board recorder then offered in evidence two voluntary statements made by plaintiff on September 9 and 21, 1955, to an agent of the Office of Special Investigations, in which plaintiff admitted that when he was a teenager he had once submitted passively to the performance of an act of fellatio upon him by a homosexual, that he had in 1951 upon inquiry by a prospective recruit advised where the recruit could find a homosexual who would commit fellatio upon him, that he had twice had the act of fellatio performed upon him in Raleigh, North Carolina, at times prior to his psychiatric examination in 1952, and on three more occasions in Atlanta, Georgia, in 1953, and stated that since that time he had not engaged in any homosexual activities. These two statements of plaintiff were admitted in evidence by the board over the objections of plaintiff's counsel that they were confessions without any evidence in corroboration.

At the request of plaintiff's counsel, the plaintiff was on March 8, 1956, given a psychiatric examination prior to the board proceedings, pursuant to the terms of AFR 35-66, at the Mental Hygiene Clinic, Fort Jackson, South Carolina. The purpose of the psychiatric study was to determine whether or not plaintiff had homosexual tendencies. The examining psychiatrist, Captain W. S. Mizell, made the following report:

> Psychiatric evaluation of this 46 year old, white, male, Air Force Master Sergeant does not reveal amoral or "abnormal moral tendencies." Although he admits having allowed some acts of fellatio to be performed on him during past years, examination shows that he does not possess habitual nor uncontrollable homosexual tendencies in the true psychodynamic sense. In view of the fact that this man's past history of participation in homosexual episodes came to light as result of routine security clearance, that he was investigated and cleared, and that he was previously investigated and cleared, and finally that he has consciously refrained from such acts in recent years, the previous willingness to participate in such acts is considered to have been overcome. Psychiatric evaluation at this time does not reveal any

overt homosexual tendencies nor any condition which would contraindicate this man's retention in Military Service.

Recommend that he be retained in Military Service.

This report was received in evidence by the board as an exhibit in behalf of the plaintiff.

Plaintiff was sworn and examined in his own behalf before the board. He denied the accusations against him in the statements in evidence of Hedgepeth, Howard and Adams. He testified that he had had fellatio committed upon him once at the age of 17 years by a male motorist who had picked him up as a hitchhiker, twice in 1949 by homosexuals in Raleigh, North Carolina, when he had been drinking heavily, and twice in 1953 by the male proprietor of the floral shop in Atlanta, Georgia, when plaintiff was intoxicated. He stated that except for those five occasions, he had never participated in any homosexual acts in any way, and that in the case of all five exceptions he was the passive participant. He stated that he would never participate in such acts again and that he had permanently stopped drinking intoxicants, having had only two beers in the last eighteen months.

Four Air Force enlisted men who had been associated with plaintiff in the service testified that plaintiff had never discussed homosexual matters in their presence, nor engaged in any abnormal conduct in that respect, and that plaintiff's reputation for morality was good. In addition, the board received in evidence about 25 letters from former associates and friends in and out of military service, attesting to plaintiff's good character. It was also shown in evidence that on several occasions throughout his various enlistments, plaintiff had received good conduct medals or citations, the last one in July or August 1955.

The transcript of proceedings of the board of officers shows that there was no evidence that plaintiff participated in any acts of homosexuality after 1953, or after his reenlistment on August 21, 1954. Plaintiff's testimony before the board stands unrebutted that he had completely refrained from such conduct since 1953. All of the evidence presented to the board concerning misconduct of the plaintiff was in the possession of the Air Force prior to plaintiff's reenlistment on August 21, 1954, except plaintiff's two statements made in September 1955, and those two statements were in all material respects like the previously-mentioned statements of plaintiff taken by the Air Force agent in Korea in March and April 1954.

11. After the closing of proof and presentation of oral arguments by plaintiff's counsel, the board of officers on March 29, 1956, made the following findings and recommendations:

> Findings: That Master Sergeant Jesse F. Murray, AF 14073711, did engage in passive homosexual activities when 17 years old and later twice during 1949 and twice in 1953.

> Recommendations: Recommended that: 1. Respondent be discharged from the USAF under the provisions of AFR 35-66. 2. Respondent be furnished a General Discharge certificate.

> Minority Recommendation:

>> First Lieutenant Frank P. Della Posta, Legal Member of the board, concurs in the findings of this board, but does not join in the recommendation that the respondent be granted a General Discharge, since it is inconsistent with the factual determinations.

>> In view of present Air Force policy, as enunciated in AFR 35-66, that the respondent's efficiency and past favorable service record should not be reflected in the board's final recommendation, this officer recommends that an Undersirable Discharge be given to the respondent.

12. By letter dated April 27, 1956, the commanding general of the Shaw Air Force Base, who had appointed the board of officers to hear plaintiff's case, advised the Director of Military Personnel, United States Air Force, Washington, D.C., as follows:

> 1. Recommend airman be separated under the provisions of AFR 35-66 and furnished an Undesirable Discharge Certificate.

> 2. I do not concur with the recommendation of the board that airman be given a General Discharge Certificate as it has been continuously emphasized that the manner of his performance of duty does not affect the type of discharge which will be effected

(reference paragraph 2c, AFR 35-66; your letter dated 10 March 1955, Subject: "Disposition of Cases Under Provisions of AFR 35-66"; and your message AFPMP 125134, 29 November 1955). This information has been brought to the attention of my Commanders.

3. Evidence indicates airman has participated in numerous acts of homosexuality (passively) during the period 1948 thru 1953. No recent acts are known. In accordance with paragraph 2b(2), AFR 35-66, this is defined as a Class II case.

4. In view of the circumstances involved trial by court-martial is deemed inappropriate.

5. AFR 39-21 is not applicable as there is no evidence of willful concealment of any homosexual acts prior to current enlistment of 21 August 1954.

6. The question is posed as to whether this administrative action against the subject airman can be revived inasmuch as he has been discharged and immediately reenlisted since commission of the homosexual acts.

7. Nevertheless, I feel his retention could possibly be inimical to the interests of the United States since he holds a sensitive position by virtue of his noncommissioned officer status (paragraph 6b, AFR 35-62) and has been exposed to the expressed acts as stated herein. In the event airman cannot be separated under the provisions of AFR 35-66, recommend action be taken in accordance with paragraph 6c(3), AFR 35-66.

8. This case was delayed due to the hospitalization of airman and the detailed administrative action necessary.

13. On May 2, 1956, upon recommendation of the Air Force Personnel Board, the Secretary of the Air Force directed that plaintiff be administratively discharged under the provisions of AFR 35-66 and that he be issued a general discharge certificate.

By special orders issued by the commanding officer of the Shaw Air Force Base on May 7, 1956, plaintiff was discharged from the Air Force "under honorable conditions," effective May 9, 1956, under the authority of AFR 35-66.

14. At the time of plaintiff's reenlistment on August 21, 1954, he was paid a reenlistment bonus of $ 947.82, granted to him by the Air Force in consideration of his reenlistment for six years. At the time of plaintiff's discharge on May 9, 1956, plaintiff had served 1 year, 8

months, and 19 days of his six-year enlistment, leaving unserved 4 years, 3 months, and 11 days. The Air Force prorated $ 271.62 of the entire bonus payment to the time served by plaintiff in the six-year enlistment, and charged plaintiff with liability to refund the balance of $ 676.20 for the unserved part of the enlistment.

At the time of his discharge on May 9, 1956, the Air Force computed that plaintiff had accumulated leave credit in the amount of $ 276.25, and accrued pay and allowances in the sum of $ 115.29, or a total of $ 391.54. This total sum was withheld by defendant and applied in reduction of the above-mentioned claim of $ 676.20, leaving a balance of $ 284.66, which sum has not been paid by plaintiff to defendant and is the amount of recovery sought by defendant in its counterclaim.

15. On June 13, 1956, plaintiff applied to the Air Force Discharge Review Board for a review of his discharge on May 9, 1956, seeking an honorable discharge and deletion of all reference to AFR 35-66. His case was heard by this board on October 19, 1956. Plaintiff was present and testified at the hearing, and was represented by counsel.

The Air Force Discharge Review Board decided on October 23, 1956, that plaintiff's appeal should be denied.

16. Under date of November 5, 1956, plaintiff forwarded his application, with supporting brief and statement of facts, to the Air Force Board for Correction of Military Records, in which he requested "Change of discharge to honorable discharge and deletion of all reference to AFR 35-66 as authority for separation. Payment of accrued leave, accrued pay and other improper deductions from pay."

By letter dated February 4, 1957, this Air Force board advised plaintiff that "a careful consideration by the Board of your military record, together with such facts as have been presented by you, fails to establish a showing of probable error or injustice in your case. Therefore, in the absence of additional material evidence tending to show the commission of an error or injustice, no further action on your application is contemplated."

17. At the proceedings of the board of officers at Shaw Air Force Base, in the hearing before the Air Force Discharge Review Board, and in his brief attached to his application to the Air Force Board for

Correction of Military Records, plaintiff maintained the position that plaintiff could not be legally discharged from a current enlistment on the basis of misconduct that had occurred in a previous enlistment.

18. On May 6, 1956, the Air Force conducted a physical examination of plaintiff for the purpose of his discharge from the service. The report of examination showed that plaintiff had had a laminectomy performed upon his spine in 1955, that plaintiff had a 50 percent limitation of motion of his back, and that he should be subjected to no heavy lifting, prolonged standing, or excessive fatigue. Plaintiff was not processed by the Air Force for determination of the extent of his disability, or whether plaintiff was entitled to disability retirement and to disability retired pay. Subsequent to his discharge on May 9, 1956, the Veterans Administration made a finding that plaintiff had a service-connected disability of 60 percent, and plaintiff has received disability compensation from that agency.

19. By agreement of the respective parties, and with the approval of the trial commissioner, the trial of this case, both as to the petition and the counterclaim, was limited to the issues of law and fact pertaining to the right of either party to recover, reserving the determination of the amount of recovery, if any, for future proceedings.

CONCLUSION OF LAW

Upon the foregoing findings of fact, which are made a part of the judgment herein, the court concludes as a matter of law that the plaintiff is entitled to recover and judgment will be entered to that effect. The amount of recovery will be determined pursuant to Rule 38(c).

In accordance with the opinion of the court and on a memorandum report of the commissioner as to the amount due thereunder, it was ordered on March 2, 1962, that judgment for plaintiff be entered for $ 15,998.82.

Royal Indemnity Company, Appellee,
v.
E. Louis Werner, Jr., Appellant.

No. 92-1595EM
UNITED STATES COURT OF APPEALS
FOR THE EIGHTH CIRCUIT
979 F.2d 1299
September 14, 1992, Submitted
November 12, 1992, Filed

For ROYAL INDEMNITY COMPANY, Plaintiff - Appellee:
Robert E. Tucker, 314-621-5757, KORTENHOF & ELY, 1015
Locust Street, Suite 500, St. Louis, MO 63101, 314-621-5757. Peter
Boone Hoffman, KORTENHOF & ELY, 1015 Locust Street, Suite
500, St. Louis, MO 63101, 314-621-5757.

For E. LOUIS WERNER, JR., Defendant - Appellant: Robert S.
Allen, Gary Michael Smith, LEWIS & RICE, 611 Olive Street, Suite
1400, St. Louis, MO 63101, 314-444-7600.

Before JOHN R. GIBSON, BEAM, and MORRIS SHEPPARD
ARNOLD, Circuit Judge.

MORRIS SHEPPARD ARNOLD, Circuit Judge.

When two limited partnerships in which appellant had invested
became unprofitable, he and other investors sued Irving Cohen, their
general partner, for securities fraud. After summary judgment was
entered in favor of Cohen, he filed a suit for malicious prosecution
against appellant and the other plaintiffs in the fraud suit. Appellant
had purchased a homeowner's insurance policy ("Homeowner's
Policy") and a personal liability policy ("VIP Policy") from appellee,
both of which covered claims brought against him for damages due
to "personal injury . . . caused by an occurrence" that happened
"during the policy period." Both policies included "malicious
prosecution" in the definition of "personal injury." Appellant
demanded that Royal Indemnity defend and indemnify him in the
malicious prosecution suit, and appellee refused on the ground that

the relevant "occurrence" happened outside the policy period. Appellee then sought a declaratory judgment that it had no duty to defend or indemnify. The district court agreed with appellee and this appeal followed.

Appellant purchased his policies after he brought the fraud suit but before it was decided. The insurer argues that the "occurrence" causing the "personal injury," if any, was the filing of that suit and that no coverage is provided since the occurrence arose outside the policy period. Appellant, on the other hand, posits that the relevant occurrence was the termination of the fraud suit, since under Missouri law no "personal injury" arises until that time. Appellant relies here on the familiar rule that a malicious prosecution action could not accrue until the relevant suit terminated in his opponent's favor. *See Euge v. LeMay Bank & Trust Co.*, 386 S.W.2d 398, 399 (Mo. 1965); *Walkenhorst v. Lowell H. Liston & Co.*, 752 S.W.2d 825, 827 (Mo. App. 1988). (There was a suggestion that Arizona law might be applicable here, but, if so, there is only a false conflict of laws, since Arizona law is the same as Missouri's. *See Bradshaw v. State Farm Mut. Auto. Ins. Co.*, 157 Ariz. 411, 758 P. 2d 1313, 1319 (Ariz. 1988)).

The cases on this question were analyzed by the district court in a lucid and well-reasoned opinion. As the district judge noted, almost all of the courts that have considered the matter have accepted the insurer's argument, even in the face of policy language that offered stronger support for appellant's position than does that contained in the policy relevant here. Many of these cases emphasize that a contrary rule might well enable plaintiffs to lull an unwary insurer into extending coverage after they perceive an impending difficulty from a suit in which they are already engaged. *See, e.g., Southern Md. Agric. Ass'n, Inc. v. Bituminous Casualty Corp.*, 539 F. Supp. 1295, 1302 (D. Md. 1982); *Zurich Ins. Co. v. Peterson*, 188 Cal. App. 3d 438; 232 Cal. Rptr. 807, 812 (Ct. App. 1986); *S. Freedman & Sons, Inc. v. Hartford Fire Ins. Co.*, 396 A.2d 195, 199 (D.C. 1978); *Patterson Tallow Co. v. Royal Globe Ins. Co.*, 89 N.J. 24, 444 A.2d 579, 585 (N.J. 1982). We believe that the Supreme Court of Missouri would be persuaded by the reasoning of these cases. We note, too, that we think it improbable that the term "personal injury" is used in a technical sense to speak of a time when a cause of action has fully matured. It is more likely intended to describe the time when harm begins to ensue, when injury occurs to the person, that is, in this case, when the relevant law suit is filed.

For the reasons indicated, we affirm the judgment of the district court.

DISSENT

JOHN R. GIBSON, Circuit Judge, dissenting.

I respectfully dissent.

In a sense, the court's opinion today runs contrary to the rule announced in our earlier decision involving the very malicious prosecution action with which we now deal. In *Cohen v. Lupo*, 927 F.2d 363 (8th Cir.), *cert. denied*, 116 L. Ed. 2d 142, 112 S. Ct. 180 (1991), we stated:

> The nucleus of operative fact necessary to maintain an action for malicious prosecution includes the conclusion of the underlying action. Whether Cohen would be victorious in the *Bastien* litigation could not have been determined until the conclusion of that case.

> . . .

> In Missouri, malicious prosecution requires proof that: (1) the underlying offending lawsuit was initiated or maintained without probable cause; . . . [and] (3) the proceeding terminated in favor of the defendant. . . .

Id. at 365.

While the court today recognizes this rule, its holding ignores it. Certainly, the maintenance of the action is a continuing wrong, and the definition of occurrence in the policy includes "exposure to conditions, which results during the policy period" in personal injury. "Personal injury," however, in turn is defined to include injury arising out of malicious prosecution; there was no malicious prosecution injury, and no claim to be covered by the policy until the *Bastien* litigation concluded. In *Roess v. St. Paul Fire and Marine Insurance Co.*, 383 F. Supp. 1231, 1235 (M.D. Fla. 1974), and *Security Mutual Casualty Co. v. Harbor Insurance Co.*, 65 Ill. App. 3d 198, 382 N.E.2d 1, 6, 21 Ill. Dec. 707 (Ill. App. 1978), *rev'd on other grounds*, 77 Ill. 2d 446, 397 N.E.2d 839, 34 Ill. Dec. 167 (Ill. 1979), courts held there was coverage under similar circumstances.

The court displays a great solicitude toward "an unwary insurer". The insurers, however, choose the language for their policies. They may include malicious prosecution or not, and further may require policy applicants to provide information on pending lawsuits to use in determining whether to insure such risks. Of the several common law torts enumerated in the definition of personal injury, only malicious prosecution may involve conduct that extends over a period of time, but requires termination of a lawsuit to reach fruition as a claim. In the record before us, Royal obtained information from Werner that he had no unusual hobbies, traveled 60 days per year and owned a

dachshund and a cockapoo. [1] If an insurer can require such information, it certainly could have required information about pending lawsuits, and upon this information could have made an educated decision to write the policy or decline it.

> 1 We so interpret a questionnaire, which actually reads "Dauchsand" and "Kocapo".

I would reverse the judgment of the district court and hold that there was coverage under the policy.

**RUSSELL STOVER and
MARGE STOVER,
Husband and Wife, Plaintiffs,
v.
EAGLE PRODUCTS, INC.,
Defendant.**

Case No. 93-4047-SAC
UNITED STATES DISTRICT COURT
FOR THE DISTRICT OF KANSAS
896 F. Supp. 1085
August 17, 1995

For RUSSELL STOVER, husband, MARGE STOVER, wife, plaintiffs: Gavin Fritton, Wallace, Saunders, Austin, Brown & Enochs, Chartered, Overland Park, KS. G. Michael Fatall, Sanders & Simpson, P.C., Kansas City, MO.

For EAGLE PRODUCTS INC, defendant: James P. Nordstrom, Donald Patterson, Fisher, Patterson, Sayler & Smith, Topeka, KS.

Sam A. Crow, U.S. District Judge

MEMORANDUM AND ORDER

In this diversity of citizenship, products liability action, the plaintiffs, Russell and Marge Stover, claim that they have suffered economic loss due to the breaches of the implied warranty of fitness for a particular purpose and of the implied warranty of merchantability by the defendant, Eagle Products, Inc, a seller of dog food. The Stovers also contend that Eagle Products is liable under a theory of strict liability. The Stovers claim that Eagle Products' feed product was low in calcium, causing certain defects and abnormalities in their dogs which they raised for sale. The Stovers seek damages in the amount of $ 300,000.

This case comes before the court upon the following motions filed by Eagle Products:

1. Motion for Summary Judgment (Dk. 107).

2. Motion to Strike Affidavit (Dk. 114).

Eagle Products' motion for summary judgment is primarily a challenge on the issue of causation--Have the plaintiffs presented sufficient evidence for a rational factfinder to conclude that there was a causal relationship between the Stovers' use of Eagle Products' dog food and the defects and abnormalities in the Stovers' dogs? Specifically, Eagle Products argues that the testimony of the plaintiffs' experts does not meet the standards of admissibility under the Federal Rules of Evidence and therefore it is entitled to summary judgment. Eagle Products also argues that the Stovers' claim based upon a breach of the implied warranty of fitness for a particular purpose fails as a matter of law.

Eagle Products' motion to strike challenges the April 5, 1995, affidavit of the plaintiffs' expert, Dr. Frederick W. Oehme. Dr. Oehme is a licensed veterinarian and an expert in veterinary toxicology at Kansas State University in Manhattan, Kansas. Eagle Products contends that the affidavit fails to comply with D. Kan. Rule 206(c) or Fed. R. Civ. P. 56(e). Eagle Products argues that the post-deposition affidavit is merely a sham--drafted in an obvious attempt to evade summary judgment.

The Stovers oppose Eagle Products' motion for summary judgment and motion to strike. The Stovers contend that Dr. Oehme is a qualified expert and that his opinion is sufficient to survive Eagle Products' attack. The Stovers suggest that Eagle Products' arguments challenging Dr. Oehme's opinions go to the weight, rather than the admissibility of the evidence. The Stovers contend that the issue of causation is one for the jury and that Eagle Products' motion should be denied.

The Stovers contend that Eagle Products' motion to strike is basically an invitation by the defendant for the court to sit as the trier of fact. The Stovers argue that Eagle Products has failed to demonstrate that Dr. Oehme is not qualified or that there are insufficient facts to support his opinion.

Brief Summary of the Facts [1]

1 In light of the court's decision, it appears unnecessary to at this juncture to use the court's limited resources to set forth the uncontroverted facts in

exacting detail. The court has simply set forth a short summary of the facts necessary to explain the court's decision.

In January of 1989, the Stovers began their puppy operation with two small dogs. Marge Stover primarily managed the operation. Eventually the breeding stock was built to a population of approximately three hundred, including fourteen toy breeds, bishons, Chihuahuas, Japanese Chins, **dachshunds**, Maltese, papillions, Pekingese, pomeranians, toy poodles, pugs, Shih Tzus, shelties, yorkies, westies, cockers and basset hounds. Marge Stover became licensed by the State of Kansas as a dog kennel keeper in 1989. As dogs were purchased to increase the number of breeding stock, none of the dogs were inspected by a veterinarian.

Initially the Stovers' dogs were fed a dog food called "K-9." Almost all of the dogs were fed by a technique allowing the dogs to eat their fill. Pups were fed a product called Eukanuba, a non-Eagle Products product. Beginning in November 1989, adult dogs were fed products manufactured by Eagle Products. The Stovers continued feeding Eagle Products to their breeding stock until January 22, 1992, when the purchase on that date was returned for a refund. The only non-Eagle Products food fed their pups was Eukanuba, which was fed to puppies at five weeks, as well as to nursing mothers.

At the time the Stovers began using Eagle Products' feed, the Stovers noticed no problems associated with the use of Eagle Products' products; losses in the kennel were acceptable and minimal. Marge Stover eventually discontinued using Eagle Products' products because the dogs were not eating it, not because of any other problem. Marge Stover had the feed analyzed, but the report revealed no toxins, aflatoxins, or mycotoxins in the feed. In March of 1992, samples of the feed were again analyzed, but no sign of aflatoxin were found.

The Stovers attribute several defects and abnormalities to the use of Eagle Products' feed. The Stovers claim that low calcium in Eagle Products' dog food caused the problems in their dogs. In an affidavit attached to the plaintiffs' response to Eagle Products' motion for summary judgment, Dr. Oehme states in part:

74

I have rendered opinions in this case in my "Expert Report" and in my deposition that the anomalies occurring at the Stover Kennels in late 1991 and early 1992 were most probably the result of calcium deficiencies in the Eagle Dog FOOd that was being fed to the dogs at the Stover Kennels during that period of time. I have stated this opinion to a reasonable degree of certainty.

. . .

It remains my opinion that the Stover's (sic) losses are the direct result of a nutritional deficit in the Eagle food product that was being fed during the time period in question."

Affidavit of Frederick W. Oehme, dated April 5, 1995.

Summary Judgment Standards

Although Kansas law supplies the elements of the Stovers' claims, [2] federal law governs the court's determination of whether Eagle Products is entitled to summary judgment. *See Richter v. Limax Intern., Inc.*, 45 F.3d 1464, 1470 (10th Cir. 1995). A court grants a motion for summary judgment if a genuine issue of material fact does not exist and if the movant is entitled to judgment as a matter of law. *Anderson v. Liberty Lobby, Inc.*, 477 U.S. 242, 250, 91 L. Ed. 2d 202, 106 S. Ct. 2505 (1986). The substantive law governing the suit dictates which facts are material or not. *Id.* at 248. "Only disputes over facts that might affect the outcome of the suit under the governing law will ... preclude summary judgment." *Id.* There are no genuine issues for trial if the record taken as a whole would not persuade a rational trier of fact to find for the nonmoving party. *Matsushita Elec. Indust. Co. v. Zenith Radio Corp.*, 475 U.S. 574, 587, 89 L. Ed. 2d 538, 106 S. Ct. 1348 (1986). "There are cases where the evidence is so weak that the case does not raise a genuine issue of fact." *Burnette v. Dow Chemical Co.*, 849 F.2d 1269, 1273 (10th Cir. 1988).

2 Eagle Products argues, and the Stovers apparently agree, that the substantive law of Kansas applies in this case. *See Phillips USA v. Allflex USA*, 869 F. Supp. 842 (D. Kan. 1994) (Kansas follows *lex loci delicti* choice of law for tort claims).

The movant's burden under Rule 56 of the Federal Rules of Civil Procedure is to lay out the basis of its motion and to "point to those portions of the record that demonstrate an absence of a genuine issue of material fact given the relevant substantive law." *Thomas v. Wichita Coca-Cola Bottling Co.,* 968 F.2d 1022, 1024 (10th Cir.), *cert. denied,* 121 L. Ed. 2d 566, 113 S. Ct. 635 (1992). "A movant is not required to provide evidence negating an opponent's claim." *Committee for First Amendment v. Campbell,* 962 F.2d 1517, 1521 (10th Cir. 1992) (citation omitted).

If the moving party meets its burden, then it becomes the nonmoving party's burden to show the existence of a genuine issue of material fact. *Bacchus Industries, Inc. v. Arvin Industries, Inc.,* 939 F.2d 887, 891 (10th Cir. 1991); *see Martin v. Nannie and the Newborns, Inc.,* 3 F.3d 1410, 1414 (10th Cir. 1993) ("If the moving party meets this burden, the non-moving party then has the burden to come forward with specific facts showing that there is a genuine issue for trial as to elements essential to the non-moving party's case."). When the nonmoving party will have the burden of proof at trial, "'Rule 56(e) ... [then] requires the nonmoving party to go beyond the pleadings and by her own affidavits or by the 'depositions, answers to interrogatories, and admissions on file,' designate 'specific facts showing that there is a genuine issue for trial.'" *Mares v. ConAgra Poultry Co., Inc.,* 971 F.2d 492, 494 (10th Cir. 1992) (quoting *Celotex Corp. v. Catrett,* 477 U.S. 317, 324, 91 L. Ed. 2d 265, 106 S. Ct. 2548 (1986)). "Unsubstantiated allegations carry no probative weight in summary judgment proceedings." *Phillips v. Calhoun,* 956 F.2d 949, 951 (10th Cir. 1992) (citations omitted); *see Martin,* 3 F.3d at 1414 (non-moving party cannot rest on the mere allegations in the pleadings). "Speculation does not create a *genuine* issue of fact; instead, it creates a false issue, the demolition of which is a primary goal of summary judgment." *Hedberg v. Indiana Bell Telephone Co., Inc.,* 47 F.3d 928, 929 (7th Cir. 1995); *see Vega v. Kodak Caribbean, Ltd.,* 3 F.3d 476, 479 (1st Cir. 1993) ("Optimistic conjecture, unbridled speculation, or hopeful surmise will not suffice."). The court views the evidence of record and draws inferences from it in the light most favorable to the nonmoving party. *Burnette v. Dow Chemical Co.,* 849 F.2d at 1273.

More than a "disfavored procedural shortcut," summary judgment is an important procedure "designed 'to secure the just, speedy and inexpensive determination of every action.' Fed. R. Civ. P. 1." *Celotex Corp. v. Catrett*, 477 U.S. 317, 327, 91 L. Ed. 2d 265, 106 S. Ct. 2548 (1986). At the same time, a summary judgment motion is not the chance for a court to act as the jury and determine witness credibility, weigh the evidence, or decide upon competing inferences. *Windon Third Oil and Gas v. Federal Deposit Ins.*, 805 F.2d 342, 346 (10th Cir. 1986), *cert. denied*, 480 U.S. 947, 94 L. Ed. 2d 791, 107 S. Ct. 1605 (1987).

Expert Testimony under Rules 702 and 703

Rule 702 of the Federal Rules of Evidence states:

> If scientific, technical, or other specialized knowledge will assist the trier of fact to understand the evidence or to determine a fact in issue, a witness qualified as an expert by knowledge, skill, experience, training, or education, may testify thereto in the form of an opinion or otherwise.

Rule 703 of the Federal Rules of Evidence states:
> The facts or data in the particular case upon which an expert bases an opinion or inference may be those perceived by or made known to the expert at or before the hearing. If of a type reasonably relied upon by experts in the particular field in forming opinions or inferences upon the subject, the facts or data need not be admissible in evidence.

" A trial judge has broad discretion in determining the competency of an expert witness." *Kloepfer v. Honda Motor Co.* 898 F.2d 1452, 1458 (10th Cir. 1990); *see Broadcort Capital Corp. v. Summa Medical Corp.*, 972 F.2d 1183, 1194-95 (10th Cir. (1992) (trial court did not abuse its discretion in finding that witness' general experience, education and training did not qualify him as an expert in the securities area).

In *Daubert v. Merrell Dow Pharmaceuticals, Inc.*, 509 U.S.   113 S. Ct. 2786, 125 L. Ed. 2d 469 (1993), the Supreme Court held that the Federal Rules of Evidence, not *Frye*, provide the standard for admitting expert scientific testimony in a federal trial. In *Frye v. United States*, 54 App. D.C. 46, 47, 293 F. 1013 (1923), the court had developed a "general acceptance" test to determine the admissibility of expert testimony--under the *Frye* rule, expert opinion based on a scientific technique is inadmissible unless the technique is "generally accepted" as reliable in the relevant scientific community. The Supreme Court held that "nothing in the text of [Rule 702] establishes "general acceptance as an absolute requisite to admissibility." 125 L. Ed. 2d at 480.

> That the *Frye* test was displaced by the Rules of Evidence does not mean, however, that the Rules themselves place no limits on the admissibility of purportedly scientific evidence. Nor is the trial judge disabled from screening such evidence. To the contrary, under the Rules the trial judge must ensure that any and all scientific testimony or evidence admitted is not only relevant, but reliable.
>
> The primary locus of this obligation is Rule 702, which clearly contemplates some degree of regulation of the subjects and theories about which an expert may testify. "If scientific, technical, or other specialized knowledge will assist the trier of fact to understand the evidence or to determine a fact in issue" an expert "may testify thereto." The subject of an expert's testimony must be "scientific . . . knowledge." The adjective "scientific" implies a grounding in the methods and procedures of science. Similarly, the word "knowledge" connotes more than subjective belief or unsupported speculation. The term "applies to any body of known facts or to any body of ideas inferred from such facts or accepted as truths on good grounds." *Webster's Third New International Dictionary* 1252 (1986). Of course, it would be unreasonable to conclude that the subject of scientific testimony must be "known" to a certainty; arguably, there are no certainties in science. . . But, in order to qualify as "scientific knowledge," an inference or assertion must be derived by the scientific method. Proposed testimony must be supported by appropriate validation--i.e., "good grounds," based on what is known. In short, the requirement that an expert's testimony pertain to "scientific knowledge" establishes a standard of evidentiary reliability.
>
> Rule 702 further requires that the evidence or testimony "assist the trier of fact to understand the evidence or to determine a fact in issue." This condition goes primarily to relevance. "Expert testimony which does not relate to any issue in the case is not relevant and, ergo, non-helpful." 3 Weinstein & Berger P 702[02], p. 702-18.

125 L. Ed. 2d at 480-481 (footnotes omitted).

> Faced with a proffer of expert scientific testimony, then, the trial judge must determine at the outset, pursuant to Rule 104(a),

whether the expert is proposing to testify to (1) scientific knowledge that (2) will assist the trier of fact to understand or determine a fact in issue. This entails a preliminary assessment of whether the reasoning or methodology underlying the testimony is scientifically valid and of whether that reasoning or methodology properly can be applied to the facts in issue.

125 L. Ed. 2d at 482 (footnotes omitted).

In deciding whether an expert's testimony is scientific knowledge that will assist the trier of fact to understand or determine a fact in issue, the district courts may consider any of the following non-exclusive list of factors:

> (1) Is the theory or technique capable of being (and has been) tested? ("The criterion of scientific status of a theory is its falsifiability, or refutability, or testability.");

> (2) Whether the theory or technique has been subjected to peer review and publication?;

> (3) In the case of a particular scientific technique, the court ordinarily should consider the known or potential rate of error, and the existence and maintenance of standards controlling the technique's operation;

> (4) Finally, "general acceptance" can yet have a bearing on the inquiry. "A 'reliability assessment does not require, although it does permit, explicit identification of a relevant scientific community and express determination of a particular degree of acceptance within that community.'" 125 L. Ed. 2d at 483 (quoting *United States v. Downing* 753 F.2d 1224, 1238). "Widespread acceptance can be an important factor in ruling particular evidence admissible, and a 'known technique that has been able to attract only minimal support within the community,' *Downing,* supra, at 1238, may properly be viewed with skepticism."

125 L. Ed. 2d at 483. The Supreme Court emphasized that the inquiry envisioned by Rule 702 is a flexible one. 125 L. Ed. 2d at 483-484.

"The 'touchstone' of admissibility is helpfulness to the trier of fact." *Werth v. Makita Elec. Works, Ltd.,* 950 F.2d 643, 648 (10th Cir. 1991). "Moreover, 'a lack of specialization does not affect the admissibility of the [expert's] opinion but only its weight,' *Wheeler v. John Deere Co.,*

935 F.2d 1090, 1100 (10th Cir. 1991), although 'an expert must have skill in the matter to which the subject relates.' *Id.* (quoting *Petition of Central Kansas Elec. Co-op, Inc.*, 224 Kan. 308, 582 P.2d 228, 236 (1978)). "An expert must, however, stay within the reasonable confines of his subject area and cannot render expert opinions of an entirely different field or discipline." *Wheeler*, 935 F.2d at 1100.

An expert, relying upon his experience and knowledge of causation factors, may express an opinion which draws a rational conclusion as to causation. *Orth v. Emerson Elec. Co., White-Rodgers Div.*, 980 F.2d 632, 637 (10th Cir. 1992). "Absolute certainty is not required." *Id.*

Theories of Recovery

In the pretrial order, the Stovers contend that Eagle Products is liable under one or more of the following legal theories: (1) breach of the implied warranty of fitness of purpose; (2) breach of the implied warranty of merchantability; or (3) strict liability.

Implied Warranty of Fitness for a Particular Purpose

Eagle Products contends that this claim is easily dispensed as there is no evidence to support the Stovers' implied warranty of fitness for a particular purpose. Eagle Products argues that there is no evidence that it supplied dog food for any purpose other than the feeding of the Stovers' dogs. Because the feeding of dogs is the ordinary use of its products, the Stovers' claim based upon the implied warranty of fitness for a particular purpose fails as a matter of law. Instead, the Stovers must pursue a claim based upon breach of the implied warranty of merchantability. The Stovers do not directly respond to each of these arguments, but "concede that the breach of implied warranty of merchantability is mutually exclusive of the breach of implied warranty of fitness of purpose."

Eagle Products is entitled to summary judgment on the Stovers' claim based upon the implied warranty of fitness for a particular purpose. " The provisions of K.S.A. 84-2-315, covering the warranty of fitness for a *particular purpose,* are frequently confused with the implied warranty of merchantability which covers fitness for *ordinary purposes.* The warranty for a *particular purpose* is narrower, more specific, and more precise" than the implied warranty of merchantability." *Smith v.*

Stewart, 233 Kan. 904, 667 P.2d 358, Syl. P 3, 667 P.2d 358 (1983); *see Duffee by and Through Thornton v. Murray Ohio Mfg.*, 866 F. Supp. 1321, 1322-1323 (D. Kan. 1994). "When goods are acquired for the *ordinary purposes* for which such goods are generally used, no implied warranty of fitness for a *particular purpose* arises. A use for ordinary purposes falls within the concept of merchantability." *Smith*, 233 Kan. 904, 667 P.2d 358, Syl. P 4. As Eagle Products suggests, using dog food to feed dogs is the ordinary purpose of the product. *See, e.g., Duffee*, 866 F. Supp. at 1323 ("A child riding and braking his bicycle are not unusual, but customary uses of a children's bicycle."). Consequently, the Stovers' claim for breach of the implied warranty of fitness for a particular purpose fails as a matter of law.

Implied Warranty of Merchantability/Strict Liability

Eagle Products contends that it is entitled to judgment as a matter of law on the Stovers' remaining claims: breach of the implied warranty of merchantability and strict liability. Eagle Products contends that the Stovers have failed to prove a causal connection between low calcium in Eagle Products' dog food and the defects and abnormalities in the Stovers' dogs. Eagle Products contends that the opinions of Stovers' experts are deficient in the following respects: (1) they are unable to state any conclusion to a reasonable degree of certainty; (2) the methodology used by the plaintiffs' experts is deficient as a matter of law; (3) the facts relied upon by the plaintiffs' experts in reaching their opinions are not the type relied upon by experts in the particular field in forming opinions; Eagle Products essentially asks the court to assume its role as "gatekeeper" to exclude the testimony of Dr. Oehme. *See Robinson v. Missouri Pacific R. Co.,* 16 F.3d 1083, 1088 (10th Cir. 1994) ("The Supreme Court's recent decision in *Daubert v. Merrell Dow Pharmaceuticals, Inc.,* U.S. , 113 S. Ct. 2786, 125 L. Ed. 2d 469 (1993), reinforces the trial court's special role as gatekeeper with respect to expert evidence and opinion."); or (4) Dr. Oehme's affidavit, attached to the Stovers' response to Eagle Products' motion for summary judgment is a sham and should be stricken.

Analysis

"Regardless of the theory upon which recovery is sought for injury in a products liability case, proof that a defect in the product caused the injury is a prerequisite to recovery." *Wilcheck v. Doonan Truck & Equipment, Inc.,* 220 Kan. 230, 235, 552 P.2d 938 (1976); *see, e.g., Duffee, By & Through Thornton v. Murray Ohio Mfg.,* 879 F. Supp. 1078, 1083 (D. Kan. 1995) (no proof that defendant's lack of warnings has a causal connection with the accident); *Lane v. Redman Mobile Homes, Inc.,* 5 Kan. App. 2d 729, 624 P.2d 984, Syl. P 2, 624 P.2d 984, *rev. denied,* 229 Kan. 670 (1981) (rule applies to negligence, breach of implied warranties and strict liability claims). " The cause of an injury is that 'which in natural and continuous sequence, unbroken by an efficient intervening cause, produces the injury and without which the injury would not have occurred, the injury being the natural and probable consequence of the wrongful act.'" *Voelkel v. General Motors Corp,* 846 F. Supp. 1468, 1475 (D. Kan.) (quoting *Wilcheck,* 220 Kan. at 235), *on reconsideration,* 846 F. Supp. 1482 (D. Kan.), *aff'd,* 43 F.3d 1484 (10th Cir. 1994). "Proof of injury during use of the product, without more, is insufficient to establish that a defect in the product caused the injury." *Voelkel,* 846 F. Supp. at 1475 (citing *Wilcheck,* 220 Kan. at 235-36).

When advancing theories of breach of implied warranty of merchantability and strict liability in a products liability case, the plaintiff must prove three elements common to these theories: "(1) There must be a defective product; (2) the defect must have existed at the time the product left the manufacturer's possession or control; and (3) the defect must have caused the injury sustained by the plaintiffs." *Lane,* 5 Kan. App. 2d at 729 Syl. P 2; *See, e.g., Mays v. Ciba-Geigy Corp.,* 233 Kan. 38, 53, 661 P.2d 348 (1983) (A prima facie strict liability case includes proof that the product's condition was unreasonably dangerous and that the condition existed when it left the defendant's control); *Black v. Don Schmid Motor, Inc.,* 232 Kan. 458, 657 P.2d 517, Syl. P 5, 657 P.2d 517 (1983) (For an implied warranty claim, the buyer must show the goods were defective and the defect existed at the time of sale). "The elements to each of the plaintiff's different legal theories can be proved by direct or circumstantial evidence." *Voelkel,* 846 F. Supp. at 1476.

Eagle Products contends that the plaintiffs have at best demonstrated a loose temporal relationship between the use of its products and the defects and abnormalities in the Stovers' dogs. While Eagle Products raises numerous valid points, the court will not grant summary judgment on the record before it. Eagle Products' arguments notwithstanding, Dr. Oehme's April 5, 1995, affidavit causes the court to have serious doubt as to the propriety of concluding, as a matter or law, that the plaintiffs have failed to present sufficient facts upon which a rational factfinder could conclude that Eagle Products' feed caused a portion of the Stovers' losses. [3]

> 3 Eagle Products correctly argues that a party may not use a sham affidavit simply to create a genuine issue of material fact precluding summary judgment. *See Durtsche v. America Colloid Co.*, 958 F.2d 1007, 1010, n.2 (10th Cir. 1992); *Franks v. Nimmo,* 796 F.2d 1230 (10th Cir. 1986); *Barber v. Hallmark Cards, Inc.*, No. 93-4087- SAC, 1994 U.S. Dist. LEXIS 14955, at * 14-19 (D. Kan. Sept. 14, 1994) (discussing sham affidavits and striking portions of plaintiff's affidavit). The court is simply unwilling at this point in time to conclude on the record before it that Dr. Oehme's affidavit is a sham.

The court believes that the better and more prudent course is to deny, without prejudice, Eagle Products' motion for summary judgment and motion to strike affidavit. Dr. Oehme's affidavit was prepared after he was deposed in October of 1994. Although the pretrial order states that discovery shall be complete on or before January 31, 1995, the court authorizes Eagle Products to depose Dr. Oehme with regard to April 5, 1995, affidavit. Within ten days of the date of this order, Eagle Products shall indicate to the court in writing whether it intends to depose Dr. Oehme and the date he is to be deposed. Within thirty days of the date Dr. Oehme is deposed, Eagle Products may filed a second or renewed motion for summary judgment on the plaintiffs' remaining claims. If no motion is filed, the case will simply proceed to trial.

The court recognizes that this procedure will require the parties to invest additional time and resources. The court also recognizes that none of the parties requested this alternative relief. The court believes, however, that this procedure will ultimately be beneficial to both the court and the parties. This procedure affords each party the opportunity to re-evaluate their respective positions in light of Dr. Oehme's deposition concerning his April 5, 1995, affidavit.

Moreover, even if summary judgment is not granted, this procedure may speed the court's assessment of the admissibility of the plaintiffs' evidence at trial. *See* Fed. R. Evid. 104(a); *Daubert,* 125 L. Ed. 2d at 482.

IT IS THEREFORE ORDERED that Eagle Products' motion for summary judgment (Dk. 107) is granted in part and denied in part without prejudice. Eagle Products is granted summary judgment on the Stovers' claim based upon the implied warranty of fitness for a particular purpose. Eagle Products' motion for summary judgment on the Stovers' remaining claims is denied without prejudice.

IT IS FURTHER ORDERED that Eagle Products' motion to strike (Dk. 114) is denied without prejudice.

Dated this 17th day of August, 1995, Topeka, Kansas.

Sam A. Crow, U.S. District Judge

MICHAEL GARCIA, Petitioner,
-against-
ISRAEL RIVERA, Respondent.

07 Civ. 2535 (PAC) (AJP)

UNITED STATES DISTRICT COURT FOR THE
SOUTHERN DISTRICT OF NEW YORK

August 16, 2007, Decided

Michael Garcia, Petitioner, Pro se, Coxsackie, NY.

ANDREW J. PECK, United States Magistrate Judge.

REPORT AND RECOMMENDATION

ANDREW J. PECK, United States Magistrate Judge:

To the Honorable Paul A. Crotty, United States District Judge:

Pro se petitioner Michael Garcia seeks a writ of habeas corpus from his February 23, 2004 conviction, after a bench trial in Supreme Court, New York County, of second degree attempted assault, third degree criminal possession of a weapon, third degree criminal mischief, three counts of third degree assault, three counts of endangering the welfare of a child, and aggravated cruelty to animals, and sentence of "concurrent and consecutive sentences aggregating to 7 1/2 to 15 years." (See Dkt. No. 1: Pet. Att.: Garcia 1st Dep't Br. at 1.) Garcia's habeas petition raises the same five grounds that he raised on direct appeal: (1) "[t]he [trial] court abused its discretion as a matter of law by sua sponte considering attempted second-degree assault as a lesser included offense of attempted first-degree assault" (Pet. P 13, incorporating Pet. Att.: Garcia 1st Dep't Br. at 31-41); (2) Garcia's "conviction for the felony of aggravated cruelty to animals violates due process" (id. at 42-48, citation omitted); (3) "proof of third-degree criminal mischief was insufficient" (id. at 49-55); (4) "the sentencing court improperly adjudicated [Garcia] a second violent felony offender" (id. at 56-57); and (5) Garcia's "aggregate 7 1/2 to

15 year sentence is excessive and should be reduced in the interests of justice" (id. at 57-58).

For the reasons set forth below, Garcia's habeas petition should be DENIED.

FACTS

The Prosecution Case at Trial

On August 2, 2003, petitioner Michael Garcia resided with his girlfriend Emelie Martinez in her three-bedroom apartment at 549 FDR Drive in Manhattan. (Dkt. No. 7: Trial Transcript ["Tr."] 205-07, 435-36.) Martinez's three children, 9 year old Juan, 8 year old Crystal and 5 year old Emaleeann, also lived in the apartment, along with Jesus Rabassa, an 18-year-old homosexual high school student. (Tr. 204-07, 302-03, 435-37.) Martinez and her three children owned two dogs, a cat, and three goldfish; Martinez had purchased the goldfish a year and a half before the incident. (Tr. 204-05, 378-79, 436-37.)

At approximately 3:00 a.m., Martinez awoke to Garcia standing over her, holding a fish tank. (Tr. 208, 295, 297-98, 309.) When Martinez asked Garcia what he was doing, Garcia threw the fish tank into the television, breaking both, and told Martinez, "'That could have been you.'" (Tr. 208-09, 298-301.) Garcia also "yanked" out items from Martinez's home theater system and damaged Juan's VCR, the receiver and a portion of a nearby glass wall unit. (Tr. 209-15, 263-64, 273, 310, 499, 512.) Garcia accused Martinez of cheating on him with one of her neighbors and with Rabassa. (Tr. 217, 301-02, 304.)

As they argued over Garcia's accusations, Juan stepped out of his room and Emaleeann and Crystal stood behind him "screaming and crying." (Tr. 209, 306.) Garcia turned to Juan and asked, "'Would you like to see something?'" (Tr. 209, 305-06, 374, 513.) Garcia stomped on one of the goldfish, killing it. (Tr. 209, 306, 374, 512-13.)

Martinez spent some time calming down her children and putting them back to bed. (Tr. 313.) Martinez and Garcia cleaned up the mess, then went to sleep. (Tr. 309, 311-13.)

Martinez and Garcia woke up around 9:00 a.m. and resumed arguing. (Tr. 218, 314-15.) At about 11:00 a.m., Martinez borrowed twenty dollars from Rabassa and went to the supermarket with Garcia. (Tr. 218-19, 314-15.) They argued about whether Garcia was having "sexual contact" with Martinez's friend. (Tr. 220-21, 223, 315-16, 318-19, 321.) When they returned to the apartment building, in the elevator Garcia threw a gallon of milk at Martinez's head. (Tr. 224, 228, 268-69, 321-25, 514.) Martinez ducked and the milk container hit the elevator wall. (Tr. 224, 228, 325.) Martinez looked down and Garcia forced Martinez's head up by shoving his knuckles under her chin and grabbing her neck. (Tr. 224-25, 321-27.)

Martinez cried as she and Garcia entered the apartment. (Tr. 225, 440.) When her children asked her what was wrong, Martinez responded that Garcia hit her. (Tr. 225-26, 229.) Garcia said that he had not hit Martinez and they argued again. (Tr. 226.) Garcia calmed down and told Martinez that he wanted to speak with her in the bedroom. (Tr. 226, 231, 327.) When Martinez entered the bedroom, Garcia closed the door, grabbed Martinez by her right hand and threw her onto the bed. (Tr. 226-27, 231, 328.) Garcia punched Martinez multiple times in her head and face and said, "'You said I hit you. Now you got a reason to say I hit you.'" (Tr. 231-32, 328.) One of the punches cut the inside of Martinez's mouth, causing her to bleed. (Tr. 232-34.) The blow to her mouth occasionally causes Martinez to mispronounce words and slur her speech. (Tr. 232-33.) Garcia's punches also caused bumps on Martinez's head and swelling on the left side of her face. (Tr. 234-36.)

After Garcia "stood away," Martinez went to the bathroom to clean up. (Tr. 236, 338-39, 441.) Garcia came into the bathroom and ordered Martinez to go back to the bedroom. (Tr. 238, 339, 342.) Garcia closed the bedroom door, climbed onto Martinez, placed his knees on her chest, and began choking her with his right hand. (Tr. 238-40, 342-43.) Martinez had trouble breathing and initially was unable to call for help. (Tr. 241, 342-45, 444.) When Martinez sat up, she "started throwing up blood." (Tr. 265, 343, 444, 515.) Garcia took a "gravity knife" [1] out of his left pocket but dropped it as Martinez struggled to free herself. (Tr. 239-40, 261, 290-93, 343-47.) Martinez yelled out her son's name. (Tr. 240-42, 345-47, 378, 440.) Garcia threw Martinez onto a computer chair next to the bed and began "mushing" her head forcibly to the side. (Tr. 240-42, 343, 347-50.) Martinez pleaded, "'Michael, stop. The kids.'" (Tr. 243.)

1 The difference between a gravity knife and a switch blade is that a switchblade opens by pressing a button while a gravity knife opens by a "snapping motion"; also, a gravity knife could be left "sort of in a halfway position where it's slightly open making a V between the handle and the blade, and it could rest in that position." (Tr. 615-16.)

After hearing Martinez scream, Juan and Rabassa entered the room and Juan jumped on Garcia's back and began biting and scratching Garcia. (Tr. 242-43, 350, 443-45, 515.) Garcia grabbed Juan and flung him "like a rag doll against the wall." (Tr. 243-44.) Rabassa told Garcia to stop hitting Martinez. (Tr. 444-45, 520.) Garcia struck Rabassa several times causing him to fall to the ground. (Tr. 244, 350, 445, 496-98, 520.)

Rabassa ran downstairs to a neighbor's apartment and called 911. (Tr. 454-56.) Juan also called 911. (Tr. 523-24, 530-31.) Martinez ran out of the bedroom and her daughters Crystal and Emaleean clung onto her. (Tr. 246-49, 445, 454.) Garcia tried to pull them off and ripped Crystal's dress. (Tr. 247-49.) Martinez and her daughters ran out of the apartment. (Tr. 249, 362-63, 454.) After realizing that Juan was not with her, Martinez went back to the apartment to get her son. (Tr. 249, 253, 363, 454.) Martinez's dog, Rusty, tried to grab onto Garcia, but Garcia grabbed Rusty by the neck and slammed him to the floor. (Tr. 250-51, 515, 522-25.) Garcia poured water into the broken television. (Tr. 524.) Shortly afterwards, Garcia fled the apartment as well. (Tr. 255.) Garcia looked for Rabassa at a neighbor's house and threatened to "kill him" and Martinez. (Tr. 456-57.)

At approximately 11:45 a.m., responding to a radio report of an assault, Police Officer Olajumoke Ajasa and her partner, Officer Nozile, arrived at the apartment. (Tr. 255, 395.) Officer Judith Hernandez arrived a few moments later. (Tr. 290, 403-04, 591, 610.) Martinez was inside the apartment and was "nervous, scared" and "shaking." (Tr. 397.) Martinez's mouth was swollen and she had blood on her shirt and feet. (Tr. 397, 593.) Martinez told the police what had happened and gave the police Garcia's name and description. (Tr. 256-57, 399, 404, 411-14, 420-21, 593-94.) The police observed that the large-screen television was broken, the VCR and a wall unit were damaged, and debris from the broken fish tank was on the floor. (Tr. 398, 419, 591-92.) Officer Hernandez prepared a complaint report. (Tr. 607.) The officers left after about ten to fifteen minutes. (Tr. 409, 610.)

At around 2:00 p.m., Officers Ajasa, Nozile and Hernandez returned to Martinez's apartment with Officer Richard Black and Sergeant Vance. (Tr. 400-01, 409-10, 418-19, 423-24, 609.) The officers interviewed Martinez again and also interviewed Rabassa. (Tr. 401, 424, 430.) Officer Hernandez recovered a "silver[] gravity pocket knife" in the bedroom. (Tr. 422, 597-98.) The blade was clean but there was blood on the floor and the bed. (Tr. 426-29, 606.)

Later that day, Martinez and Rabassa went to Beth Israel Hospital. (Tr. 257, 340, 411, 480-82.) Rabassa had scratches and bruises on his back and face, a "sharp pain" in his neck and a swollen right eye. (Tr. 480-82, 489-94.) Rabassa was diagnosed with a mild concussion, temporarily wore a neck brace, and had headaches for two to three days. (Tr. 480-82.) Martinez's body was bruised and her mouth was swollen. (Tr. 233, 239, 277-81.) Martinez took Juan to the hospital the following day because he was complaining of a headache and a backache. (Tr. 257-58, 525-26.)

Martinez purchased the television Garcia damaged in May 2002 for $ 1,699.97. (Tr. 210, 215.) Martinez produced a post-dated store receipt for her television and home theater system. (Tr. 210, 213-15.) Martinez testified that a repairman gave her an estimate of $ 700 to professionally repair the television screen, but she could not afford to fix it. (Tr. 212, 270-71, 334, 336.) The rest of the home theater system cost $ 599.98. (Tr. 215.) The receiver was covered by a warranty, and Martinez had it fixed free of charge. (Tr. 212.) Martinez purchased the wall unit at a P.C. Richard's store in May 2003 for $ 1,500. (Tr. 215, 335.) Martinez testified that a furniture company estimated that the wall unit would cost $ 500 to repair. (Tr. 336.) Martinez purchased the fish, fish tank, stand, gravel, motor and other equipment at a Petland store for approximately $ 80. (Tr. 216.) Martinez also testified that the VCR cost $ 60. (Tr. 215-16, 337.)

The Defense Case at Trial and Reservation of Motions

The defense rested without calling any witnesses or presenting any evidence. (Tr. 624.)

Because it was a bench trial, Justice Kahn directed, without objection by the parties, that the defense motion for a trial order of dismissal be made in combination with the summations. (Tr. 624.) The parties also agreed to conduct the "precharge conference" together with closing arguments. (Tr. 624-25.) After hearing closing arguments, Justice Kahn adjourned the case for about a week to consider the motion arguments and the verdict. (Tr. 726.)

Verdict and Sentence

On January 30, 2004, Justice Kahn rendered her decision on the parties' motions and her verdict. (Tr. 727-42.)

First, Justice Kahn held that the court had the authority to sua sponte "charge itself on the lesser-included offense under Count One of Attempted Assault in the Second Degree, under Penal Law 120.05(1)." (Tr. 728-31.) Justice Kahn granted the defense motion for a trial order of dismissal of the first degree attempted assault charge. (Tr. 732.)

Justice Kahn denied the defense motion to dismiss the third degree criminal possession of a weapon charge. (Tr. 732-34.) Justice Kahn dismissed the second degree criminal mischief charge, but found it "perfectly appropriate for the Court to consider a lesser-included offense of Criminal Mischief in the Third Degree and lesser-included offense of Criminal Mischief in the Fourth Degree . . ." (Tr. 734-37.)

Justice Kahn denied the defense motion to dismiss as "unconstitutionally vague" the aggravated cruelty to animals count. (Tr. 737-39.)

Justice Kahn proceeded to announce her verdict in the bench trial. She found Garcia guilty of second degree attempted assault, third degree criminal possession of a weapon, third degree criminal mischief, three counts of third degree assault (on Martinez, Rabassa and Juan), three counts of endangering the welfare of a child (for each of Martinez's three children), and one count of aggravated cruelty to animals. (Tr. 739-41.)

At the start of the sentencing hearing, Garcia's counsel asked Justice Kahn to clarify the verdict. (Dkt. No. 7: 2/23/04 Sentencing Transcript ["S."] at 2.) Defense counsel asked whether Justice Kahn's verdict as to the second-degree assault count was based upon the milk-throwing incident in the elevator or the knife-removal incident in the bedroom. (S. 2-3.) Justice Kahn responded that her verdict on that count was based not on the elevator incident, but rather on "all of the defendant's conduct inside the apartment, including his beating of [Martinez] with his fists before he ever pulled the knife and then his pulling the knife later on." (S. 3-4.) Justice Kahn added that the prosecution had "charged the case and indicted the case" on the basis of "everything that happened inside the apartment." (S. 4.)

Defense counsel also asked Justice Kahn to clarify her basis for the aggravated cruelty to animals verdict. (S. 4.) Justice Kahn responded that "there was legally sufficient proof and proof beyond a reasonable doubt to establish that the second clause of the statute was met." (S. 4.)

Defense counsel moved pursuant to C.P.L. § 330.30 to set aside the verdict on the attempted second degree assault, criminal mischief and aggravated cruelty to animals counts based on insufficiency of the evidence. (S. 4-5.) Justice Kahn denied Garcia's motion to set aside the verdict. (S. 8-10.) As to the attempted second degree assault and criminal mischief counts, Justice Kahn stated that she could "rely on all of the evidence in the case to see whether or not a lesser included offense is supported by the evidence," and "that's what [she] found." (S. 8.) As to the value of the damaged merchandise with respect to the criminal mischief charge, Justice Kahn stated that she considered not only Martinez's testimony of the purchase prices and repair estimates, but also the photographs of the property, particularly of the damaged 47-inch television screen. (S. 8.) As to the aggravated cruelty to animals count, Justice Kahn realized that "we are traveling in new territory" since "there is not a lot of case law interpreting the aggravated cruelty to animal statute." (S. 9.) However, Justice Kahn stated that the evidence was sufficient to show both extreme pain and sadism, whether towards the goldfish or towards Juan. (S. 9-10.) Justice Kahn found that "the defendant's behavior was sadistic crushing the fish with his heel into the carpeting, and certainly was sadistic vis-a-vis the little nine year-old boy [Juan] who watched it, who the defendant called him into the room to watch it. . . . I think you can probably presume that severe pain was caused to the fish, too." (S. 9-10.) Justice Kahn added that she would issue "a written opinion explaining the reasons [she] denied the motion to dismiss on Constitutional grounds," which she would "provide to both sides as soon as it's available." (S. 9.) Justice Kahn's written opinion is discussed at pages 11-12 below.

Turning to sentencing, Justice Kahn found Garcia to be a second predicate violent felony offender, having previously been convicted of third degree criminal possession of a weapon. (S. 14-16.) Justice Kahn sentenced Garcia to 2 to 4 years for the second degree attempted assault. (S. 28-29.) Justice Kahn sentenced Garcia to 3- 1/2 to 7 years for third degree criminal possession of a weapon, "to run consecutively to all other counts." (S. 30.) Justice Kahn also sentenced Garcia to 2 to 4 years for third degree criminal mischief, "to be served consecutively to all other counts." (S. 30.) For the three third degree assault counts, Justice Kahn sentenced Garcia to one year. (S. 30-31.) Similarly, Garcia was sentenced to one year for the three endangering the welfare of a minor counts. (S. 31.) As to the "aggravated cruelty to animals under Agriculture & Markets Law 353-A," Justice Kahn sentenced Garcia to 2 years incarceration, to run "consecutively to all other counts." (S. 31-32.)

Justice Kahn concluded that "[t]his is a total of 7- 1/2 to 15 years to be served by [Garcia] in State prison." (S. 32.)

Justice Kahn's Written Decision on the Aggravated Cruelty to Animals Charge

Justice Kahn issued her written decision on March 11, 2004. People v. Garcia, 3 Misc. 3d 699, 777 N.Y.S.2d 846 (Sup. Ct. N.Y. Co. 2004). Justice Kahn held "that the definition of 'animal' within the statute, 'every living creature except a human being,' is plain and unambiguous," and "conforms with generally accepted definitions of this term." Id., 3 Misc. 3d at 705, 777 N.Y.S.2d at 850-51. As to goldfish, Justice Kahn explained:

> Goldfish are small orange fish often bred by human beings to live in fish tanks. It is not uncommon to see this tiny member of the carp family as a child's pet, dutifully maintained and cared for by its young human owner. A goldfish is almost always named and

spoken to as any household pet might be. Moreover, the demise of a goldfish, as with any pet, often causes its young owner much distress, requiring significant consolation, and necessitates a burial or other dignified disposition of the animal's remains.

The statutory definition of "companion animal" uses ordinary terms to express ideas which find adequate interpretation in common usage and understanding. Both a potential offender of ordinary intelligence and a police officer would be adequately informed of the nature of the offense prohibited by the statute. In this case, all three of the goldfish in the aquarium had names given to them by Juan Torres and his siblings. In fact, the children anthropomorphically named their pet goldfish after themselves. Both Juan Torres and his mother regularly cleaned the fish tank and fed the fish. After defendant destroyed the aquarium, Juan's mother rushed to scoop the fish off the floor and place them into a bowl of water, but defendant killed the fish named "Junior" (Juan's nickname) before she could complete her task. These facts clearly establish that the goldfish were household pets. It is beyond cavil that a person of ordinary intelligence, including a police officer charged with enforcing the law, would know that the common household pet known as a goldfish is a companion animal intended to be protected under the statute, and that, in particular, Juan Torres' goldfish was such a companion animal.

Id. 3 Misc. 3d at 706, 777 N.Y.S.2d at 851-52 (citations omitted).

Justice Kahn's written opinion concluded that:

As Agriculture and Markets Law § 353-a is not unconstitutionally vague as applied to defendant, there is at least one person to whom the statute is properly applied, and defendant's as-applied and facial challenge to the statute must fail. Accordingly, defendant's motion is denied in its entirety.

Id., 3 Misc. 3d at 708, 777 N.Y.S.2d at 852-53 (citations omitted).

Garcia's Direct Appeal

Represented by new counsel (the Center for Appellate Litigation), Garcia's appeal to the First Department claimed that: (1) "[t]he [trial] court abused its discretion as a matter of law by sua sponte considering attempted second-degree assault as a lesser included offense of attempted first-degree assault" (Dkt. No. 1: Pet. Att.: Garcia 1st Dep't Br. at 31-41); (2) Garcia's "conviction for the felony of aggravated cruelty to animals violates due process" (id. at 42-48);

(3) "proof of third-degree criminal mischief was insufficient" (id. at 49-55); (4) "the sentencing court improperly adjudicated [Garcia] a second violent felony offender" (id. at 56-57); and (5) Garcia's "aggregate 7 1/2 to 15 year sentence is excessive and should be reduced in the interests of justice" (id. at 57-58).

On March 28, 2006, the First Department affirmed and modified Garcia's conviction, vacating the conviction for second degree attempted assault, replacing the second violent felony offender adjudication with a second felony offender adjudication, and reducing the seven and one-half to fifteen year aggregate sentence to a five and one-half to eleven year aggregate sentence, People v. Garcia, 29 A.D.3d 255, 812 N.Y.S.2d 66 (1st Dep't 2006).

Recognizing that the scope of Agriculture & Markets Law § 353-a(1) "is a question of first impression for the Appellate Division," People v. Garcia, 29 A.D.3d at 257, 812 N.Y.S.2d at 68, the First Department's opinion addressed it at length. The opening paragraph of the First Department's decision started with a lesson about the history of domestic animals:

> The earliest known domestic animal appears to be the dog, a companion to mankind as early as 15000 b.c. Goats, sheep, pigs and cows followed in domestication in the next 10,000 years. Horses, however, did not succumb to the lure of mankind's presence until 4000 b.c. The domestication of fish is believed to have begun much later, in China during the Tang Dynasty, around 620 a.d. The common goldfish (Carassius Auratus), a member of the carp family that was first domesticated in China, is now the most commonly kept aquarium fish. The goldfish's leap from domesticated fish to family pet and companion may have happened as early as 1368 during the Ming Dynasty. The goldfish's popularity in the West began as the first public aquarium opened in London in 1853. Keeping goldfish as companions and pets in the United States has been popular since that time.
>
> Agriculture and Markets Law § 353-a(1), "Aggravated Cruelty To Animals," represents the Legislature's recognition that man's inhumanity to man often begins with inhumanity to those creatures that have formed particularly close relationships with mankind.

People v. Garcia, 29 A.D.3d at 257, 812 N.Y.S.2d at 68.

The First Department rejected Garcia's arguments that a goldfish is not domesticated and that "there is no reciprocity or mutuality of feeling between a fish and its owner," holding:

> The defendant's contention that all household pets are equal but some are more equal than others is manifestly not derived from the statute. The Legislature simply did not require a reciprocity of affection in the definition of "companion animal." To the contrary, the statutory language is consistent with the People's contention that, "domesticated" is commonly understood to mean "to adapt (an animal or plant) to life in intimate association with and to the advantage of humans." Thus, a goldfish such as the one herein is a domesticated rather than a wild animal within the common meaning of the term. Moreover, the goldfish was, as the statute requires, "normally maintained in or near the household of the owner or person who cares for [it]." Indeed, acknowledging that the goldfish is one of the most common household pets, defense counsel stipulated at trial that there are "millions of fish owners throughout the country."

> The defendant's argument that goldfish are not domesticated animals because given the opportunity they would leave home is without merit. While this trait arguably distinguishes fish from dogs and, probably to a lesser extent cats, it fails to take into account that many other animals commonly considered pets, such as hermit crabs, gerbils, hamsters, guinea pigs and rabbits, would depart for less confining venues and greener pastures if given the opportunity. Loyalty, if that is what it is, is merely another characteristic urged by defendant -- but not included by the Legislature -- as a defining feature of a companion animal.

> Moreover, Agriculture and Markets Law § 353-a(2) provides that "[n]othing contained in this section shall be construed to prohibit or interfere in any way with anyone lawfully engaged in hunting, trapping, or *fishing*. . . ." (emphasis added.) This provision would be superfluous if a fish could not be considered a companion animal.

> While the defendant maintains that the statute's definition of "companion animal" is unconstitutionally vague, we find, as did the trial court, the statute sufficiently clear to apprise a person of ordinary intelligence that the sort of conduct in which the defendant engaged comes within the statute's prohibition.

> The defendant further asserts that because the fish's death was instantaneous, it was not accompanied by "extreme pain" or accomplished with "especial[]" depravity or sadism, and that therefore the killing was not accomplished with any heightened level of cruelty. The trial court correctly observed that the legislative

history of the statute indicates that the crime was established in recognition of the correlation between violence against animals and subsequent violence against human beings. Thus, it must be inferred that the Legislature's concern was with the state of mind of the perpetrator rather than that of the victim.

People v. Garcia, 29 A.D.3d at 260-61, 812 N.Y.S.2d at 70 (citations omitted).

The First Department reversed Garcia's conviction for second degree attempted assault (as a lesser included of first degree attempted assault) because the factual basis for Justice Kahn's consideration of the lesser charge "represented a significant departure from the prosecution's theory of the case against the defendant and requires reversal." People v. Garcia, 29 A.D.3d at 262, 812 N.Y.S.2d at 71.

Regarding Garcia's claim that his conviction for third degree criminal mischief [2] was not supported by sufficient evidence to establish that he damaged property in an amount in excess of $ 250.00, the First Department agreed with Justice Kahn's conclusion and held:

> In a criminal mischief case, the amount of damage is generally measured by the reasonable cost of repairing the damaged property, provided it can be repaired. The repair cost may be established by expert testimony. It may be established by documentation. It may not be established by hearsay.

> In the case at bar, there was no expert testimony or documentation as to repair costs. The only documentary evidence was Martinez's receipt showing that the television had cost $ 1,700 when new, 13 months earlier. Her testimony about repair estimates was hearsay. . .
>
> .

> The defendant argues that the photographs here do not illuminate the record beyond the witnesses' trial testimony, but show (1) cracked glass, (2) Juan holding a new goldfish bowl in front of a white sheet, and (3) broken television-screen glass on a floor. Indeed, the People concede that "nothing in the photographs, standing alone, could establish an exact repair value." However, the People contend that the photographs "did confirm the magnitude of the repairs required, and did establish that the costs would be far from trivial." The People also observe that the estimates about which Martinez gave hearsay testimony meet the statutory threshold even if they are discounted by almost 80%, and that "[m]oreover, common sense dictates that repairs of the magnitude required in this case cannot be made in New York City for under $ 250." We

find the People's argument persuasive and accordingly conclude that there was ample evidentiary support for the trial court's conclusion that repair costs of at least $ 250 were proved.

People v. Garcia, 29 A.D.3d at 263-64, 812 N.Y.S.2d at 72-73 (citations omitted).

2 Penal Law § 145.05(2) states: "[a] person is guilty of criminal mischief in the third degree when, with the intent to damage property of another person, and having no right to do so nor any reasonable ground to believe that he or she has such right, he or she . . . damages property of another person in an amount exceeding two hundred fifty dollars."

The First Department also addressed Garcia's contention that his adjudication as a second violent felony offender must be vacated:

Finally, the People concede that the defendant's adjudication as a second violent felony offender must be vacated because he was not convicted of any violent felony in this case. However, since the sentences imposed were all lawful for a non-violent second felony offender and the trial court stated its intention to sentence defendant to the maximum possible term, there is no need for resentencing. We perceive no basis for reducing the sentence, except as indicated.

People v. Garcia, 29 A.D.3d at 264, 812 N.Y.S.2d at 73 (citation omitted).

The First Department modified Garcia's conviction and sentence,

to the extent of vacating the conviction for attempted assault in the second degree, and replacing the second violent felony offender adjudication with a second felony offender adjudication, reducing the aggregate sentence to 5 1/2 to 11 years, and otherwise affirmed.

People v. Garcia, 29 A.D.3d at 264, 812 N.Y.S.2d at 73.

The New York Court of Appeals denied leave to appeal on July 13, 2006. People v. Garcia, 7 N.Y.3d 789, 821 N.Y.S.2d 818 (2006).

Ortiz's Federal Habeas Corpus Petition

Garcia's pro se habeas petition simply incorporates his First Department brief, raising claims that: (1) "[t]he [trial] court abused its discretion as a matter of law by sua sponte considering attempted second-degree assault as a lesser included offense of attempted first-degree assault" (Dkt. No. 1: Pet. P 13, incorporating Pet. Att.: Garcia 1st Dep't Br. at 31-41); (2) Garcia's "conviction for the felony of aggravated cruelty to animals violates due process" (id. at 42-48); (3) "proof of the third-degree criminal mischief was insufficient" (id. at 49-55); (4) "the sentencing court improperly adjudicated [Garcia] a second violent felony offender" (id. at 56-57); and (5) Garcia's "aggregate 7 1/2 to 15 year sentence is excessive and should be reduced in the interests of justice" (id. at 57-58).

ANALYSIS

I. THE AEDPA REVIEW STANDARD [3]

3 For additional decisions by this Judge discussing the AEDPA review standard in language substantially similar to that in this entire section of this Report & Recommendation, see, e.g., Haynesworth v. Fischer, 06 Civ. 13329, 2007 U.S. Dist. LEXIS 5623, 2007 WL 2219422 at *8-11 (S.D.N.Y. Aug. 3, 2007) (Peck, M.J.); Ortiz v. Ercole, 07 Civ. 2178, 2007 U.S. Dist. LEXIS 52702, 2007 WL 2086456 at *8-11 (S.D.N.Y. July 23, 2007) (Peck, M.J.); Lopez v. Miller, 05 Civ. 7060, 2007 U.S. Dist. LEXIS 51145, 2007 WL 2032839 at *4-7 (S.D.N.Y. July 17, 2007) (Peck, M.J.); Morris v. Sears, 06 Civ. 2476, 2007 U.S. Dist. LEXIS 46983, 2007 WL 1875665 at *6-10 (S.D.N.Y. June 29, 2007) (Peck, M.J.); Harrison v. Walsh, 06 Civ. 13328, 2007 U.S. Dist. LEXIS 39616, 2007 WL 1576265 at *12-15 (S.D.N.Y. June 1, 2007) (Peck, M.J.); Brown v. Greene, 06 Civ. 4824, 2007 U.S. Dist. LEXIS 34460, 2007 WL 1379873 at *8-11 (S.D.N.Y. May 11, 2007) (Peck, M.J.); Cassie v. Graham, 06 Civ. 5536, 2007 U.S. Dist. LEXIS 6770, 2007 WL 506754 at *12-15 (S.D.N.Y. Jan. 31, 2007) (Peck, M.J.); Morales v. Artus, 05 Civ. 3542, 2006 U.S. Dist. LEXIS 93422, 2006 WL 3821488 at *13-16 (S.D.N.Y. Dec. 28, 2006) (Peck, M.J.) (citing my prior decisions); Bryant v. Fischer, 05 Civ. 0437, 2005 U.S. Dist. LEXIS 32759, 2005 WL 3418282 at *10-14 (S.D.N.Y. Dec. 14, 2005) (Peck, M.J.); Olivo v. Thorton, 05 Civ. 3237, 2005 U.S. Dist. LEXIS 31231, 2005 WL 3292542 at *5-8 (S.D.N.Y. Dec. 6, 2005) (Peck, M.J.) (citing my prior decisions), report & rec. adopted, 2006 U.S. Dist. LEXIS 38683, 2006 WL 1636742 (S.D.N.Y. June 12, 2006) & 2006 U.S. Dist. LEXIS 67355, 2006 WL 2689889 (S.D.N.Y. Sept. 19, 2006); Boyd v. Smith, 03 Civ. 5401, 2004 U.S. Dist. LEXIS 25324, 2004 WL 2915243 at *5-7 (S.D.N.Y. Dec. 17, 2004) (Peck, M.J.) (citing my prior decisions); Montalvo v. Annetts, 02 Civ. 1056, 2003

U.S. Dist. LEXIS 22619, 2003 WL 22962504 at *12-14 (S.D.N.Y. Dec. 17, 2003) (Peck, M.J.) (citing my prior decisions); Larrea v. Bennett, 01 Civ. 5813, 2002 U.S. Dist. LEXIS 10067, 2002 WL 1173564 at *14 (S.D.N.Y. May 31, 2002) (Peck, M.J.), report & rec. adopted, 2002 U.S. Dist. LEXIS 14463, 2002 WL 1808211 (S.D.N.Y. Aug. 6, 2002), aff'd, 368 F.3d 179 (2d Cir. 2004); Mendez v. Artuz, 98 Civ. 2652, 2000 U.S. Dist. LEXIS 8841, 2000 WL 722613 at *22 (S.D.N.Y. June 6, 2000) (Peck, M.J.), report & rec. adopted, 2000 U.S. Dist. LEXIS 11527, 2000 WL 1154320 (S.D.N.Y. Aug. 14, 2000), aff'd, 303 F.3d 411, 417 (2d Cir. 2002), cert. denied, 537 U.S. 1245, 123 S. Ct. 1353, 155 L. Ed. 2d 218 (2003); Fluellen v. Walker, 97 Civ. 3189, 2000 U.S. Dist. LEXIS 8839, 2000 WL 684275 at *10 (S.D.N.Y. May 25, 2000) (Peck, M.J.), aff'd, 41 Fed. Appx. 497 (2d Cir. 2002), cert. denied, 538 U.S. 978, 123 S. Ct. 1787, 155 L. Ed. 2d 666 (2003).

Before the Court can determine whether petitioner is entitled to federal habeas relief, the Court must address the proper habeas corpus review standard under the Antiterrorism and Effective Death Penalty Act ("AEDPA").

In enacting the AEDPA, Congress significantly "modifie[d] the role of federal habeas courts in reviewing petitions filed by state prisoners." Williams v. Taylor, 529 U.S. 362, 403, 120 S. Ct. 1495, 1518, 146 L. Ed. 2d 389 (2000). The AEDPA imposed a more stringent review standard, as follows:

> (d) An application for a writ of habeas corpus on behalf of a person in custody pursuant to the judgment of a State court shall not be granted with respect to any claim that was adjudicated on the merits in State court proceedings unless the adjudication of the claim --
>
>> (1) resulted in a decision that was contrary to, or involved an unreasonable application of, clearly established Federal law, as determined by the Supreme Court of the United States; or
>>
>> (2) . . . was based on an unreasonable determination of the facts in light of the evidence presented in the State court proceeding.

28 U.S.C. § 2254(d)(1)-(2). [4]

4 See also, e.g., Henry v. Poole, 409 F.3d 48, 67 (2d Cir. 2005), cert. denied, 547 U.S. 1040, 126 S. Ct. 1622, 164 L. Ed. 2d 334 (2006); Howard v. Walker, 406 F.3d 114, 121-22 (2d Cir. 2005); Cox v. Donnelly, 387 F.3d

193, 197 (2d Cir. 2004); Dallio v. Spitzer, 343 F.3d 553, 559-60 (2d Cir. 2003), cert. denied, 541 U.S. 961, 124 S. Ct. 1713, 158 L. Ed. 2d 402 (2004); Eze v. Senkowski, 321 F.3d 110, 120 (2d Cir. 2003) ("AEDPA changed the landscape of federal habeas corpus review by 'significantly curtail[ing] the power of federal courts to grant the habeas petitions of state prisoners.'") (quoting Lainfiesta v. Artuz, 253 F.3d 151, 155 (2d Cir. 2001), cert. denied, 535 U.S. 1019, 122 S. Ct. 1611, 152 L. Ed. 2d 625 (2002)).

The "contrary to" and "unreasonable application" clauses of § 2254(d)(1) have "independent meaning." Williams v. Taylor, 529 U.S. at 404-05, 120 S. Ct. at 1519. [5] Both, however, "restrict[] the source of clearly established law to [the Supreme] Court's jurisprudence." Williams v. Taylor, 529 U.S. at 412, 120 S. Ct. at 1523. [6] "That federal law, as defined by the Supreme Court, may either be a generalized standard enunciated in the [Supreme] Court's case law or a bright-line rule designed to effectuate such a standard in a particular context." Kennaugh v. Miller, 289 F.3d at 42. "A petitioner cannot win habeas relief solely by demonstrating that the state court unreasonably applied Second Circuit precedent." Yung v. Walker, 341 F.3d at 110; accord, e.g., DelValle v. Armstrong, 306 F.3d at 1200.

5 Accord, e.g., Henry v. Poole, 409 F.3d at 68; Howard v. Walker, 406 F.3d at 122; Parsad v. Greiner, 337 F.3d 175, 181 (2d Cir.), cert. denied, 540 U.S. 1091, 124 S. Ct. 962, 157 L. Ed. 2d 798 (2003); Jones v. Stinson, 229 F.3d 112, 119 (2d Cir. 2000); Lurie v. Wittner, 228 F.3d 113, 125 (2d Cir. 2000), cert. denied, 532 U.S. 943, 121 S. Ct. 1404, 149 L. Ed. 2d 347 (2001); Clark v. Stinson, 214 F.3d 315, 320 (2d Cir. 2000), cert. denied, 531 U.S. 1116, 121 S. Ct. 865, 148 L. Ed. 2d 778 (2001).

6 Accord, e.g., Carey v. Musladin, 127 S. Ct. 649, 654, 166 L. Ed. 2d 482 (2006) ("Given the lack of holdings from the Court regarding this [issue], it cannot be said that the state court 'unreasonabl[y] appli[ed] clearly established Federal law.'"); Yarborough v. Alvarado, 541 U.S. 652, 659, 124 S. Ct. 2140, 2147, 158 L. Ed. 2d 938 (2004) ("We look for 'the governing legal principle or principles set forth by the Supreme Court at the time the state court renders its decision.'"); Wiggins v. Smith, 539 U.S. 510, 519, 123 S. Ct. 2527, 2534, 156 L. Ed. 2d 471 (2003); Lockyer v. Andrade, 538 U.S. 63, 72, 123 S. Ct. 1166, 1172, 155 L. Ed. 2d 144 (2003) ("Section 2254(d)(1)'s 'clearly established' phrase 'refers to the holdings, as opposed to the dicta, of [the Supreme] Court's decisions as of the time of the relevant state-court decision.'"); Howard v. Walker, 406 F.3d at 122; Tueros v. Greiner, 343 F.3d 587, 591 (2d Cir. 2003), cert. denied, 541 U.S. 1047, 124 S. Ct. 2171, 158 L. Ed. 2d 739 (2004); Parsad v. Greiner, 337 F.3d at

181; DelValle v. Armstrong, 306 F.3d 1197, 1200 (2d Cir. 2002); Yung v. Walker, 341 F.3d 104, 109-110 (2d Cir. 2003); Kennaugh v. Miller, 289 F.3d 36, 42 (2d Cir.), cert. denied, 537 U.S. 909, 123 S. Ct. 251, 154 L. Ed. 2d 187 (2002); Loliscio v. Goord, 263 F.3d 178, 184 (2d Cir. 2001); Sellan v. Kuhlman, 261 F.3d 303, 309 (2d Cir. 2001).

As to the "contrary to" clause:

> A state-court decision will certainly be contrary to [Supreme Court] clearly established precedent if the state court applies a rule that contradicts the governing law set forth in [Supreme Court] cases. . . . A state-court decision will also be contrary to [the Supreme] Court's clearly established precedent if the state court confronts a set of facts that are materially indistinguishable from a decision of [the Supreme] Court and nevertheless arrives at a result different from [Supreme Court] precedent.

Williams v. Taylor, 529 U.S. at 405-06, 120 S. Ct. at 1519-20. [7]

> 7 Accord, e.g., Brown v. Payton, 544 U.S. 133, 125 S. Ct. 1432, 1438-39, 161 L. Ed. 2d 334 (2005); Bell v. Cone, 543 U.S. 447, 452-53, 125 S. Ct. 847, 851, 160 L. Ed. 2d 881 (2005); Price v. Vincent, 538 U.S. 634, 640, 123 S. Ct. 1848, 1853, 155 L. Ed. 2d 877 (2003); Lockyer v. Andrade, 123 S. Ct. at 1173-74; Hawkins v. Costello, 460 F.3d 238, 242 (2d Cir. 2006), cert. denied, 127 S. Ct. 1267, 167 L. Ed. 2d 92 (2007); Henry v. Poole, 409 F.3d at 68; Howard v. Walker, 406 F.3d at 122; Rosa v. McCray, 396 F.3d 210, 219 (2d Cir.), cert. denied, 546 U.S. 889, 126 S. Ct. 215, 163 L. Ed. 2d 201 (2005); Tueros v. Greiner, 343 F.3d at 591; DelValle v. Armstrong, 306 F.3d at 1200; Yung v. Walker, 341 F.3d at 109; Kennaugh v. Miller, 289 F.3d at 42; Loliscio v. Goord, 263 F.3d at 184; Lurie v. Wittner, 228 F.3d at 127-28.

In Williams, the Supreme Court explained that "[u]nder the 'unreasonable application' clause, a federal habeas court may grant the writ if the state court identifies the correct governing legal principle from [the Supreme] Court's decisions but unreasonably applies that principle to the facts of the prisoner's case." Williams v. Taylor, 529 U.S. at 413, 120 S. Ct. at 1523. [8] However, "[t]he term 'unreasonable' is . . . difficult to define." Williams v. Taylor, 529 U.S. at 410, 120 S. Ct. at 1522. The Supreme Court made clear that "an unreasonable application of federal law is different from an incorrect application of federal law." Id. [9] Rather, the issue is "whether the state court's application of clearly established federal law was objectively unreasonable." Williams v. Taylor, 529 U.S. at 409, 120 S. Ct. at 1521. [10] "Objectively unreasonable" is different from "clear error." Lockyer v. Andrade, 538 U.S. at 75, 123 S. Ct. at 1175 ("The gloss of clear error fails to give proper deference to state courts by conflating error (even clear error) with unreasonableness."). However, the Second Circuit has explained "that while '[s]ome increment of incorrectness beyond error is required . . . the increment need not be great; otherwise, habeas relief would be limited to state court decisions so far off the mark as to suggest judicial incompetence.'" Jones v. Stinson, 229 F.3d at 119 (quoting Francis S. v. Stone, 221 F.3d 100, 111 (2d Cir. 2000)). [11] "[T]he range of reasonable judgment can depend in part on the nature of the relevant rule." Yarborough v. Alvarado, 541 U.S. at 663, 124 S. Ct. at 2149. [12]

8 Accord, e.g., Brown v. Payton, 544 U.S. at 141, 125 S. Ct. at 1439; Wiggins v. Smith, 539 U.S. at 520, 123 S. Ct. at 2534-35; Lynn v. Bliden, 443 F.3d 238, 246 (2d Cir. 2006), cert. denied, 127 S. Ct. 1383, 167 L. Ed. 2d 168 (2007); Howard v. Walker, 406 F.3d at 122; Parsad v. Greiner, 337 F.3d at 181.

9 See also, e.g., Yarborough v. Alvarado, 541 U.S. at 664, 124 S. Ct. at 2150; Wiggins v. Smith, 539 U.S. at 520, 123 S. Ct. at 2535; Price v. Vincent, 538 U.S. at 641, 123 S. Ct. at 1853 ("As we have explained: '[A] federal habeas court may not issue the writ simply because that court concludes that the state-court decision applied [a Supreme Court case] incorrectly.'") (quoting Woodford v. Visciotti, 537 U.S. 19, 24-25, 123 S. Ct. 357, 360, 154 L. Ed. 2d 279 (2002)); Lockyer v. Andrade, 538 U.S. at 75, 123 S. Ct. at 1175; Hawkins v. Costello, 460 F.3d at 243; Lynn v. Bliden, 443 F.3d at 246; Henry v. Poole, 409 F.3d at 68; Howard v. Walker, 406 F.3d at 122; Rosa v. McCray, 396 F.3d at 219; Cox v. Donnelly, 387 F.3d at 197; Eze v. Senkowski, 321 F.3d at 124-25; DelValle v. Armstrong, 306 F.3d at 1200 ("With regard to issues of law, therefore, if the state court's decision was not an unreasonable application of, or contrary to, clearly established federal law as defined by Section 2254(d), we may not grant habeas relief even if in our judgment its application was erroneous.").

10 Accord, e.g., Yarborough v. Alvarado, 541 U.S. at 664, 124 S. Ct. at 2150; Wiggins v. Smith, 539 U.S. at 520-21, 123 S. Ct. at 2535; Price v. Vincent, 538 U.S. at 641, 123 S. Ct. at 1853; Lockyer v. Andrade, 538 U.S. at 75, 123 S. Ct. at 1174-75; Woodford v. Visciotti, 537 U.S. at 25-27, 123 S. Ct. at 360-61; Mosby v. Senkowski, 470 F.3d 515, 519 (2d Cir. 2006); Hawkins v. Costello, 460 F.3d at 243; Lynn v. Bliden, 443 F.3d at 246;

Henry v. Poole, 409 F.3d at 68; Howard v. Walker, 406 F.3d at 122; Cox v. Donnelly, 387 F.3d at 197; Eze v. Senkowski, 321 F.3d at 125; Ryan v. Miller, 303 F.3d 231, 245 (2d Cir. 2002); Loliscio v. Goord, 263 F.3d at 184; Lurie v. Wittner, 228 F.3d at 128-29.

11 Accord, e.g., Lynn v. Bliden, 443 F.3d at 246; Henry v. Poole, 409 F.3d at 68; Howard v. Walker, 406 F.3d at 122; Rosa v. McCray, 396 F.3d at 219; Cox v. Donnelly, 387 F.3d at 197, 200-01; Eze v. Senkowski, 321 F.3d at 125; Ryan v. Miller, 303 F.3d at 245; Yung v. Walker, 341 F.3d at 110; Loliscio v. Goord, 263 F.3d at 184.

12 The Supreme Court explained:

> [T]he range of reasonable judgment can depend in part on the nature of the relevant rule. If a legal rule is specific, the range may be narrow. Applications of the rule may be plainly correct or incorrect. Other rules are more general, and their meaning must emerge in application over the course of time. Applying a general standard to a specific case can demand a substantial element of judgment. As a result, evaluating whether a rule application was unreasonable requires considering the rule's specificity. The more general the rule, the more leeway courts have in reaching outcomes in case by case determinations.

Yarborough v. Alvarado, 541 U.S. at 663, 124 S. Ct. at 2149; accord, e.g., Hawkins v. Costello, 460 F.3d at 243.

Moreover, the Second Circuit has held "that a state court determination is reviewable under AEDPA if the state decision unreasonably failed to extend a clearly established, Supreme Court defined, legal principle to situations which that principle should have, in reason, governed." Kennaugh v. Miller, 289 F.3d at 45. [13]

13 Accord, e.g., Tueros v. Greiner, 343 F.3d at 591; Yung v. Walker, 341 F.3d at 109; see Yarborough v. Alvarado, 541 U.S. at 665-66, 124 S. Ct. at 2150-51 ("The petitioner contends that if a habeas court must extend a rationale before it can apply to the facts at hand then the rationale cannot be clearly established at the time of the state-court decision. There is force to this argument. Section 2254(d)(1) would be undermined if habeas courts introduced rules not clearly established under the guise of extensions to existing law. At the same time, the difference between applying a rule and extending it is not always clear. Certain principles are fundamental enough that when new factual permutations arise, the necessity to apply the earlier rule will be beyond doubt.") (citations omitted).

Under the AEDPA, in short, the federal courts "must give the state court's adjudication a high degree of deference." Yung v. Walker, 341 F.3d at 109; accord, e.g., Bell v. Cone, 543 U.S. at 455, 125 S. Ct. at 853; Mosby v. Senkowski, 470 F.3d at 519.

Even where the state court decision does not specifically refer to either the federal claim or to relevant federal case law, the deferential AEDPA review standard applies:

> For the purposes of AEDPA deference, a state court "adjudicate[s]" a state prisoner's federal claim on the merits when it (1) disposes of the claim "on the merits," and (2) reduces its disposition to judgment. When a state court does so, a federal habeas court must defer in the manner prescribed by 28 U.S.C. § 2254(d)(1) to the state court's decision on the federal claim -- even if the state court does not explicitly refer to either the federal claim or to relevant federal case law.

Sellan v. Kuhlman, 261 F.3d at 312; accord, e.g., Bell v. Cone, 543 U.S. at 455, 125 S. Ct. at 853 ("Federal courts are not free to presume that a state court did not comply with constitutional dictates on the basis of nothing more than a lack of citation."); Early v. Packer, 537 U.S. 3, 8, 123 S. Ct. 362, 365, 154 L. Ed. 2d 263 (2002) (State court not required to cite Supreme Court cases, or even be aware of them, to be entitled to AEDPA deference, "so long as neither the reasoning nor the result of the state-court decision contradicts them."); Mosby v. Senkowski, 470 F.3d at 519; Hawkins v. Costello, 460 F.3d at 243; Lynn v. Bliden, 443 F.3d at 246; Howard v. Walker, 406 F.3d at 122; Rosa v. McCray, 396 F.3d at 220; Wade v. Herbert, 391 F.3d 135, 140 (2d Cir. 2004) (Appellate Division held claim was "'without merit.'" "Such a summary determination, even absent citation of federal case law, is a 'determination on the merits' and as such requires the deference specified by § 2254." Moreover, "[I]f any reasonable ground was available [for the state court's decision], we must assume that the [state] court relied on it."); Francolino v. Kuhlman, 365 F.3d 137, 141 (2d Cir.) (Where "the Appellate Division concluded its opinion by stating that it had 'considered and rejected defendants' remaining claims,'" AEDPA deference applies.), cert. denied, 543 U.S. 872, 125 S. Ct. 110, 160 L. Ed. 2d 120 (2004); Jenkins v. Artuz, 294 F.3d 284, 291 (2d Cir. 2002) ("In Sellan, we found that an even more concise Appellate Division disposition -- the word 'denied' -- triggered AEDPA deference.").

Where the state court decision is not clear as to whether it rests on federal law or state procedural law, the Second Circuit in Jimenez v. Walker, 458 F.3d 130, 145-46 (2d Cir. 2006), cert. denied, 127 S. Ct. 976, 166 L. Ed. 2d 740 (2007), instructed that the court must "examine the three clues laid out in Coleman, Quirama and Sellan" -- that is, "(1) the face of the state-court opinion, (2) whether the state court was aware of a procedural bar, and (3) the practice of state courts in similar circumstances." Jimenez v. Walker, 458 F.3d at 145 & n.16. Using these three factors, the court should classify the

> decision as either:
> (1) fairly appearing to rest primarily on federal law or to be interwoven with federal law or
>
> (2) fairly appearing to rest primarily on state procedural law.

> Absent a clear and express statement of reliance on a state procedural bar, the Harris presumption applies to decisions in the first category and deems them to rest on the merits of the federal claim. Such decisions are not procedurally barred and must be afforded AEDPA deference as adjudications "on the merits" under 28 U.S.C. § 2254(d). The Harris presumption does not apply to decisions in the second category, which show themselves to rest on an independent state procedural bar. Nor does it apply to decisions in the first category which contain a clear statement of reliance on a state procedural bar. No AEDPA deference is due to these decisions, but the state may successfully assert that habeas relief is foreclosed provided that the independent state procedural bar is adequate to support the judgment and that neither cause and prejudice nor a fundamental miscarriage of justice is shown.

> The effect of these rules is to present federal habeas courts with a binary circumstance: we either apply AEDPA deference to review a state court's disposition of a federal claim or refuse to review the claim because of a procedural bar properly raised. The middle ground . . . does not exist.

Jimenez v. Walker, 458 F.3d at 145-46 (citations & fns. omitted); accord, e.g., Hawkins v. Costello, 460 F.3d at 242 ("In Jimenez v. Walker, we recently made clear that when a state court rejects a petitioner's claim as either unpreserved or without merit, the conclusive presumption is that the adjudication rested on the merits."). Of course, "[i]f there is no [state court] adjudication on the merits [and no procedural bar], then the pre-AEDPA, de novo standard of review applies." Cotto v. Herbert, 331 F.3d 217, 230 (2d Cir. 2003); see also Jimenez v. Walker, 458 F.3d at 145 n.17.

Finally, "[i]f [the] court finds that the state court engaged in an unreasonable application of established law, resulting in constitutional error, it must next consider whether such error was harmless." Howard v. Walker, 406 F.3d at 122.

In addition to the standard of review of legal issues, the AEDPA provides a deferential review standard for state court factual determinations: "a determination of a factual issue made by a State court shall be presumed to be correct." 28 U.S.C. § 2254(e)(1); accord, e.g., Lynn v. Bliden, 443 F.3d at 246-47; Rosa v. McCray, 396 F.3d at 220. "The petitioner bears the burden of 'rebutting the presumption of correctness by clear and convincing evidence.'" Parsad v. Greiner, 337 F.3d at 181 (quoting § 2254(e)(1)); accord, e.g., Lynn v. Bliden, 443 F.3d at 246-47.

II. GARCIA'S FIRST AND FOURTH HABEAS CLAIMS ARE MOOT

Because Garcia's habeas petition merely incorporates his First Department brief (see pages 16-17 above), he has raised two claims on which he already prevailed before the First Department.

Garcia's first habeas claim is that "[t]he [trial] court abused its discretion as a matter of law by sua sponte considering attempted second-degree assault as a lesser included offense of attempted first-degree assault." (Dkt. No. 1: Pet. P 13, incorporating Pet. Att.: Garcia 1st Dep't Br. at 31-41.) The First Department agreed and vacated Garcia's second degree attempted assault conviction. People v. Garcia, 29 A.D.3d 255, 264, 812 N.Y.S.2d 66, 73 (1st Dep't 2006) (quoted at page 14 above). Thus, Garcia's first habeas claim should be DENIED as moot. Warney v. McGinnis, No. 04-CV-6202, 2006 WL 2482017 at *1 (W.D.N.Y. Aug. 25, 2006) ("Since the underlying conviction has been vacated [by the state court, petitioner's] habeas claims have been rendered moot" and are dismissed.); Wilson v. Goord, 00 Civ. 4849, 2004 U.S. Dist. LEXIS 1513, 2004 WL 226149 at *6 (S.D.N.Y. Feb. 6, 2004) (Habeas claim regarding coerced guilty plea denied as moot where Appellate Division previously granted petitioner's motion to vacate that guilty plea.); Delgado v. Duncan, No. 02-CV-4929, 2003 U.S. Dist. LEXIS 24123, 2003 WL 23185682 at *5 (E.D.N.Y. Nov. 4, 2003) (Weinstein, D.J.) ("Petitioner claims that his conviction for seventh degree criminal possession of a controlled substance should be dismissed as an inclusory concurrent count. Petitioner received relief on this claim from the Appellate Division, which vacated his conviction of this crime and dismissed the count from the indictment. The claim as raised in this habeas proceeding is denied as moot."); Eatmon v. Kelly, No. CIV-86-1072, 1991 WL 129803 at *1-2 (E.D.N.Y. June 30, 1991) (Habeas petition dismissed as moot where the state court already reversed the subject conviction.).

Similarly, Garcia's fourth habeas claim is that "the sentencing court improperly adjudicated [Garcia] a second violent felony offender." (Pet. P 13, incorporating Garcia 1st Dep't Br. at 56-57.) The State conceded this claim before the First Department, which vacated his second violent felony offender adjudication (replacing it with a second felony offender adjudication). People v. Garcia, 29 A.D.3d at 264, 812 N.Y.S.2d at 73 (quoted at page 16 above). Thus, again, since Garcia obtained the relief he seeks before the First Department, his fourth habeas claim should be DENIED as moot.

III. GARCIA'S CONVICTION FOR AGGRAVATED CRUELTY TO ANIMALS DOES NOT VIOLATE DUE PROCESS

A. Garcia's Second Habeas Claim Is Not Cognizable On Habeas Review

The Supreme Court has reiterated "many times that 'federal habeas corpus relief does not lie for errors of state law.'" Estelle v. McGuire, 502 U.S. 62, 67, 112 S. Ct. 475, 480, 116 L. Ed. 2d 385 (1991). The role of a federal habeas court is not to "reexamine state-court determinations on state-law questions. In conducting habeas review, a federal court is limited to deciding whether a conviction violated the Constitution, laws, or treaties of the United States." Estelle v. McGuire, 502 U.S. at 67-68, 112 S. Ct. at 480; accord, e.g., Haynesworth v. Fischer, 06 Civ. 13329, 2007 U.S. Dist. LEXIS 56233, 2007 WL 2219422 at *15 (S.D.N.Y. Aug. 3, 2007) (Peck,

M.J.); Harris v. Woods, 05 Civ. 5582, 2006 U.S. Dist. LEXIS 24608, 2006 WL 1140888 at *36-38 & n.42 (S.D.N.Y. May 1, 2006) (Peck, M.J.) (citing cases), report & rec. adopted, 05 Civ. 5582, 2006 U.S. Dist. LEXIS 47432, 2006 WL 1975990 (S.D.N.Y. July 10, 2006); Gittens v. Thomas, 02 Civ. 9435, 2003 U.S. Dist. LEXIS 9087, 2003 WL 21277151 at *2 (S.D.N.Y. May 30, 2003); James v. Artuz, 97 Civ. 2792, 2000 U.S. Dist. LEXIS 4606, 2000 WL 375240 at *1 (S.D.N.Y. Apr. 12, 2000), aff'd, 29 Fed. Appx. 654 (2d Cir.), cert. denied, 536 U.S. 966, 122 S. Ct. 2678, 153 L. Ed. 2d 850 (2002); D'Amico v. Johnson, 92 Civ. 4702, 1993 U.S. Dist. LEXIS 18194, 1993 WL 541658 at *1 (S.D.N.Y. Dec. 23, 1993).

Although using the term "due process" in his petition (Dkt. No. 1: Pet. Att.: Garcia 1st Dep't Br. at 42), the gist of Garcia's second habeas claim is that the state court misinterpreted Agriculture & Markets Law Section 353-a(1). Interpretation of Agriculture & Markets Law Section 353-a(1), however, is purely a state law issue. This Court cannot "re-examine" the state court's decision, as this claim exclusively rests on state law.

B. In Any Event, Garcia's Second Habeas Claim Is Meritless

Garcia argues that his conviction of aggravated cruelty to animals under Agriculture & Markets Law Section 353-a(1) violated due process (i) because a pet goldfish is not a "companion animal" as defined by the statute (Dkt. No. 1: Pet. Att.: Garcia 1st Dep't Br. at 42-47), and (ii) because the killing of the pet goldfish was not accomplished with aggravated cruelty (id. at 47-48). Agriculture & Markets Law § 353-a(1) states:

> A person is guilty of aggravated cruelty to animals when, with no justifiable purpose, he or she intentionally kills or intentionally causes serious physical injury to a companion animal with aggravated cruelty. For purposes of this section, "aggravated cruelty" shall mean conduct which: (i) is intended to cause extreme physical pain; or (ii) is done or carried out in an especially depraved or sadistic manner.

Agriculture & Markets Law § 350(5) defines "'[c]ompanion animal' or 'pet' [to] mean[] any dog or cat, and shall also mean any other domesticated animal normally maintained in or near the household of the owner or person who cares for such other domesticated animal," and not including a "farm animal." Section 350(1) defines "'[a]nimal,' as used in this article, [as] includ[ing] every living creature except a human being." Agriculture & Markets Law § 353-a(2) provides that "[n]othing contained in this section shall be construed to prohibit or interfere in any way with anyone lawfully engaged in hunting, trapping, or fishing. . . ."

The pet goldfish clearly falls under the statute's definition of "companion animal." Martinez purchased the goldfish a year and a half before the incident. (See page 2 above.) Martinez and her children maintained the goldfish in an aquarium in her home. (See pages 2, 11 above.) Martinez's children named the goldfish after themselves, and helped Martinez regularly clean the fish tank and feed the fish. (See page 11 above.) The goldfish therefore was a domesticated animal that was maintained in its owner's household, as required by the statute.

Additionally, Agriculture & Markets Law § 353-a(2) specifically excludes the behavior of "anyone lawfully engaged in . . . fishing." As the First Department noted, Garcia's reading of the law would render this section of the statute superfluous if fish could not be considered to be companion animals. (See page 14 above.)

The state courts also properly found that Garcia killed the goldfish with "aggravated cruelty" because he killed the goldfish in an "especially depraved or sadistic manner." First, Garcia threw the fish tank into the television, breaking both the fish tank and the television. (See page 2 above.) Garcia specifically caught Martinez's 9-year old son's attention and stomped on and killed the goldfish right in front of him. (See page 3 above.) This behavior is consistent with behavior of other defendants convicted of aggravated cruelty to animals. See People v. DeGiorgio, 36 A.D.3d 1007,1009, 827 N.Y.S.2d 342, 344 (3d Dep't) (finding that defendant acted in an especially depraved and sadistic manner where he attacked a twelve year old, eighteen pound **dachshund**, and "kicked the dog while wearing boots, picked it up by its neck and shook it, banged the dog's head against a door and threw it down basement stairs onto a cement floor"), appeal denied, 8 N.Y.3d 921, 834 N.Y.S.2d 511, 866 N.E.2d 457 (2007); People v. Knowles, 184 Misc. 2d 474, 478-79, 709 N.Y.S.2d 916, 920 (Sup. Ct. Rensselaer Co. 2000) (finding that defendant acted in an especially depraved and sadistic manner where he kicked an eight month old dog down a walkway and threw it up against a brick wall). Because the state court properly found that the goldfish was a companion animal that Garcia killed in an especially depraved and sadistic manner, Garcia's claim that his conviction for aggravated cruelty to animals violates due process is meritless.

Garcia's second habeas claim should therefore be DENIED.

IV. THE EVIDENCE WAS SUFFICIENT TO PROVE THIRD DEGREE CRIMINAL MISCHIEF

A. Legal Principles Governing Sufficiency of the Evidence Habeas Claims [14]

14 For additional decisions authored by this Judge discussing the sufficiency of the evidence standard in habeas cases in language substantially similar to this section of this Report & Recommendation, see, e.g., Harrison v. Walsh, 06 Civ. 13328, 2007 U.S. Dist. LEXIS 39616, 2007 WL 1576265 at *18-19 (S.D.N.Y. June 1, 2007) (Peck, M.J.); Cassie v. Graham, 06 Civ. 5536, 2007 U.S. Dist. LEXIS 6770, 2007 WL 506754 at *18 (S.D.N.Y. Jan. 31, 2007) (Peck, M.J.); Murray v. Greene, 06 Civ. 3677, 2006 U.S. Dist. LEXIS 92341, 2006 WL 3751294 at *10-11 (S.D.N.Y. Dec. 21, 2006) (Peck, M.J.); A.S. Goldmen, Inc. v. Phillips, 05 Civ. 4385 & 05 Civ. 5496, 2006 U.S. Dist. LEXIS 45342, 2006 WL 1881146 at *58-59 (S.D.N.Y. July 6, 2006) (Peck, M.J.); Rosario v. Walsh, 05 Civ. 2684, 2006 U.S. Dist. LEXIS 33385, 2006 WL 1431410 at *19-20 (S.D.N.Y. May 25, 2006) (Peck, M.J.), report & rec. adopted, 2006 U.S. Dist. LEXIS 45726, 2006 WL 1880958 (S.D.N.Y. July 5, 2006); Nelson v. Sears, 05 Civ. 10341, 2006 U.S. Dist. LEXIS 13220, 2006 WL 775123 at *9-10 (S.D.N.Y. Mar. 28, 2006) (Peck, M.J.); Olivo v. Thorton, 05 Civ. 3237, 2005 U.S. Dist. LEXIS 31231, 2005 WL 3292542 at *14 (S.D.N.Y. Dec. 6, 2005) (Peck, M.J.), report & rec. adopted, 2006 U.S. Dist. LEXIS 38683, 2006 WL 1636742 (S.D.N.Y. June 12, 2006); Roman v. Filion, 04 Civ. 8022, 2005 U.S. Dist. LEXIS 11292, 2005 WL 1383167 at *31-33 (S.D.N.Y. June 10, 2005) (Peck, M.J.); Castro v. Fisher, 04 Civ. 0346, 2004 U.S. Dist. LEXIS 13976, 2004 WL 1637920 at *23-25 (S.D.N.Y. July 23, 2004) (Peck, M.J.) (citing my prior decisions), report & rec. adopted, 2004 U.S. Dist. LEXIS 22527, 2004 WL 2525876 (S.D.N.Y. Nov. 8, 2004); Besser v. Walsh, 02 Civ. 6775, 2003 U.S. Dist. LEXIS 15758, 2003 WL 22093477 at *10-13 (S.D.N.Y. Sept. 10, 2003) (Peck, M.J.) (citing my prior decisions), report & rec. adopted, 2003 U.S. Dist. LEXIS 21361, 2003 WL 22846044 (Dec. 2, 2003); Hediam v. Miller, 02 Civ. 1419, 2002 U.S. Dist. LEXIS 24482, 2002 WL 31867722 at *11-14 (S.D.N.Y. Dec. 23, 2002) (Peck, M.J.) (citing my prior decisions).

"'[T]he Due Process Clause of the Fourteenth Amendment protects a defendant in a criminal case against conviction 'except upon proof beyond a reasonable doubt of every fact necessary to constitute the crime' with which he is charged.'" Jackson v. Virginia, 443 U.S. 307, 315, 99 S. Ct. 2781, 2787, 61 L. Ed. 2d 560 (1979) (quoting In re Winship, 397 U.S. 358, 364, 90 S. Ct. 1068, 1073, 25 L. Ed. 2d 368 (1970)). However, "a properly instructed jury may occasionally convict even when it can be said that no rational trier of fact could find guilt beyond a reasonable doubt." Jackson v. Virginia, 443 U.S. at 317, 99 S. Ct. at 2788. Accordingly, "in a challenge to a state criminal conviction brought under 28 U.S.C. § 2254 -- if the settled procedural prerequisites for such a claim have otherwise been satisfied -- the applicant is entitled to habeas corpus relief if it is found that upon the record evidence adduced at the trial no rational trier of fact could have found proof of guilt beyond a reasonable doubt." Jackson v. Virginia, 443 U.S. at 324, 99 S. Ct. at 2791-92. [15]

15 Accord, e.g., Fama v. Comm'r of Corr. Servs., 235 F.3d 804, 811 (2d Cir. 2000); Einaugler v. Supreme Court, 109 F.3d 836, 839 (2d Cir. 1997).

The petitioner bears a very heavy burden:

[T]he standard for appellate review of an insufficiency claim placed a "very heavy burden" on the appellant. Our inquiry is whether the jury, drawing reasonable inferences from the evidence, may fairly and logically have concluded that the defendant was guilty beyond a reasonable doubt. In making this determination, we must view the evidence in the light most favorable to the government, and construe all permissible inferences in its favor.

United States v. Carson, 702 F.2d 351, 361 (2d Cir.) (citations omitted), cert. denied, 462 U.S. 1108, 103 S. Ct. 2456, 2457, 103 S. Ct. 2457, 77 L. Ed. 2d 1335 (1983). [16]

16 Accord, e.g., Fama v. Comm'r of Corr. Servs., 235 F.3d at 811 ("petitioner bears a very heavy burden in convincing a federal habeas court to grant a petition on the grounds of insufficiency of the evidence"); United States v. Middlemiss, 217 F.3d 112, 117 (2d Cir. 2000); United States v. Autuori, 212 F.3d 105, 114 (2d Cir. 2000) ("a defendant shoulders a 'heavy

burden' in challenging the sufficiency of evidence supporting a conviction"); United States v. Kinney, 211 F.3d 13, 16 (2d Cir. 2000), cert. denied, 531 U.S. 1079, 121 S. Ct. 778, 148 L. Ed. 2d 676 (2001); United States v. Bicaksiz, 194 F.3d 390, 398 (2d Cir. 1999) (The defendant "bears a 'very heavy burden' in challenging the sufficiency of the evidence that led to his conviction. In considering any such challenge, we view all proof in the light most favorable to the government and draw all reasonable inferences in the government's favor.") (citations omitted), cert. denied, 528 U.S. 1161, 120 S. Ct. 1175, 145 L. Ed. 2d 1083 (2000); United States v. Russo, 74 F.3d 1383, 1395 (2d Cir.), cert. denied, 519 U.S. 927, 117 S. Ct. 293, 136 L. Ed. 2d 213 (1996); United States v. Rosa, 11 F.3d 315, 337 (2d Cir. 1993) ("[T]he defendant who makes a sufficiency challenge bears a heavy burden."), cert. denied, 511 U.S. 1042, 114 S. Ct. 1565, 128 L. Ed. 2d 211 (1994); United States v. Strauss, 999 F.2d 692, 696 (2d Cir. 1993) (burden on defendant claiming insufficiency is "very heavy" and all inferences must be drawn in the government's favor).

The habeas court's review of the jury's findings is limited:

[T]his inquiry does not require a court to "ask itself whether it believes that the evidence at the trial established guilt beyond a reasonable doubt." Instead, the relevant question is whether, after viewing the evidence in the light most favorable to the prosecution, any rational trier of fact could have found the essential elements of the crime beyond a reasonable doubt. This familiar standard gives full play to the responsibility of the trier of fact fairly to resolve conflicts in the testimony, to weigh the evidence, and to draw reasonable inferences from basic facts to ultimate facts.

Jackson v. Virginia, 443 U.S. at 318-19, 99 S. Ct. at 2789 (citations omitted). [17]

17 Accord, e.g., United States v. Middlemiss, 217 F.3d at 117; United States v. Kinney, 211 F.3d at 16; United States v. Russo, 74 F.3d at 1395 (quoting United States v. Martinez, 54 F.3d 1040, 1042-43 (2d Cir.), cert. denied, 516 U.S. 1001, 116 S. Ct. 545, 133 L. Ed. 2d 448 (1995)); Mallette v. Scully, 752 F.2d 26, 31 (2d Cir. 1984).

The Jackson v. Virginia "standard must be applied with explicit reference to the substantive elements of the criminal offense as defined by state law." Jackson v. Virginia, 443 U.S. at 324 n.16, 99 S. Ct. at 2792 n.16; accord, e.g., Green v. Abrams, 984 F.2d 41, 44-45 (2d Cir. 1993) ("In considering a petition for a writ of habeas corpus based on insufficient evidence to support a criminal conviction in the state courts, a federal court must look to state law to determine the elements of the crime.").

B. Application of the Standard to Garcia's Conviction of Third Degree Criminal Mischief

Garcia argues that because there was no expert testimony, documentary proof or non-hearsay evidence to show that the amount of the repair costs for Martinez's television and wall unit exceeded $ 250, there was insufficient evidence to prove that Garcia committed third degree criminal mischief. (Dkt. No. 1: Pet Att.: Garcia 1st Dep't Br. at 49.) Penal Law § 145.05(2) states that "[a] person is guilty of criminal mischief in the third degree when, with intent to damage property of another person, and having no right to do so nor any reasonable ground to believe that he or she has such right, he or she . . . damages property of another person in an amount exceeding two hundred fifty dollars."

In the present case, both Martinez and the police officers testified that the large screen television, the VCR, a wall unit, and the fish tank were all badly damaged. (See pages 6-7 above.) Martinez purchased the television for $ 1,699.97, the home theater system for $ 599.98, the wall unit for $ 1,500, the fish tank for $ 80, and the VCR for approximately $ 60. (See pages 6-7 above.) The trial court examined photographs of Martinez's damaged property. (See page 9 above.) Martinez testified that repairmen had given her an estimate of $ 700 to professionally repair the television screen and $ 500 to repair the wall unit. (See pages 6-7 above.) Although the evidence of the repair estimate was hearsay, Martinez's and the officers' testimony and the photographs, along with common sense, demonstrate that Martinez's high cost possessions (large screen TV and wall unit) were badly damaged by Garcia's actions. This Court finds, therefore, that there was sufficient evidence to support the state court's finding that Martinez suffered more than $ 250 worth of damage to her belongings which cost about $ 4,000. See People v. Hoppe, 184 A.D.2d 582, 582, 584 N.Y.S.2d 860, 861 (2d Dep't 1992) ("[W]e have reviewed the photographs of the damage introduced at trial and find that they demonstrate beyond a reasonable doubt that the value of the damage exceeded $ 250, the statutory amount required to prove criminal mischief in the third degree."). The evidence was sufficient (albeit barely) to prove that Garcia committed third degree criminal mischief. Consequently, Garcia's third habeas claim is meritless.

Garcia's third habeas claim should be DENIED.

V. GARCIA'S EXCESSIVE SENTENCE CLAIM DOES NOT PROVIDE A BASIS FOR FEDERAL HABEAS RELIEF

Garcia's fifth habeas claim asserts that his "aggregate 7 1/2 to 15 year sentence is excessive and should be reduced" because "the physical injuries, the property damage, and the death of the goldfish simply do not warrant that length of time upstate." (Dkt. No. 1: Pet. P 13, incorporating Garcia 1st Dep't Br. at 57-58.) In fact, his sentence no longer is 7- 1/2 to 15 years. Because the First Department vacated Garcia's second degree attempted assault conviction, the First Department reduced Garcia's sentence to 5- 1/2 to 11 years. People v. Garcia, 29 A.D.3d 255, 812 N.Y.S.2d 66 (1st Dep't 2006) (discussed at pages 14-16 above).

Garcia's excessive sentence claim is quickly disposed of. An excessive sentence claim does not provide a basis for habeas relief, because "[n]o federal constitutional issue is presented where, as here, the sentence is within the range prescribed by state law." White v. Keane, 969 F.2d 1381, 1383 (2d Cir. 1992). [18]

[18] Accord, e.g., Ortiz v. Ercole, 07 Civ. 2178, 2007 U.S. Dist. LEXIS 52702, 2007 WL 2086456 at *16 (S.D.N.Y. July 23, 2007) (Peck, M.J.); Rosario v. Walsh, 05 Civ. 2684, 2006 U.S. Dist. LEXIS 33385, 2006 WL 1431410 at *24 (S.D.N.Y. May 25, 2006) (Peck, M.J.), report & rec. adopted, 2006 U.S. Dist. LEXIS 45726, 2006 WL 1880958 (S.D.N.Y. July 5, 2006); Hardison v. Artus, 06 Civ. 0322, 2006 U.S. Dist. LEXIS 29445, 2006 WL 1330064 at *15 (S.D.N.Y. May 16, 2006) (Peck, M.J.), report & rec. adopted, 2006 U.S. Dist. LEXIS 43222, 2006 WL 1763678 (S.D.N.Y. June 23, 2006); Harris v. Woods, 05 Civ. 5582, 2006 U.S. Dist. LEXIS 24608, 2006 WL 1140888 at *39 (S.D.N.Y. May 1, 2006) (Peck, M.J.), report & rec. adopted, 2006 U.S. Dist. LEXIS 47432, 2006 WL 1975990 (S.D.N.Y. July 10, 2006); Bryant v. Fischer, 05 Civ. 0437, 2005 U.S. Dist. LEXIS 32759, 2005 WL 3418282 at *25-26 (S.D.N.Y. Dec. 14, 2005) (Peck, M.J.); Yapor v. Mazzuca, 2005 U.S. Dist. LEXIS 6597, 2005 WL 894918 at *27-28 (S.D.N.Y. Apr. 19, 2005) (Peck, M.J.), report & rec. adopted, 2005 U.S. Dist. LEXIS 15997, 2005 WL 1845089 (S.D.N.Y. Aug. 3, 2005); Peakes v. Spitzer, 04 Civ. 1342, 2004 U.S. Dist. LEXIS 10905, 2004 WL

1366056 at *13 (S.D.N.Y. June 16, 2004)(Peck, M.J.), report & rec. adopted, 2004 U.S. Dist. LEXIS 14063, 2004 WL 1656568 (S.D.N.Y. July 23, 2004); Rodriguez v. Senkowski, 03 Civ. 3314, 2004 U.S. Dist. LEXIS 3975, 2004 WL 503451 at *38 (S.D.N.Y. Mar. 15, 2004) (Peck, M.J.); McPherson v. Greiner, 02 Civ. 2726, 2003 U.S. Dist. LEXIS 18718, 2003 WL 22405449 at *17 (S.D.N.Y. Oct. 22, 2003) (Peck, M.J.); Briggs v. Phillips, 02 Civ. 9340, 2003 U.S. Dist. LEXIS 10921, 2003 WL 21497514 at *7 (S.D.N.Y. June 30, 2003) (Peck, M.J.); Wilson v. Senkowski, 02 Civ. 0231, 2003 U.S. Dist. LEXIS 7583, 2003 WL 21031975 at *13 (S.D.N.Y. May 7, 2003) (Peck, M.J.); Naranjo v. Filion, 02 Civ. 5449, 2003 U.S. Dist. LEXIS 6287, 2003 WL 1900867 at *13 (S.D.N.Y. Apr. 16, 2003) (Peck, M.J.); Ferguson v. Walker, 00 Civ. 1356, 2002 U.S. Dist. LEXIS 18864, 2002 WL 31246533 at *10 (S.D.N.Y. Oct. 7, 2002) (Swain, D.J. & Peck, M.J.); Bryant v. Bennett, 00 Civ. 5692, 2001 U.S. Dist. LEXIS 2151, 2001 WL 286776 at *6 (S.D.N.Y. Mar. 2, 2001) (Peck, M.J.); Solomon v. Artuz, 00 Civ. 0860, 2000 U.S. Dist. LEXIS 8837, 2000 WL 863056 at *7 (S.D.N.Y. June 28, 2000) (Peck, M.J.); Foreman v. Garvin, 99 Civ. 9078, 2000 U.S. Dist. LEXIS 8219, 2000 WL 631397 at *13 (S.D.N.Y. May 16, 2000) (Peck, M.J.); Thomas v. Greiner, 111 F. Supp. 2d 271, 278 n.8 (S.D.N.Y. 2000) (Preska, D.J. & Peck, M.J.); Thomas v. Senkowski, 968 F. Supp. 953, 956 (S.D.N.Y. 1997) ("It is well established that, when a sentence falls within the range prescribed by state law, the length of the sentence may not be raised as grounds for federal habeas relief."); see also, e.g., Townsend v. Burke, 334 U.S. 736, 741, 68 S. Ct. 1252, 1255, 92 L. Ed. 1690 (1948) (severity of sentence generally not reviewable on habeas).

In this case, it is undisputed that Garcia's sentence was within the range prescribed by state law. Third degree criminal possession of a weapon is a class D felony, carrying a maximum sentence of four to seven years imprisonment. Penal Law §§ 265.02, 70.06(3)(d). Garcia was sentenced to 3- 1/2 to 7 years. (S. 30.) Third degree criminal mischief is a class E felony, carrying a maximum sentence of three to four years imprisonment. Penal Law §§ 145.05, 70.06(3)(e). Garcia was sentenced to 2 to 4 years. (S. 30.) Aggravated cruelty to animals is a class E felony, carrying a maximum sentence of two years imprisonment. Penal Law § 55.10(1)(b); Agriculture & Markets Law § 353-a(3). Garcia was sentenced to 2 years. (S. 31-32.) Third degree assault is a class A misdemeanor and each of the three counts carry a maximum sentence of one year imprisonment. Penal Law §§ 120.00, 70.15(1). Garcia was sentenced to 1 year. (S. 30-31.) Endangering the welfare of a child also is a class A misdemeanor and each of the three counts carry a maximum sentence of one year imprisonment. Penal Law §§ 260.10, 70.15(1). Garcia was sentenced to 1 year (S. 31.)

Because Garcia's sentence is within the statutory range, it is not reviewable on habeas corpus by this Court as "excessive."

CONCLUSION

For the reasons discussed above, Garcia's habeas petition should be DENIED and a certificate of appealability should not issue.

FILING OF OBJECTIONS TO THIS REPORT AND RECOMMENDATION

Pursuant to 28 U.S.C. § 636(b)(1) and Rule 72(b) of the Federal Rules of Civil Procedure, the parties shall have ten (10) days from service of this Report to file written objections. See also Fed. R. Civ. P. 6. Such objections (and any responses to objections) shall be filed with the Clerk of the Court, with courtesy copies delivered to the chambers of the Honorable Paul A. Crotty, 500 Pearl Street, Room 735, and to my chambers, 500 Pearl Street, Room 1370. Any requests for an extension of time for filing objections must be directed to Judge Crotty (with a courtesy copy to my chambers). Failure to file objections will result in a waiver of those objections for purposes of appeal. Thomas v. Arn, 474 U.S. 140, 106 S. Ct. 466, 88 L. Ed. 2d 435 (1985); IUE AFL-CIO Pension Fund v. Herrmann, 9 F.3d 1049, 1054 (2d Cir. 1993), cert. denied, 513 U.S. 822, 115 S. Ct. 86, 130 L. Ed. 2d 38 (1994); Roldan v. Racette, 984 F.2d 85, 89 (2d Cir. 1993); Frank v. Johnson, 968 F.2d 298, 300 (2d Cir.), cert. denied, 506 U.S. 1038, 113 S. Ct. 825, 121 L. Ed. 2d 696 (1992); Small v. Secretary of Health & Human Servs., 892 F.2d 15, 16 (2d Cir. 1989); Wesolek v. Canadair Ltd., 838 F.2d 55, 57-59 (2d Cir. 1988); McCarthy v. Manson, 714 F.2d 234, 237-38 (2d Cir. 1983); 28 U.S.C. § 636(b)(1); Fed R. Civ. P. 72, 6(a), 6(e).

DATED: New York, New York

August 16, 2007

Respectfully submitted,
Andrew J. Peck

United States Magistrate Judge

JUNE BAKER WORD, PLAINTIFF
v.
CHRISTIAN COUNTY KENTUCKY et al., DEFENDANTS

CIVIL ACTION NO. 5:07-CV163-R
UNITED STATES DISTRICT COURT FOR THE
WESTERN DISTRICT OF KENTUCKY
October 4, 2007

June Baker Word, Plaintiff, Pro se, Hopkinsville, KY.

Thomas B. Russell, Judge.

MEMORANDUM OPINION

The plaintiff, June Baker Word, filed this civil action against Christian County Kentucky; Steve Tribble, Christian County Judge Executive; and Freida Gilford, Director of the Christian County Animal Shelter. Since Plaintiff is proceeding *in forma pauperis,* this Court must review the instant action pursuant to 28 U.S.C. § 1915(e) and *McGore v. Wrigglesworth,* 114 F.3d 601 (6th Cir. 1997). The Court will dismiss Plaintiff's complaint for the reasons set forth below.

I. SUMMARY OF CLAIMS

Plaintiff used a court-supplied general complaint form to initiate this lawsuit. Under the section of the form directing Plaintiff to state the grounds for filing her case in federal court (including any federal and/or U.S. Constitutional provisions), Plaintiff states: "Abuse of my rights as an elderly person. I am 81 years old and have had my property stolen." In the "statement of claim" section of the form complaint, Plaintiff explains her claim as follows:

> Now that my daughter's state appeals have been exhausted, I am reinstating my suit to recover my animals taken from me via her false charge of animal abuse. While we have no proof of this, several animal professionals have told us Mrs. Gilford made this charge to get our pure breds. My animals include:

4 dogs-Max, a Neopolitan Mastiff which she sent to the Humane Society; Tess, Australian Shepherd/Collie Mix, Dylan, pure bred

Pembroke Welsh; Katrina, pure bred miniature **Daschund**

12 cats-Ariel and Samantha, yellow tigers; Miranda Blue, very large gray-white mix; Cassie, very small Russian Blue mix; Amelia, Sebastian, Bobby, all black; Percy, buff long hair mix; C.S. and Lionel, black and white mixes; Miss Fi, gray Tiger; and Felix, pure bred Himalayan

1-rabbit

1-guinea pig

As relief Plaintiff states that she is seeking the following:

a. Return all of my animals to me-reverse all adoptions and/or fosterings without any charge for care; and

b. County Judge Tribble and Mrs. Gilford pay me $ 500,000 for the pain I have suffered having my babies snatched from me. Also for the deaths of one much loved cat and one precious rabbit from negligence by shelter personnel, Mrs. Gilford especially. These animals are like children to me. I was forced to break my commitment to them and we have been denied each others' company for 16 months already. This is cruelty to an 81-year old woman and to the animals that loved and trusted me.

II. ANALYSIS

Upon initial review of the complaint, this Court must dismiss a case if it determines that the action is frivolous or malicious, fails to state a claim upon which relief may be granted, or seeks monetary relief from a defendant who is immune from such relief. 28 U.S.C. § 1915(e)(2)(B). A claim is legally frivolous when it lacks an arguable basis either in law or in fact. *Neitzke v. Williams,* 490 U.S. 319, 325, 109 S. Ct. 1827, 104 L. Ed. 2d 338 (1989). The Court may, therefore, dismiss a claim as frivolous where it is based on an indisputably meritless legal theory or where the factual contentions are clearly baseless. *Id.* at 327. When determining whether a plaintiff has stated a claim upon which relief can be granted, the Court must construe the complaint in the light most favorable to the plaintiff, accept all factual allegations as true, and determine whether the complaint contains "enough facts to state a claim to relief that is plausible on its face." *Bell Atl. Corp. v. Twombly,* --U.S.--, 127 S. Ct. 1955, 1974, 167 L.

Ed. 2d 929 (2007). "A plaintiff's obligation to provide the grounds of his entitlement to relief requires more than labels and conclusions, and a formulaic recitation of the elements of a cause of action will not do." *Id.* at 1964-65. Additionally, even though a complaint need not contain "detailed" factual allegations, its "[f]actual allegations must be enough to raise a right to relief above the speculative level on the assumption that all the allegations in the complaint are true." *Id.*

Although Plaintiff states that the basis of her claim is elder abuse/discrimination, nowhere does Plaintiff actually allege that her age was the motivating factor behind Defendants' decision to seize the animals. To the contrary, Plaintiff suggests that the animals were removed because Defendant Gilford wanted the pure breeds for her own financial gain. Therefore, at most, Plaintiff has alleged the wrongful taking of her property.

The Supreme Court has held that where adequate remedies are provided by state law, the negligent or intentional loss or destruction of personal property does not state a claim cognizable under the Due Process Clause. *Hudson v. Palmer,* 468 U.S. 517, 533, 104 S. Ct. 3194, 82 L. Ed. 2d 393 (1984); *Parratt v. Taylor,* 451 U.S. 527, 101 S. Ct. 1908, 68 L. Ed. 2d 420 (1981), *rev'd on other grounds by, Daniels v. Williams,* 474 U.S. 327, 106 S. Ct. 662, 88 L. Ed. 2d 662 (1986). In order to assert a claim for deprivation of property without due process pursuant to 42 U.S.C. § 1983, a plaintiff must allege that the state post-deprivation procedures are inadequate to remedy the deprivation. *Parratt,* 451 U.S. at 543-44. The law of this Circuit is in accord. For example, in *Vicory v. Walton,* 721 F.2d 1062 (6th Cir. 1983), the court held that "in § 1983 damage suits claiming the deprivation of a property interest without procedural due process of law, the plaintiff must plead and prove that state remedies for redressing the wrong are inadequate." *Id.* at 1066. The Sixth Circuit has found that Kentucky's statutory remedy for such losses is adequate within the meaning of *Parratt. See Wagner v. Higgins,* 754 F.2d 186, 191-92 (6th Cir. 1985). The same rationale applies to claims under the Fifth Amendment Takings Clause; that is, no taking has occurred absent a showing that available remedies have been pursued and have failed to provide adequate compensation. *Hudson v. Palmer,*

468 U.S. 517, 539, 104 S. Ct. 3194, 82 L. Ed. 2d 393 (1984) (O'Connor, J., concurring).

Here, Plaintiff has failed to allege that there are inadequate state remedies available through which she can either seek return of or compensation for the fair market value of the animals. [1] As such, Plaintiff cannot maintain a federal cause of action against Defendants for taking the animals. Therefore, the Court must dismiss this action for failure to state a claim.

1 The Court is mindful that many pet owners, like Plaintiff, consider their pets to be much more than mere property. However, under Kentucky state law dogs and cats are considered to be items of property, and state law provides for compensation for the wrongful/unauthorized destruction of such animals based on the fair market value of the animal. *See Duff v. Louisville & Nashville Railroad Co.*, 219 Ky. 238, 292 S.W. 814 (1927); *Ammon v. Welty*, 113 S.W.3d 185, 187 (Ky. Ct. App. 2002) ("The affection an owner has for, and receives from, a beloved dog is undeniable. It remains, however, that a dog is property, not a family member . . . The loss of love and affection resulting from the loss or destruction of personal property is not compensable.").

The Court will enter an Order consistent with this Memorandum Opinion.

Date: October 4, 2007

Thomas B. Russell, Judge

United States District Court

MURRILL L. MCLEAN, Plaintiff,
v.
PHILIP A. BROADFOOT,
Chief of Police of the City of Danville,
Defendant.

4:10CV00019
UNITED STATES DISTRICT COURT FOR
THE WESTERN DISTRICT OF VIRGINIA,
DANVILLE DIVISION
May 13, 2011

For Murrill L. McLean, Plaintiff: Henry Lavander Marsh , III, LEAD ATTORNEY, HILL TUCKER MARSH & JACKSON, RICHMOND, VA.

For Philip A. Broadfoot, Chief of Police of the City of Danville, Defendant: James A. L. Daniel, Martha G. White Medley, LEAD ATTORNEYS, DANIEL VAUGHAN MEDLEY & SMITHERMAN PC, DANVILLE, VA; Janine Marie Jacob, LEAD ATTORNEY, DANIEL, MEDLEY & KIRBY, P.C., DANVILLE, VA.

Jackson L. Kiser, Senior United States District Judge.

MEMORANDUM OPINION

Before me is a Motion for Summary Judgment filed on March 4th, 2011 by Defendant Philip Broadfoot, who is the Chief of the Danville Police Department. Mot. for Summ. J., Mar. 4, 2011, ECF No. 12; Def.'s Br. in Supp., Mar. 4, 2011, ECF No. 13. Under the Scheduling Order issued in this case, the Plaintiff, Murrill McLean, had fourteen days to submit his response. Pretrial Order 2, June 30, 2010, ECF No. 6 (providing that, "[b]riefs in opposition must be filed within 14 days of the date of service of the movant's brief...EXCEPT FOR GOOD CAUSE SHOWN, IF BRIEFS IN OPPOSITION TO THE MOTIONS ARE NOT FIELD, IT WILL BE DEEMED THAT THE MOTION IS WELL TAKEN") (bold text and capital letters in the original). Twenty-four days later, the Plaintiff filed a

Motion for Extension of Time to Respond and a Proposed Response. Mot. for Extension, Mar. 28, 2011, ECF No. 16. Unfortunately, everything beyond the first two pages of the eight page Proposed Response concerned another case with which Plaintiff's counsel is involved in the Eastern District of Virginia. See Proposed Resp. 3-8, Mar. 28, 2011, ECF No. 16-1. Furthermore, the Plaintiff never noticed his Motion for an Extension of Time for a hearing despite being reminded to do so by the Clerk's Office. The Scheduling Order provides that "[i]t shall be the obligation of the moving party to bring the motion on for hearing by notice." Pretrial Order 2. Over the next two days, the Defendant filed two Responses in Opposition to the Plaintiff's Motion for an Extension of Time. Def.'s Resp. in Opp'n I, Mar. 29, 2011, ECF No. 19; Def.'s Resp. in Opp'n II, Mar. 30, 2011, ECF No. 20. It was not until April 1st, fifteen days beyond the fourteen day deadline, that the Plaintiff submitted a meaningful Response. Pl.'s Resp., Apr. 1, 2011, ECF No. 21-1. Along with that second Response, Plaintiff's counsel submitted a Reply to the Defendant's two Responses in Opposition. Pl.'s Reply, Apr. 1, 2011, ECF No. 21. On May 5th, 2011 the Court held a hearing on both the Defendant's Motion for Summary Judgment and the Plaintiff's Motions for an Extension of Time. For the reasons explained herein, the Court GRANTS the Plaintiff's Motions for an Extension of Time, but HOLDS Plaintiff's counsel in civil contempt for his two violations of the Scheduling Order and IMPOSES A FINE of FIVE HUNDRED DOLLARS upon Plaintiff's counsel. The Court further GRANTS the Defendant's Motion for Summary Judgment on the Title VII claim and DECLINES to exercise supplemental jurisdiction over the Plaintiff's Virginia Human Rights Act claim.

FACTS

This case arises out of a contentious police shooting incident that occurred in the summer of 2009. Compl. 2-3, May 21, 2010, ECF No. 1. The parties agree that on June 8th, 2009, Officer Murrill McLean, the Plaintiff, was attempting to serve warrants at a house in north Danville. Compl. 2; Answer 1, June 30, 2010, ECF No. 4. While doing so, the Plaintiff was approached by a **dachshund** that had a history of attacking people in the community. Compl. 2; Answer 2. The Plaintiff admits that, in light of the dog's aggressive behavior, he shot the **dachshund**. Compl. 2; Aff. of Def. 5, Mar. 4, 2011, ECF No. 13-1. An investigation ensued amid rising tension and controversy. Compl. 3; Answer 2. The Defendant initially supported the Plaintiff, but later changed his position and said that the Plaintiff had acted improperly. Compl. 3; Aff. of Def. 3-5. On July 1st, 2009, the Defendant suspended the Plaintiff with pay and put him on notice of his intent to terminate him. July 1 Letter, Mar. 4, 2011, ECF No. 13-4. On July 10th, 2009, the Defendant terminated the Plaintiff, citing that the Plaintiff's "accounts of the event are factually incorrect and misleading" and his "reasoning for using deadly force was based on [an] overwhelming fear of contracting rabies," which "impairs [his] ability to make sound judgments." July 10 Letter, Mar. 4, 2011, ECF No. 13-5; Compl. 3. It is the details of these incidents over which the two sides disagree.

The first and most major disagreement is over what, exactly, happened on June 8th in north Danville. According to the Plaintiff, while attempting to serve warrants, he "was approached by a vicious dog from an adjacent driveway." Aff. of Pl., Mar. 28, 2011, ECF No. 16-2; Compl. 2. The Plaintiff made verbal attempts to scare the dog away, whereupon "the dog lunged to attack [him]." Aff. of Pl. 2; Compl. 2. The dog apparently "lunged at [him] a second time," prompting the Plaintiff to shoot the **dachshund**. Aff. of Pl. 2; Compl. 2. The Defendant demands strict proof of the Plaintiff's version of events. Answer 2.

In his affidavit, the Defendant provides more details about the findings made during the course of the investigation. Immediately after the shooting, the Plaintiff's two supervisors, Lieutenant Eanes and Corporal Chivvis, came to the scene. Aff. of Pl. 2. The Plaintiff was instructed to prepare a report of what occurred and Lieutenant Eanes was told to take pictures of the scene. Id. The Plaintiff's first statement indicates that he "pulled into the driveway at the residence and noticed a dog barking in the driveway." Pl.'s First Incident Report, Mar. 4, 2011, ECF No. 13-2. The Plaintiff went to the front door of the house, no one answered, at which time the Plaintiff avers:

> ...I turned to go back to my vehicle. The dog ran up behind me
> growling and lunged as I turned to leave. I felt certain that if I had
> hesitated for a moment the dog would have attacked and would
> have been too close to me to shoot. I barely had time to draw my
> weapon and fire hitting the animal at the foot of the steps
> approximately 2 to 3 feet from me. It spun once or twice then ran
> to the side of [the residence] where it died.

Id. The pictures taken by Lieutenant Eanes "depicted a dead

dachshund lying on the ground near three wooden steps."
Aff. of Def. 3. There was no blood on these wooden steps, which
were located at the side of the residence. Id. at 4.

Two days later, on June 10th, both the Plaintiff and another one of
his supervisors, Captain Jones, were asked to write detailed reports
about the shooting. Id. at 2. In that second report the Plaintiff states
that the dog was in the neighbor's driveway when he arrived, not the
driveway of the residence where he was attempting to serve the
warrants. Pl.'s Second Incident Report, Mar. 4, 2011, ECF No. 13-3.
Upon arrival, the Plaintiff alleges that the following events took
place:

> I went up 3 stairs to the front porch, which has trees on both sides
> of it and knocked on the front door. After waiting a few minutes I
> decided to leave, then from behind me as I turned I heard the
> growling of a dog at the foot of the steps, the animal showed his
> teeth and hunkered down, I was boxed in, the door I was knocking
> on was behind me and about three feet to the left of me another
> door and wall. While still standing at the door on the porch that was
> only 6 feet wide, I told it to "get" and it lunged forward towards me
> to attack. I had my metal clipboard with warrants in my left hand
> and had only seconds to un-holster. The dog was only two to three
> feet from me at this time and it started to lunge towards me and I
> fired one shot hitting the animal.

Id. Captain Jones also interviewed the Plaintiff and prepared a report
for the Defendant. Aff. of Def. 3. The next day, on June 11th, the
Defendant returned from a few days' vacation and spoke with the
Plaintiff by telephone and reviewed Captain Jones' report. Id. Based
on the aforementioned two sources, the Defendant believed that the
Plaintiff "was trapped and had very little time to react," prompting

him to shoot the dog on the residence's wooden side steps. Id. The Defendant even admits that "[b]ased on the information provided to me at the time, I publicly supported [the Plaintiff] and his actions." Id. The Plaintiff contends that, at this point, the internal investigation ended with the conclusion that he "had acted properly in defending [him]self against an attack by a vicious dog." Aff. of Pl. 2. It appears that the Plaintiff would characterize anything beyond this point as "continuous questioning, only to look for a pretext to fire [the Plaintiff]." Pl.'s Resp. 5, Apr. 1, 2011, ECF No. 21-1. Whether this difference in labeling creates a genuine issue of material fact is another matter. See Wards Co., Inc. v. Stamford Ridgeway Assocs., 761 F.2d 117, 120 (2d Cir. 1985) ("[c]ontorted semanticism must not be permitted to create an issue where none exists"); Kinsey v. Cendant Corp., 521 F.Supp.2d 292, 306 (S.D.N.Y. 2007) (semantic distinction was insufficient to create a genuine issue of material fact); Harmon v. Baltimore and Ohio R. Co., 560 F.Supp. 914, 916 (D.D.C. 1983) (same).

Later in the day on June 11th, the Defendant learned from news stories that there was blood on the porch steps of the house at which the shooting occurred. Aff. of Def. 3. The Defendant found this odd, since the pictures taken by Lieutenant Eanes showed no sign of blood on the wooden side steps. Id. This also seemed to contradict the Plaintiff's first report, in which the Plaintiff averred that he "fire[d] hitting the animal at the foot of the steps approximately 2 to 3 feet from [him]." Pl.'s First Incident Report. Perplexed, the Defendant visited the residence the next day, June 12th. Aff. of Def. 3. It was at this time that the Defendant saw that the residence had two sets of stairs, one in front with six brick steps and one on the side with three wooden steps. Id. The Defendant began to have questions about where the shooting actually occurred at this point, but apparently was unable to meet with the Plaintiff, who was out of the office on National Guard training. Id. at 4; Aff. of Pl. 2.

The Defendant met with the Plaintiff on June 24th and "specifically sought to clarify the location where the shooting had occurred." Aff. of Def. 4. The Plaintiff told the Defendant that the shooting happened at the front brick steps, not the side wooden steps, as the Defendant originally thought. Id. The Defendant then returned to the residence and spoke with the owner, who showed the Defendant the blood on the lowest step of the front brick steps. Id. The Defendant concluded that the Plaintiff had more space between him and the dog than he reported and that this increased space "offered more time to assess the situation and attempt to diffuse the situation without employing deadly force." Id.

The next day, on June 25th, Officer Brown went to the residence with a crime scene officer on the Defendant's orders. Id. at 5. Officer Brown and the crime scene officer measured the area and took photographs, "which further supported our conclusions of June 24, 2009 that [the Plaintiff] had more time to assess the situation and determine a more appropriate means of response than initially reported." Id. Officer Brown also interviewed the Plaintiff a few days later, on July 1st. Id. The Plaintiff apparently gave Officer Brown two inconsistent accounts of what happened back on June 8th. Id. At the culmination of his investigation, Officer Brown determined that the Defendant "used poor judgment in the decision to shoot the dog" and that the Plaintiff's series of statements were inconsistent. Id. Officer Brown reported these findings to the Defendant and recommended that the Plaintiff be terminated. Id. The Defendant "likewise concluded that terminating [the Plaintiff] was appropriate because [his] accounts of the event were factually incorrect and misleading and his overwhelming fear of contracting rabies interfered with his ability to make sound judgments with regard to the use of force." Id.

Along with the Plaintiff's first attempt to respond to the Defendant's Motion for Summary Judgment, which was itself ten days beyond the deadline, the Plaintiff included an affidavit. The bulk of the Plaintiff's affidavit appears to have been copied and pasted from the Complaint. Compare Aff. of Pl. 2-3 (paragraphs 6-16) with Compl. 2-3 (paragraphs 8-18). Interestingly, the Plaintiff does not dispute in his affidavit that he gave misleading information to the Defendant during the course of the investigation. The Plaintiff's affidavit also fails to address distance and time to react, key issues which the Defendant discussed at length in his affidavit. Aff. of Def. 3-5. In the Plaintiff's second Response to the Defendant's Motion for Summary Judgment, filed twenty-nine days after the Defendant's Motion, the Plaintiff asserts that the primary material fact in dispute is "whether plaintiff made inconsistent statements during the investigation into the complaint of his shooting of the dog." Pl.'s Resp. 3. The Plaintiff further avers that "[t]he allegation that plaintiff made inconsistent statements was a pretext." Id. This is the extent of the Plaintiff's refutation of the Defendant's allegation that the Plaintiff misled him and his investigators during the internal investigation following the shooting.

Although the Plaintiff does not rebut the Defendant's sworn statement that he gave misleading information during the investigation, he notes that "[n]ever before in the history of the City of Danville Police Department has an officer been terminated after being cleared of any wrongdoing by the Defendant." Aff. of Pl. 2. The Plaintiff further avers that "[n]o action was taken against Lieutenant Eanes, even though [the Defendant] found his report to be erroneous" and points out that Lieutenant Eanes is white. Id. In his affidavit, the Defendant insists that he has terminated six Police Department employees for lying during the course of an internal investigation since becoming chief in May 2003. Aff. of Def. 7. The Defendant further avers that:

> In several of [these] incidents...while the conduct itself may not have been egregious on its own, and may have only resulted in a reprimand or time off without pay had the employee been forthright about his/her conduct, the fact that the employee gave false information during the course of an internal investigation or tried to hide the conduct, led to the employee's termination.

Id. The Defendant has also provided copies of various Police Department regulations, its code of ethics, and its reasons for discipline and dismissal. Use of Force Policy, Mar. 4, 2011, ECF No. 13-6; Regulations, Mar. 4. 2011, ECF No. 13-7; Code of Ethics, Mar. 4, 2011, ECF No. 13-8; Reasons for Discipline and Dismissal, Mar. 4, 2011, ECF No. 13-9. All of these documents were either signed by the Plaintiff or provide that the Plaintiff, as an officer, is obligated to familiarize himself with them. Use of Force Policy 7; Regulations 4; Code of Ethics 1; Reasons for Discipline and Dismissal 1. According to the Defendant, it was the Plaintiff's poor judgment and lack of candor that resulted in his discharge. Aff. of Def. 6. The Plaintiff, by contrast, alleges that the Defendant's "decision to terminate my employment was not based on evidence, but based on racial discrimination." Aff. of Pl. 3.

Addressing the merits, the Defendant argues that he is entitled to summary judgment because he is not the Plaintiff's "employer" within the meaning of Title VII, rather the City of Danville would be the Plaintiff's Title VII "employer." Def.'s Br. in Supp. 6-7. Furthermore, the Plaintiff cannot establish a prima facie case under the framework of McDonnell Douglas Corp. v. Green, 411 U.S. 792, 802, 93 S. Ct. 1817, 36 L. Ed. 2d 668 (1973) because he cannot show that he was treated less favorably than disciplined employees from outside the protected class. Id. at 8-11. Even if he did establish a prima facie case, the Defendant has articulated a legitimate, non-discriminatory reason for dismissing the Plaintiff. Id. at 11-14. As for any claims arising out of the Virginia Human Rights Act, the Defendant reasserts his argument that he is not the Plaintiff's employer and thus cannot be liable under the Act. Id. at 15-17.

The Plaintiff counters that the Defendant was indeed the Plaintiff's employer, since he was the final decision-maker. Pl.'s Resp. 4. The Plaintiff does not respond to the Defendant's McDonnell Douglas Corp.-based arguments, but instead elects to proceed under the Desert Palace, Inc. v. Costa mixed-motive framework in which the Plaintiff will have to produce at least circumstantial evidence that race motivated the adverse employment action. Id. at 4-5; Desert Palace, Inc. v. Costa, 539 U.S. 90, 123 S. Ct. 2148, 156 L. Ed. 2d 84 (2003). The Plaintiff claims that he "has put forth, at a minimum, circumstantial evidence of [the Defendant]'s discriminatory intent and that an impermissible factor such as race motivated the adverse employment action." Pl.'s Resp. at 4. The Plaintiff further concedes that the Defendant has proffered a permissible reason for terminating the Defendant, but alleges that the reason was pretextual. Id. at 5. Finally, the Plaintiff argues that by violating Title VII, the Defendant has necessarily also violated the state Human Rights Act. Id. at 5.

On the issue of the late filings, in the initial Motion for an Extension of Time to Respond the Plaintiff states that he "inadvertently did not note the receipt of Defendant's Motion for Summary Judgment." Mot. for Extension 1. He further submits that his Response alleges no new facts and that the "Defendant will not be prejudiced by the granting of the extension." Id. The Defendant argues that it is well settled that inadvertence does not constitute excusable neglect. Def.'s Resp. in Opp'n I 2. Furthermore, the Defendant submits that it would prejudice him for the Court to allow the Plaintiff to violate the deadlines when the Defendant has scrupulously complied with the Scheduling Order. Id. at 4. As such, the Defendant asks that his Motion for Summary Judgment be deemed well taken, as provided in the Scheduling Order. Def.'s Resp. in Opp'n II 1; Pretrial Order 2.

In his Reply, Plaintiff's counsel admits that he did not begin preparing his Response to the Summary Judgment Motion until March 27th, nine days beyond the deadline. Pl.'s Reply 1. Plaintiff's counsel contends that his secretary filed the wrong document the next day. Id. at 2. Counsel appears to imply that because Defense counsel responded to his Motion for an Extension of Time in one day, the defense should have ample time to prepare for the motion hearing and will not be prejudiced by the Plaintiff's extraordinarily late filing. Id. In mitigation, when the case was first filed Plaintiff's counsel was part of a three person firm. Id. Two of those attorneys have since left counsel's firm, leaving him with more cases than he can handle. Id. at 2-3. Compounding counsel's problem are his duties as a state senator, which limit the amount of time he can devote to the practice of law. Id. Plaintiff's counsel submits that the "Plaintiff should not be penalized because of the transition of his representation." Id. at 3.

APPLICABLE LAW

Summary judgment is appropriate where there is no genuine issue of material fact and the movant is entitled to judgment as a matter of law. Fed. R. Civ. P. 56(c); George & Co. LLC v. Imagination Entertainment Ltd., 575 F.3d 383, 392 (4th Cir. 2009). On a Motion for Summary Judgment, the facts are taken in the light most favorable to the non-moving party, but only insofar as there is a genuine dispute about those facts. Scott v. Harris, 550 U.S. 372, 380, 127 S. Ct. 1769, 167 L. Ed. 2d 686 (2007). The movant has the initial burden of pointing out to the Court where the deficiency lies in the non-movants's case that would make it impossible for a reasonable fact-finder to bring in a verdict in the non-movants's favor. Celotex Corp. v. Catrett, 477 U.S. 317, 323, 106 S. Ct. 2548, 91 L. Ed. 2d 265

(1986). A movant-defendant may show that he is entitled to judgment as a matter of law by demonstrating that the non-movant plaintiff could not prove an essential element of his case. Id. at 322-23. It is then up to the non-movant to demonstrate to the Court that there are genuine issues of material fact and that he has made a sufficient showing on each of the essential elements of his case. Emmett v. Johnson, 532 F.3d 291, 297 (4th Cir. 2008); Hinkle v. City of Clarksburg, 81 F.3d 416, 421 (4th Cir. 1996). When the movant provides affidavits and other materials with his Motion for Summary Judgment, the non-movant must respond with affidavits, deposition testimony, or as otherwise provided in Fed. R. Civ. P. 56(c). Celotex Corp., 477 U.S. at 324; Pension Ben. Guar. Corp. v. Beverley, 404 F.3d 243, 246 (4th Cir. 2005). Mere allegations, denials, references to the Complaint, or oral argument is insufficient to rebut a movant's Motion which is supported by affidavits. Fed. R. Civ. P. 56(e)(2); Berckeley Inv. Group, Ltd. v. Colkitt, 455 F.3d 195, 201 (3d Cir. 2006); Beverley, 404 F.3d at 246. "Evidence, not contentions, avoids summary judgment." Al-Zubaidy v. TEK Industries, Inc., 406 F.3d 1030, 1036 (8th Cir. 2005). See also Goodman v. Nat'l Sec. Agency, Inc., 621 F.3d 651 (7th Cir. 2010) ("the non-moving party is required to marshal and present the court with the evidence [he] contends will prove [his] case"); Sylvia Dev. Corp. v. Calvert Cnty., 48 F.3d 810, 818 (4th Cir. 1995) (there is no genuine issue of material fact "unless the non-movant's version is supported by sufficient evidence to permit a reasonable jury to find the fact[s] in his favor"). Merely restating the allegations in the Complaint under penalty of perjury, therefore, cannot defeat a properly supported Motion for Summary Judgment. See Lujan v. Nat'l Wildlife Fed'n, 497 U.S. 871, 888, 110 S. Ct. 3177, 111 L. Ed. 2d 695 (1990) ("[t]he object of [Fed. R. Civ. P. 56(e)] is not to replace conclusory allegations of the complaint or answer with conclusory allegations of an affidavit") (citing references omitted); Law Enforcement Alliance of Am. v. USA Direct, Inc., 56 Fed.Appx. 147, 148 (4th Cir. 2003) ("[t]he nonmoving party's evidence must be probative, not merely colorable, cannot be conclusory statements...without specific evidentiary support") (internal citing references and quotation marks omitted); Fullman v. Graddick, 739 F.2d 553, 557 (11th Cir. 1984) ("mere verification of a party's own conclusory allegations is not sufficient to oppose a motion for summary judgment"); Zigmund v. Foster, 106 F.Supp.2d

352, 356 (D.Conn. 2000) ("[a]n affidavit in which the plaintiff merely restates the conclusory allegations of the complaint and denies the truth of the affidavits filed by the defendants is insufficient to create an issue of fact that would make summary judgment inappropriate") (citing reference omitted). It should further be noted that legal memoranda do not count as evidence and cannot, without more, create a genuine issue of material fact. Orson, Inc. v. Miramax Film Corp., 79 F.3d 1358, 1372 (3d Cir. 1996).

The Plaintiff alleges that he was the victim of discriminatory discipline. There are two ways the Plaintiff can overcome a motion for summary judgment on such a claim. Martin v. Scott & Stringfellow, Inc., 643 F.Supp.2d 770, 782 (E.D.Va. 2009). One option is for the Plaintiff to present "direct or circumstantial evidence that raises a genuine issue of material fact as to whether an impermissible factor such as race motivated the employer's adverse employment action." Tabor v. Freightliner of Cleveland, 388 Fed.Appx. 321, 322 (4th Cir. 2010) (citing Hill v. Lockheed Martin Logistics, 354 F.3d 277, 284 (4th Cir. 2004)). Where there is no direct evidence of discrimination, the second option is for the Plaintiff to use the burden-shifting framework established by the Supreme Court in McDonnell Douglas Corp. v. Green. Martin, 643 F.Supp.2d at 782.

Under McDonnell Douglas Corp., the Plaintiff must first make a prima facie case of discrimination. Merritt v. Old Dominion Freight Line, Inc., 601 F.3d 289, 294 (4th Cir. 2010). The Supreme Court has recognized that the wording of the four-part test is fact specific. McDonnell Douglas Corp., 411 U.S. at 802 n.13. Where disparate treatment in discipline is at issue, the Fourth Circuit has held that a plaintiff establishes a prima facie case by showing:

> (1) that he is a member of the class protected by Title VII, (2) that the prohibited conduct in which he engaged was comparable in seriousness to misconduct of employees outside the protected class, and (3) that the disciplinary measures enforced against him were more severe than those enforced against other employees.

Cook v. CSX Transp. Corp., 988 F.2d 507, 511 (4th Cir. 1993) (citing Moore v. City of Charlotte, 754 F.2d 1100, 1105-06 (4th Cir. 1985)). See also Hoyle v. Freightliner, LLC, 650 F.3d 321, 2011 U.S. App. LEXIS 6628, 2011 WL 1206658, at *11 (4th Cir. 2011). Once the

Plaintiff establishes a prima facie case of disparate treatment, the "burden of production then shifts to the employer to articulate a legitimate, non-discriminatory justification for its allegedly discriminatory action." Merritt, 601 F.3d at 294 (citing Tex. Dep't of Cmty. Affairs v. Burdine, 450 U.S. 248, 253, 101 S. Ct. 1089, 67 L. Ed. 2d 207 (1981)). If the employer is able to do this, the Plaintiff may then demonstrate that the "neutral" reasons offered by the employer are a pretext for discrimination. Merritt, 601 F.3d at 294.

ANALYSIS

I. The Plaintiff Has Consistently Failed to Follow the Scheduling Order and the Local Rules

Fortunately, this Court is not often confronted with situations where parties file briefs more than a few days late. The Plaintiff's Response here, however, is unusually late--fifteen days late. The Plaintiff's first Motion for an Extension of Time was filed ten days after the fourteen day deadline had elapsed. This first motion was not accompanied by a supporting brief, as required by the local rules. W.D.Va. Civ. R. 11(c) (providing that "[b]riefs need not accompany motions...for an extension of time to respond to or file pleadings, *unless the time has already expired*") (emphasis added). In the body of the motion, Plaintiff's counsel provided a five sentence justification for his tardiness by stating that he "inadvertently did not note the receipt of Defendant's Motion." [1] Mot. for Extension 1. Plaintiff's counsel further asserted that he alleged no new facts, that the Defendant would not be prejudiced, and that his motion should be granted "to meet the ends of justice." Id. at 1-2. He then filed a "Motion for Leave to File the Correct Response" five days later, which one can assume is also an implicit Second Motion for an Extension of Time. See Pl.'s Reply 1-2 (the first two pages appear to be both a motion and supporting brief for a time extension, setting out the reasons for the untimely Response and why the Court should consider the Plaintiff's Response).

1 W.D.Va. Civ. R. 11(c) provides that "a separate brief is not required where a motion itself contains the legal and factual argument necessary to support the motion." It is debatable whether counsel's Motion falls into this category.

Both the Federal Rules of Civil Procedure and the Supreme Court have made it clear that the criteria the District Court is to use in considering whether to grant an extension depends on whether the motion was made before or after the deadline. Fed. R. Civ. P. 6(b)(1); Lujan v. Nat'l Wildlife Fed'n, 497 U.S. 871, 895-97, 110 S. Ct. 3177, 111 L. Ed. 2d 695 (1990). When the motion comes after the deadline, as both motions have here, the party filing late must show both good cause and excusable neglect for the untimely filing. Lujan, 497 U.S. at 896. District Courts have wide discretion to grant or deny extensions and the Fourth Circuit prefers that matters be resolved on their merits. Choice Hotels Intern., Inc. v. Goodwin and Boone, 11 F.3d 469, 471-72 (4th Cir. 1993) (preference for resolution on the merits); Marryshow v. Flynn, 986 F.2d 689, 693 (4th Cir. 1993) (broad discretion). It should be noted, however, that "excusable neglect is not easily demonstrated, nor was it intended to be." Thompson v. E.I. DuPont de Nemours & Co., Inc., 76 F.3d 530, 534 (4th Cir. 1996).

Although excusable neglect is a "somewhat elastic concept" and can include negligent oversight, there are limits to what a District Court may accept as excusable neglect. Pioneer Inv. Servs. Co. v. Brunswick Assocs. Ltd. P'ship, 507 U.S. 380, 392-95, 113 S. Ct. 1489, 123 L. Ed. 2d 74 (1993).

> The determination of whether neglect is excusable is at bottom an equitable one, taking account of all relevant circumstances surrounding the party's omission, including the danger of prejudice to the nonmoving party, the length of the delay and its potential impact on judicial proceedings, the reason for the delay, including whether it was within the reasonable control of the movant, and whether the movant acted in good faith.

Bredell v. Kempthorne, 290 Fed.Appx. 564, 565 (4th Cir. 2008) (quoting Pioneer Inv. Servs. Co., 507 U.S. at 395) (internal citing references and quotation marks omitted). In this case, the real prejudice cited by the Defendant is the fact that he has complied with the deadlines while the Plaintiff has not, and that this fact should not go unnoticed. Def.'s Resp. in Opp'n I 4. The Plaintiff's delay has been unusually long. In fact, the Defendant correctly points out that it took the Plaintiff longer to respond to the Motion for Summary Judgment than he would have had to answer a complaint. Id. at 3. The original motion hearing date was already within the Scheduling Order's thirty day window between dispositive motion hearings and trial. Pretrial Order 2 ("[a]ll Rule 12 and Rule 56 motions must be heard or submitted on briefs no later than 30 days prior to trial"). Because the Defendant filed his Motion for Summary Judgment far enough in advance, it is unlikely that the Clerk's Office would have had to push the hearing date back any further, even in spite of the Plaintiff's tardiness. [2]

> 2 The hearing date was in fact moved back by three weeks and the trial by over three months because of scheduling conflicts with Plaintiff's counsel's commitments in the General Assembly, but not necessarily because of his late response.

The most important of the excusable neglect considerations is the reason for the untimely filing. Thompson, 76 F.3d at 534. The reason originally offered by Plaintiff's counsel, that he "inadvertently did not note the receipt of Defendant's Motion," does not usually constitute excusable neglect. Pioneer Inv. Servs. Co., 507 U.S. at 392; Thompson, 76 F.3d at 533; Mot. for Extension 1. The fact that Plaintiff's counsel's secretary originally filed the wrong document also falls short of excusable neglect, especially in light of the fact that Plaintiff's counsel admits that he did not begin preparing his Response until nine days after the deadline. Pl.'s Reply 1; Van Horn v. Perrine, No. 90-2142, 1991 U.S. App. LEXIS 841, 1991 WL 4655, at *1 (4th Cir. Jan. 18, 1991) (attempting to blame a secretary's errors for missing deadlines does not establish good cause); Hart v. U.S., 817 F.2d 78, 81 (9th Cir. 1987) ("[s]ecretarial negligence...is chargeable to counsel"). In what might be construed as the Plaintiff's Second Motion for an Extension, Plaintiff's counsel avers that the main reason he needed an extension was because he was busy with his duties in the General Assembly. Pl.'s Reply 3. This should not be considered a valid reason for the untimely filings, especially since Plaintiff's counsel knew or should have known that the General Assembly would be taking up the issue of redistricting in light of the recent Census. Key v. Robertson, 626 F.Supp.2d 566, 577-78 (E.D.Va. 2009) (being extremely busy does not qualify as excusable neglect). See also Shoulders v. U.S. Dept. of Agriculture, 878 F.2d 141, 143 (4th Cir. 1989) (attorney who was a member of the Virginia General Assembly and who missed a deadline to file a claim in federal court could not rely on Va. Code Ann. § 30-5, which gives General Assembly members a continuance of right in state court, to extend the deadline). Again, this explanation does not justify counsel's failure to move for an extension *before* the deadline. Counsel's final reason for the delay, that the two other lawyers in his practice left, is certainly a sympathetic one. Although perhaps a bit cruel, this is not something many courts have considered to be excusable neglect. See, e.g., Pioneer Inv. Servs. Co., 507 U.S. at 398 ("[w]e give little weight to the fact that counsel was experiencing upheaval in his law practice at the time"); Morris-Belcher v. Housing Authority of City of Winston-Salem, No. 1:04cv255, 2005 WL 1423592, at *4 (M.D.N.C. June 17, 2005) (finding that an attorney's handling cases for a disbarred lawyer and having an unmanageable caseload as a result did not constitute excusable neglect, especially since that attorney failed to explain why he did not move for an extension before the deadline).

Nonetheless, it has been recognized that District Courts have wide discretion in granting extensions and the appellate courts will only reverse for an abuse of that discretion. Marryshow, 986 F.2d at 693. In a fairly recent published opinion, it was noted that "the liberal spirit of the rules...has always been followed in the United States District Court for the Western District of Virginia." Cornett v. Weisenburger, 454 F.Supp.2d 544, 549 (W.D.Va. 2006). Fed. R. Civ. P. 16(f)(1)(C) authorizes the Court to impose a wide range of sanctions for non-compliance with the Scheduling Order. The Court's options include not considering the brief or treating the non-compliance as civil contempt meriting a fine. See Nick v. Morgan's Foods, Inc., 270 F.3d 590, 595-96 (8th Cir. 2001) (Fed. R. Civ. P. 16(f) permits a Court to impose a fine payable to the Court); Rutledge v. Town of Chatham, No. 4:10cv35, 2010 U.S. Dist. LEXIS 122273, 2010 WL 4791840, at * 2 (W.D.Va. Nov. 18, 2010) (refusing to consider the pro se plaintiff's untimely brief), aff'd per curiam sub nom. Rutledge v. Roach, No. 10-2310, 414 Fed. Appx. 568, 2011 U.S. App. LEXIS 4170, 2011 WL 755622 (4th Cir. Mar. 4, 2011); Lederer v. Hargraves Tech. Corp., 256 F.Supp.2d 467, 469-70 (W.D.N.C.

2003) (Court refused to consider a party's late response brief where the explanation for the delay was mere inadvertence). In light of the Fourth Circuit's preference that its District Courts resolve cases on their merits, this Court has considered the Plaintiff's Response, but holds Plaintiff's counsel in civil contempt for its very late filing. Choice Hotels Intern., Inc., 11 F.3d at 471-72 (preference for resolution on the merits); Fed R. Civ. P. 16(f)(1)(C); Pretrial Order 1-2 (explaining motion deadlines). The Court further holds Plaintiff's counsel in contempt for his failure to notice his Motion for an Extension of Time for a hearing. Fed. R. Civ. P. 16(f)(1)(C); Pretrial Order 2 (setting out the movant's obligation to notice his motion for a hearing). For these two violations of the Scheduling Order the Court imposes a five hundred dollar fine on Plaintiff's counsel.

II. The Plaintiff Has Sued a Proper Defendant

Although perhaps more appropriately brought up in a motion to dismiss, the Defendant's preliminary argument in his summary judgment motion is that he is not the Plaintiff's employer for Title VII purposes and thus is not the proper party here. Def.'s Br. in Supp. 6. The Defendant would be correct if this were an individual capacity suit, but it is not. The Defendant cites Huff v. Southwest Virginia Reg'l Jail Auth. for the proposition that the Defendant is the wrong party regardless of whether he is sued in his individual or official capacity. Def.'s Br. in Supp. 6 n.1 (citing Huff v. Southwest Virginia Reg'l Jail Auth., No. 1:08cv00041, 2009 U.S. Dist. LEXIS 12853, 2009 WL 395392, at *6 (W.D.Va. Feb. 17, 2009)). Specifically, the Defendant appears to rely on a two sentence paragraph from the Huff case which explains:

> The court also is not persuaded by Huff's argument that because these defendants were sued in *both* their individual *and* official capacities, her Title VII claim against them should not be dismissed. This is because the "official capacity" to which Huff refers is exactly the capacity that the Lissau court found insufficient to confer liability under Title VII.

Id. (citing Lissau v. Southern Food Serv., Inc., 159 F.3d 177 (4th Cir. 1998)). The Huff Court only cited Lissau generally for the above proposition. Although Huff is persuasive, it is not binding upon this

Court. See Gasperini v. Center for Humanities, Inc., 518 U.S. 415, 430 n.10, 116 S. Ct. 2211, 135 L. Ed. 2d 659 (1996) (each district judge "sits alone and renders decisions not binding on the others," even within the same judicial district). In the case at bar, there is no indication that the Plaintiff is attempting to hold Philip Broadfoot personally liable for Title VII violations. For example, in the Complaint the Plaintiff demands a declaratory judgment, compensatory damages of $250,000, other "appropriate reimbursement," and that the Court retain jurisdiction over this matter to ensure compliance with Title VII. Compl. 4. This is not the sort of relief typically sought from an individual defendant. Furthermore, the Complaint notes the Defendant's role as Chief of Police. Compl. 1.

Although the Fourth Circuit has made it clear that supervisors cannot be sued in their individual capacities under Title VII, this does not mean that the Plaintiff in the case at bar has sued the wrong Defendant. Lissau, 159 F.3d at 181. See also Luy v. Baltimore Police Dept., 326 F.Supp.2d 682, 687 (D.Md. 2004), aff'd per curiam, 120 Fed.Appx. 465 (4th Cir. 2005). A supervisor can be a proper defendant in a Title VII suit where he is sued in his capacity as an agent of the employer. See Hinson v. Clinch Cnty. Bd. of Educ., 231 F.3d 821, 827 (11th Cir. 2000) ("[t]he only proper individual defendants in a Title VII action would be supervisory employees in their capacity as agents of the employer"); Malone v. Shenandoah Cnty. Dept. of Soc. Servs., No. 5:04-cv-114, 2005 WL 1902857, at *2 (W.D.Va. Aug. 9, 2005) (noting that, in Title VII suits, Lissau only stands for the proposition that supervisors cannot be sued in their individual capacities and hinting that this would not preclude official capacity suits, but ultimately deciding the issue on other grounds); Zakeri v. Oliver, 19 F.Supp.2d 553, 556 (E.D.Va. 1998) (although the Fourth Circuit has not decided the issue, other circuits have held that a plaintiff can recover under Title VII by naming supervisors as agents of the employer). While this is not precisely the same principle as the individual/official capacity distinction for the purposes of sovereign immunity or § 1983 claims, it is its conceptual blood brother. Compare Busby v. City of Orlando, 931 F.2d 764, 772 (11th Cir. 1991) (discussing the relationship between official and individual capacity in the context of lawsuits brought under both 42 U.S.C. §

1983 and Title VII and concluding that "[w]e think the proper method for a plaintiff to recover under Title VII is by suing the employer, either by naming the supervisory employees as agents of the employer or by naming the employer directly") with Will v. Michigan Dept. of State Police, 491 U.S. 58, 71, 109 S. Ct. 2304, 105 L. Ed. 2d 45 (1989) (for Eleventh Amendment purposes, a suit against a state official in his official capacity is "no different from a suit against the State itself) and Kentucky v. Graham, 473 U.S. 159, 165-66, 105 S. Ct. 3099, 87 L. Ed. 2d 114 (1985) (in a § 1983 claim, an official capacity suit is "an action against an entity of which an officer is an agent" and "the real party in interest is the entity") (citing references omitted).

The Defendant offers another case from this District, Session v. Anderson, for the proposition that the individual/official capacity distinction is one without a difference for the purposes of Title VII. Session v. Anderson, No. 7:09cv138, 2010 U.S. Dist. LEXIS 12078, 2010 WL 519839, at *2 (W.D.Va. Feb. 11, 2010). In Session, a plaintiff brought a Title VII claim against a county school board and the superintendent of the county schools in her official capacity. 2010 U.S. Dist. LEXIS 12078, [WL] at *1. The Court dismissed the claim against the superintendent, finding that she was not the plaintiff's employer under Title VII. 2010 U.S. Dist. LEXIS 12078, [WL] at *2. In Session, as in Malone, the county board or department was a named defendant and so remained after the Court dismissed the claims against the supervisor. Compare Session, 2010 U.S. Dist. LEXIS 12078, 2010 WL 519839, at *1 with Malone, 2005 WL 1902857, at *2. The Malone Court best explained the rationale behind its ruling when it commented that "the Title VII claim against [the supervisor], in his official capacity, is redundant and may be dismissed since the claim is also asserted against [the county department]." Malone, 2005 WL 1902857, at *2. Since the Plaintiff's agent/official capacity suit is, in essence, an action against the City of Danville, the Plaintiff has sued a proper defendant.

III. The Plaintiff Has Produced No Evidence That His Discharge Was Racially Motivated

In his Response, the Plaintiff makes no mention of burden-shifting, but instead asserts that he "has put forth, at a minimum, circumstantial evidence of [the Defendant]'s discriminatory intent and that an impermissible factor such as race motivated the adverse employment decision." Pl.'s Resp. 4. This is the mixed motive language from Desert Palace, Inc., 539 U.S. at 101-02. Before discussing the evidence the Plaintiff has put forth, it is useful to review what constitutes "circumstantial evidence" under Desert Palace and its Fourth Circuit counterpart, Hill v. Lockheed Martin Logistics Management, Inc., 354 F.3d 277 (4th Cir. 2004). No matter the theory under which the Plaintiff proceeds:

> ...the ultimate question in every employment discrimination case involving a claim of disparate treatment is whether the plaintiff was the victim of intentional discrimination. To demonstrate such an intent to discriminate on the part of the employer, an individual alleging disparate treatment based upon a protected trait must produce sufficient evidence upon which one could find that the protected trait actually motivated the employer's decision. The protected trait must have actually played a role in the employer's decisionmaking process and had a determinative influence on the outcome.

Hill, 354 F.3d at 286 (internal citing references, quotation marks, and punctuation omitted). See also Adams v. The Trustees of the Univ. of N.C. Wilmington, 640 F.3d 550, 2011 U.S. App. LEXIS 7036, 2011 WL 1289054, at *7 (4th Cir. 2011). To be clear, Desert Palace and Hill did not give plaintiffs the option of proceeding under a truncated version of McDonnell Douglas whereby they could survive summary judgment simply by establishing a prima facie case. Diamond v. Colonial Life & Acc. Ins. Co., 416 F.3d 310, 317-18 (4th Cir. 2005). If that were so, no plaintiff would present his Title VII claim under the McDonnell Douglas framework because there would be a much easier option available to him. Id. at 319 n.5 (Desert Palace did not nullify McDonnell Douglas). By way of example, courts have found that plaintiffs have proffered circumstantial evidence of racial motives where the plaintiff has offered statistics, racially charged comments in connection with employment, or even suspicious timing in the context of unlawful retaliation cases. Austin v. Rappahannock Area Alcohol Safety Action Program, No. 3:09cv200, 2009 U.S. Dist. LEXIS 102806, 2009 WL 3669734, at *2 (E.D.Va. Nov. 4, 2009) (comments and suspicious timing); Mulvey v.

Bellsouth Telecommunications, Inc., No. 2:08-3547, 2010 U.S. Dist. LEXIS 99406, 2010 WL 3782852, at *11 (D.S.C. July 12, 2010) (suspicious timing); Martin v. Alumax of South Carolina, Inc., 380 F.Supp.2d 723, 735-36 (D.S.C. 2005) (comments); E.E.O.C. v. Jordan Graphics, Inc., 769 F.Supp. 1357, 1383 (W.D.N.C. 1991) (statistics).

As evidence of racial motives, the Plaintiff points to his assertion that "he was investigated by his immediate supervisor and was cleared of any wrongdoing" and that "[i]t was only after some time, did [the Defendant] subject [the Plaintiff] to continuous questioning, only to look for a pretext to fire [the Plaintiff]." Id. at 5. Both parties admit that the Defendant continued looking into the shooting after this point, but the Plaintiff appears to contend that this was not an "investigation" but rather "continuous questioning...to look for a pretext." Compare Id. at 5 with Aff. of Def. 6. Both parties also agree that the Defendant initially supported the Plaintiff's actions in the shooting, but later, after further "investigation"/"continuous questioning," the Defendant switched his position. Compare Aff. of Pl. 2-3 with Aff. of Def. 3-6. It is the agreement over the substance of what occurred, not the artificial difference in labeling, that matters here. See Wards Co., Inc., 761 F.2d at 120; Kinsey, 521 F.Supp.2d at 306; Harmon, 560 F.Supp. at 916.

The Defendant devotes three pages of his affidavit to explaining the reason for his change in positions. Aff. of Def. 3-6; Hill, 354 F.3d at 293 (in a discriminatory discipline case, the Court must look at the facts as they appeared to the person making the decision to discipline). See also Gibson v. Fluor Daniel Servs. Corp., 281 Fed.Appx. 177, 179 (4th Cir. 2008) ("an employer who fires an employee under the mistaken but honest impression that the employee violated a work rule is not liable for discriminatory conduct") (citing references omitted). Based on the information available to him the day he returned from vacation, the Defendant supported the Plaintiff. Id. at 2-3. Later that same day, however, the Defendant began to second guess his decision. Id. at 3. Over the course of the next two and a half weeks, the inquiry into the shooting continued, during which time the Defendant met with the Plaintiff to question him about the incident, directed a group of officers to conduct an internal investigation, and twice visited the residence where the shooting took place. Id. at 3-5. At the culmination of this inquiry, the Defendant believed he made a mistake in initially supporting the Plaintiff. Id. at 5.

The Plaintiff, on the other hand, asserts that "[a]fter a thorough and complete investigation," Lieutenant Eanes "concluded that I had acted properly." Aff. of Pl. 2. "Some time after that, complaints were made regarding the shooting," including one by a city councilman. Id. At the hearing, Plaintiff's counsel commented that "it was okay until there was a public furor about it." The Plaintiff specifically alleges that because of that pressure, the Defendant changed his position, found Lieutenant Eanes' investigation to be erroneous, and "stated publicly that [the Plaintiff] had not acted properly." Id. This resulted in the Plaintiff being discharged "after being cleared of any wrongdoing by the Defendant" while Lieutenant Eanes, who is white, was not punished at all, "even though [the Defendant] found his report to be erroneous." Id. at 3. For the purposes of comparing disciplinary action to establish pretext or discriminatory motive, however, innocently proffering a report that turns out to be erroneous differs significantly from providing intentionally misleading information. [3] Bell v. Town of Port Royal, 586 F.Supp.2d 498, 510-13 (D.S.C. 2008) (terminated police officer did not offer sufficient circumstantial evidence under Hill where he showed other officers were disciplined differently, but those officers had not engaged in the same type of misconduct as the terminated officer). Courts consistently find that an employee who intentionally gives misleading information to his employer has not met his employer's expectations and has given the employer a legitimate, non-discriminatory reason to terminate the employee. See Garrett v. Langley Federal Credit Union, 121 F.Supp.2d 887, 901 (E.D.Va. 2000) (lying to one's employer is a legitimate, non-discriminatory rationale for terminating employment); Anderson v. Duke Energy Corp., No. 3:06cv399, 2008 U.S. Dist. LEXIS 81649, 2008 WL 4596238, at *11 (W.D.N.C. Oct. 14, 2008) (dishonest employee was not meeting her employer's legitimate expectations).

---

3 From the Defendant's Affidavit, it appears that the reason Lieutenant Eanes' report and photographs were erroneous was because the Lieutenant was getting his information from the Plaintiff. See Aff. of Def. 2-3.

Not only has the Plaintiff failed to rebut the Defendant's assertion that he intentionally provided misleading information during the internal investigation, the Plaintiff almost concedes the point implicitly. See Aff. of Pl. 3 ("No action was taken against Lieutenant Eanes, even though [the Defendant] found his report to be erroneous"). When confronted with this at the hearing, Plaintiff's counsel insisted that although the Plaintiff never denied the Defendant's allegation in his affidavit, he never admitted it either. At any rate, Plaintiff's counsel advised that the Plaintiff was, as of the hearing, denying that he misled the Defendant. Under Fed. R. Civ. P. 56(e), however, this denial in oral argument is too little too late. Berckeley Inv. Group, 455 F.3d at 201; Beverley, 404 F.3d at 246.

The Plaintiff avers that it was only after "some time" that the Defendant subjected him to "continuous questioning," but the Plaintiff admits that, following the shooting, he was out of the office for training and does not dispute that he was unavailable to meet with the Defendant at that time. Aff. of Pl. 2 (out on training); Aff. of Def. 4 (the Plaintiff was deployed with the National Guard for two weeks when the Defendant returned to the office on June 11th). Furthermore, although the Plaintiff characterizes the questioning as "continuous," he offers no other instances of questioning after Lieutenant Eanes' investigation aside from the two in late June/early July, which were a week apart from one another. Aff. of Def. 4-5. Although doubtful, the Plaintiff may have offered sufficient circumstantial evidence that pressure from local politicians possibly played a role in the Plaintiff's discharge. Aff. of Pl. 2 (city councilman publicly complained about the shooting at a City Council meeting and "[s]ubsequent to pressure placed on him by certain individuals, defendant stated that the investigation was erroneous and stated publicly that [the Plaintiff] had not acted properly"). But see Hill, 354 F.3d at 291 ("an employer will be liable not for the improperly motivated person who merely influences the decision, but for the person who in reality makes the decision"); Cruz v. Town of South Boston, No. 4:06cv1, 2006 U.S. Dist. LEXIS 91550, 2006 WL 3760140, at *4 (W.D.Va. Dec. 19, 2006) ("the burden rests on the plaintiff to prove that the person who allegedly acted with discriminatory intent was the actual decisionmaker") (Kiser, J.). Most importantly, however, he has offered no evidence whatsoever, circumstantial or direct, that race was a motive in his termination. As the Defendant astutely points out, termination because of political pressure, while certainly unfair, is not actionable under Title VII. Hill, 354 F.3d at 286 (the protected trait must have motivated the adverse employment action); Def.'s Br. in Supp. 14.

IV. The Plaintiff Has Not Made a Prima Facie Case Under McDonnell Douglas

In light of the Plaintiff's failure to produce any evidence that race was a motivating factor in this disciplinary action, his second option would be to use the burden-shifting method of the McDonnell Douglas case. Laber v. Harvey, 438 F.3d 404, 430 (4th Cir. 2006); Martin, 643 F.Supp.2d at 782. Although the Plaintiff's briefs appear to indicate that he is proceeding under the mixed motive framework, at the hearing the Plaintiff seemed to abandon the mixed motive framework in favor of the burden-shifting framework. In an effort to give the Plaintiff the benefit of the doubt, then, the Court includes an analysis under McDonnell Douglas. Unfortunately, the Plaintiff is unable to establish a prima facie case using the discriminatory discipline test the Fourth Circuit formulated in Cook v. CSX Transp. Corp. and invoked very recently in Hoyle v. Freightliner, LLC. Hoyle, 650 F.3d 321, 2011 U.S. App. LEXIS 6628, 2011 WL 1206658, at *11; Cook, 988 F.2d at 511.

There is no question that the Plaintiff meets the first of Cook's three prongs. Cook, 988 F.2d at 511 (first element is that the Plaintiff is a member of a protected class). As to the second prong, the Plaintiff contends that the six other instances in which the Defendant has terminated employees for dishonesty during an internal investigation were not comparable in seriousness to the Plaintiff's situation. Id. Of those six employees, five were white and one was black. Aff. of Def. 7. Their underlying misconduct included sending harassing e-mails, alerting a citizen that the police had obtained a search warrant for his property, taking money from an office collection, covering up a single car accident involving a police cruiser, and providing false information in reports of investigation. Id. At the hearing, the Plaintiff attempted to take the focus off of whether he lied to the Defendant by arguing that the underlying conduct mentioned above is "criminal" and significantly more serious than shooting a dog.

While the argument that sending harassing e-mails or covering up an accident involving a police cruiser is more grievous than shooting someone's pet is astounding, it also fails to address the real issue here--lying to a boss or supervisor about a work-related matter. The Defendant acknowledges that:

> In several of the incidents above, while the conduct itself may not have been egregious on its own, and may have only resulted in a reprimand or time off without pay had the employee been forthright about his/her conduct, the fact that the employee gave false information during the course of an internal investigation or tried to hide the conduct, led to the employee's termination.

Id. As to both underlying conduct and, more importantly, attendant dishonesty, the Court finds that the Plaintiff's misconduct is at least as serious as the six prior instances offered by the Defendant, if not more serious than a few of them. See Tabor, 388 Fed.Appx. at 322 ("precise equivalence in culpability between employees is not the ultimate question...comparison can be made in light of the harm caused or threatened to the victim or society, and the culpability of the offender") (citing reference omitted); Cook, 988 F.2d at 511 (holding that only discipline imposed for like offenses should be compared and noting "the reality that the comparison will never involve precisely the same set of work-related offenses occurring over the same period of time and under the same sets of circumstances") (citing reference omitted). It should also be noted that this is not a case where the Defendant has changed his justification for the termination at any point. Compare July 1 Letter 1 with Aff. of Def. 6. See also E.E.O.C. v. Sears Roebuck and Co., 243 F.3d 846, 852-53 (4th Cir. 2001) (the fact that an employer has given shifting explanations for an adverse employment action is generally probative of pretext). The Plaintiff offers one more instance of employee misconduct, specifically that the Defendant found Lieutenant Eanes' internal investigation report to be erroneous. Aff. of Pl. 3. As discussed above in Section III, Lieutenant Eanes' conduct, if it could even be characterized as misconduct, was not comparable in seriousness to the Plaintiff's.

For the six instances of discipline that were similar to the facts in this case, the Plaintiff cannot meet Cook's third prong, "that the disciplinary measures enforced against him were more severe than those enforced against those other employees." Hoyle, ___ F.3d ___, 2011 U.S. App. LEXIS 6628, 2011 WL 1206658, at *11; Cook, 988 F.2d at 511. Those six other employees were fired, just like the Plaintiff. Aside from the aforementioned Lieutenant Eanes incident, the Plaintiff offers no other instances of misconduct where the sanction imposed by the Defendant was any different. The Plaintiff has therefore failed to establish a prima facie case of discriminatory discipline.

V. The Plaintiff Has Not Shown That the Proffered Reason for the Discharge Was a Pretext

The Defendant admits that he initially supported the Plaintiff, but upon further investigation he changed his position. Aff. of Def. 3-5. The Plaintiff contends that the Defendant's explanation of that change in position, that further inquiry showed that the Plaintiff had misled the chief and his officers about what occurred, is a pretext for discrimination. Pl.'s Resp. 5. Progressing to the pretext analysis presumes, of course, that the Plaintiff has made a prima facie case under McDonnell Douglas, which he has not done. [4] Cook, 988 F.2d at 511.

> 4 The pretext analysis is only applicable to cases using McDonnell Douglas' burden-shifting framework. See Diamond, 416 F.3d at 318 (distinguishing the two tests). Because the Desert Palace-style cases require some showing of discriminatory motive at the outset, a separate pretext inquiry would be redundant under that mixed-motive framework.

There is no question that the reason the Defendant offers, that the Plaintiff intentionally misled him, is an acceptable, race-neutral explanation. Garrett, 121 F.Supp.2d at 901. Assuming for the sake of discussion that the Plaintiff has established a prima facie case under McDonnell Douglas, he has still failed to demonstrate race-based pretext. The key question is whether the Plaintiff has offered any evidence that the Defendant did not believe that the Plaintiff intentionally misled him when he made the decision to terminate the Plaintiff. Holland v. Washington Homes, Inc., 487 F.3d 208, 215 (4th Cir. 2007). The Plaintiff offers some evidence that the Defendant decided to fire him after the City Council pressed the issue of the shooting, prompting the continuing inquiry to look for a reason for dismissal. Aff. of Pl. 2-3. Although probative of termination because of political pressure, this evidence has nothing to do with firing the Plaintiff because of race discrimination. To show pretext, it is incumbent upon the Plaintiff to show that the Defendant's explanation is a pretext *for discrimination*. See Bonds v. Leavitt, 629 F.3d 369, 386 (4th Cir. 2011) (Title VII plaintiffs must show that the defendant's reasons for the adverse employment action "were not the actual reasons...giv[ing] rise to a reasonable inference that [the protected trait] was the real reason"); Love-Lane v. Martin, 355 F.3d 766, 788 (4th Cir. 2004) (stressing that the pretext must be related to the defendant's protected trait). Merely showing that the Defendant has proffered *some sort* of pretext is insufficient in a Title VII case. Love-Lane, 355 F.3d at 788.

The Plaintiff also offers the example of Lieutenant Eanes as evidence of pretext. Aff. of Pl. 3. As discussed in Section III, Lieutenant Eanes' conduct was not comparable to the Plaintiff's, thus the lack of disciplinary action against the Lieutenant cannot help the Plaintiff establish a pretext for discrimination. Bell, 586 F.Supp.2d at 510-11 (under McDonnell Douglas framework, terminated police officer's evidence that two other officers were not disciplined as harshly did not demonstrate pretext where the conduct of the other two officers was not comparable to that of the terminated officer).

VI. The Court Declines to Exercise Its Supplemental Jurisdiction Over the Virginia Human Rights Act Claim

In addition to his Title VII claim, the Plaintiff alleges that the conduct of which he complains violates the Virginia Human Rights Act. Va. Code Ann. § 2.2-3901. Specifically, "an employer's violation of a federal statute or regulation prohibiting discrimination is an unlawful practice under Virginia law." Pl.'s Resp. 5. See also Grimes v. Canadian Am. Transp., Inc., 72 F.Supp.2d 629, 634 (W.D.Va. 1999) ("[t]he VHRA essentially makes any federal violation a violation of Virginia law as well") (Kiser, J.). Having determined that the Defendant is entitled to summary judgment on the Title VII claim, the Court does not need to address the possibility that the Defendant violated the state Human Rights Act. The Plaintiff's Title VII claim invokes this Court's federal question jurisdiction. Graham

v. Frank, No. 88-3196, 1989 WL 100668, at *1 (4th Cir. Aug. 28, 1989). When the case was filed, both parties were Virginia residents, which precludes them from invoking the Court's diversity jurisdiction. 28 U.S.C. § 1332; Civil Cover Sheet, May 21, 2010, ECF No. 1-1 (showing that both parties are residents of the City of Danville). Without the Title VII claim, then, the Plaintiff has no means of keeping his claim in federal court. See Waybright v. Frederick Cnty., 528 F.3d 199, 209-210 (4th Cir. 2008) (District Court properly declined to exercise supplemental jurisdiction over state law tort claims once it granted summary judgment to the defendants on the federal claims).

CONCLUSION

The Court GRANTS the Plaintiff's Motions for an Extension of Time, but HOLDS Plaintiff's counsel in CIVIL CONTEMPT for his two violations of the Scheduling Order and IMPOSES A FINE of FIVE HUNDRED DOLLARS upon Plaintiff's counsel. Because the Plaintiff has neither offered any evidence of race discrimination nor established a prima facie case, the Court GRANTS the Defendant's Motion for Summary Judgment on the Title VII claim and DECLINES to exercise supplemental jurisdiction over the Plaintiff's Virginia Human Rights Act claim. The Clerk of the Court is directed to DISMISS this case from the docket.

ENTERED this 13th day of May, 2011.

/s/ Jackson L. Kiser

Senior United States District Judge

THE CITY OF RIVIERA BEACH,
Plaintiff-Appellee,
versus
THAT CERTAIN UNNAMED GRAY, TWO-STORY VESSEL APPROXIMATELY FIFTY-SEVEN FEET IN LENGTH, her engines, tackle, apparel, furniture, equipment and all other necessaries appertaining and belonging in rem, Defendant, FANE LOZMAN, Claimant-Appellant.

No. 10-10695
UNITED STATES COURT OF APPEALS
FOR THE ELEVENTH CIRCUIT
649 F.3d 1259
August 19, 2011

For CITY OF RIVIERA BEACH, FLORIDA, Plaintiff - Appellee: Robert B. Birthisel, Michael J. Bradford, Jonah Maurice Levine, Jules Victor Massee, Hamilton Miller & Birthisel, LLP, TAMPA, FL; Michael John Dono, Hamilton Miller & Birthisel, LLP, MIAMI, FL.

For FANE LOZMAN, Claimant - Appellant: Philip J. Nathanson, The Nathanson Law Firm, CHICAGO, IL.

Before EDMONDSON and MARCUS, Circuit Judges, and FAWSETT,* District Judge.

* Honorable Patricia C. Fawsett, United States District Judge for the Middle District of Florida, sitting by designation.

OPINION

MARCUS, Circuit Judge:

Claimant-Appellant Fane Lozman appeals the district court's entry of an order of partial summary judgment and, following a two-day bench trial, an order of final judgment for Plaintiff-Appellee City of Riviera Beach ("City") in an in rem proceeding against Defendant

Unnamed Gray, Two-Story Vessel Approximately Fifty-Seven Feet in Length ("Defendant"). The City filed a complaint in admiralty against the Defendant, first, claiming that the Defendant committed the maritime tort of trespass, because the Defendant remained at the City marina after the City explicitly revoked its consent, and second, seeking to foreclose its maritime lien for necessaries (unpaid dockage provided to the Defendant by the City). On partial summary judgment, the district court concluded that it had admiralty jurisdiction over the Defendant because the Defendant was indeed a "vessel" under 1 U.S.C. § 3, and that the Defendant was liable for maritime trespass.[1] After a bench trial, the district court determined that the trespass gave rise to nominal damages of $1 and that the Defendant owed the City approximately $3,000 under the maritime lien. After thorough review, we AFFIRM the judgments of the district court in all respects.

1 On appeal, Lozman does not challenge the district court's trespass ruling (except to the extent that he claims the district court lacked jurisdiction in the first place).

I.

The relevant facts are these. Lozman purchased the Defendant vessel in 2002. After purchasing the Defendant, Lozman had it towed from a location near Fort Myers, Florida to North Beach Village, Florida, a distance of at least 200 miles. In North Bay Village, Lozman lived in the Defendant from the time of purchase until Hurricane Wilma struck in late 2005.[2] Lozman had the Defendant towed to the City marina in March 2006, where he continued to use the Defendant as his primary residence until its arrest in April 2009.

2 According to Lozman, he moved the Defendant to two different marinas in North Bay Village after he was evicted from another marina for attempting to require that marina to provide reasonable accommodation -- in the form of a wheelchair ramp -- for his disabled houseboat neighbor.

The City owns and operates a municipal marina on the Atlantic Intracoastal Waterway. The marina provides wet and dry storage for approximately 510 vessels, both commercial and recreational. The marina leases slips to vessels on both a monthly basis and at a higher daily transient rate. On March 10, 2006, Lozman and the City marina entered into a "Wet-Slip or Dry Storage Agreement" (the "Agreement"). It called for Lozman to pay a monthly dockage fee of $1,174.48 by the first of each month, and dockage was provided on a month to month basis. It is undisputed that Lozman paid the entire monthly dockage fee for the month of March 2006, although he arrived at the marina some time in the middle of the month.

Conflict -- indeed, litigious conflict -- between the City and Lozman erupted shortly after Lozman's arrival. According to Lozman, on May 10, 2006, one day before then-Governor Jeb Bush signed an anti-eminent domain bill, the City entered into an agreement with a private developer for the redevelopment of the marina. Seeking to scuttle the redevelopment agreement, Lozman filed suit in Palm Beach County Circuit Court, alleging that the City's May 10, 2006 meeting with the developer violated the Florida Sunshine Law, Fla. Stat. § 286.011, because the public was only given one day's notice of the meeting. While it is not clear from the record how that lawsuit was resolved, the redevelopment plan was ultimately postponed or abandoned, a result for which Lozman takes credit.

On August 9, 2006, the City issued Lozman a notice of eviction from the marina, and subsequently filed an eviction suit also in the Circuit Court for Palm Beach County. The City's purported reasons for the eviction were that Lozman had failed to muzzle his ten-pound **daschund** and had used unlicensed repair persons to perform work on the Defendant. In the eviction proceedings, the City argued on summary judgment that the Agreement between Lozman and the City established a nonresidential tenancy under Florida law. The Circuit Court agreed that the Agreement established a nonresidential tenancy under Florida law and was therefore governed by Florida's landlord-tenant statute. The court, however, denied the City's motion for summary judgment because Lozman had raised an issue of material fact as to whether the eviction was improper retaliation for his opposition to the redevelopment plan. On March 2, 2007, after a three-day trial, a jury returned a verdict in Lozman's favor, finding that Lozman's protected speech was a substantial or motivating factor in the City's attempt to terminate the lease, and that the attempted termination would not have occurred absent the protected speech. Lozman continued to pay the monthly dockage fee throughout the proceedings, and remained at the marina.

On June 14, 2007, a few months after Lozman's state court victory, the Riviera Beach City Council unanimously passed a resolution adopting a revised dockage agreement and accompanying Marina Rules & Regulations. The revised agreement and rules and regulations require all vessels docked at the marina and their owners to: (1) secure and maintain liability insurance to specified limits and name the marina as an additional insured; (2) show proof of valid registration or documentation; (3) be operational and capable of vacating the marina in case of an emergency; and (4) comply with the Florida Clean Vessel Act, Fla. Stat. § 327.53, which, among other things, prohibits owners of vessels or floating structures from discharging raw sewage into Florida waters.

The City marina sent numerous letters to all marina residents and customers describing the new requirements. On or about July 25, 2007, the marina sent its initial notice of the new requirements and provided residents and customers with the revised dockage agreement to be executed by September 30, 2007. The marina sent customers an additional letter on November 13, 2007, further describing the new insurance requirements. On January 25, 2008, the marina sent Lozman a letter repeating the new insurance requirements and listing deficiencies in his and the Defendant's compliance with the marina's new rules and regulations. Specifically, the letter informed Lozman that he needed to sign a revised dockage agreement, that he lacked sufficient insurance coverage for the Defendant, and that he needed to provide insurance and registration documentation to the marina. Two months later, the marina performed an assessment of the vessels' compliance with the City resolution, and determined that seventeen vessels docked at the marina, including the Defendant, were not in compliance.[3] On April 22, 2008, the marina sent Lozman a letter informing him that he had missed the deadline to execute a new agreement and procedures to enforce the City's rights would be implemented against the Defendant.

Lozman claims that he never received these letters. He does not dispute, however, that he received a letter from the marina dated March 6, 2009, which provided final notice of the marina's revocation of permission for the Defendant to remain at the marina unless (1) Lozman brought the Defendant into compliance with the City resolution's new requirements, (2) Lozman paid the outstanding balance on the account, and (3) Lozman executed the revised dockage agreement. The letter stated that "[s]hould your vessel remain and you fail to pay your account in full, execute the 'Marina Dockage Agreement,' and otherwise bring your vessel into compliance with the Agreement's provisions by April 1, 2009, the City will promptly institute legal proceedings against you and your vessel for trespass and to foreclose the City's lien on your vessel." It is undisputed that Lozman never executed the new agreement and that the Defendant remained at the marina after April 1, 2009.

Accordingly, on April 20, 2009, the City filed a two-count verified complaint in admiralty against the Defendant to foreclose its maritime liens for "necessaries" (dockage provided by the City marina to the Defendant), under 46 U.S.C. § 31342,[4] and for trespass. The United States District Court for the Southern District of Florida issued a warrant for the arrest of the Defendant under Supplemental Rule C for Certain Maritime and Admiralty Claims, which provides, in relevant part, that "[i]f the conditions for an in rem action appear to exist, the court must issue an order directing the clerk to issue a warrant for the arrest of the vessel or other property that is the subject of the action." Fed. R. Civ. P. Supp. Rule C(3)(a)(i). On the afternoon of April 20, 2009, the United States Marshal arrested the Defendant, and had it towed from the City marina to Miami, Florida, a distance of approximately eighty miles. The next day, Lozman filed, pro se,[5] an emergency motion to dismiss the complaint and return the Defendant to the marina. After a hearing on April 23, 2009, the district court denied Lozman's motion.

4 46 U.S.C. § 31342 provides:

(a) Except as provided in subsection (b) of this section, a
person providing necessaries to a vessel on the order of the
owner or a person authorized by the owner--
> (1) has a maritime lien on the vessel;
> (2) may bring a civil action in rem to enforce
> the lien; and
> (3) is not required to allege or prove in the
> action that credit was given to the vessel.
(b) This section does not apply to a public vessel.

5 Lozman proceeded pro se for the entirety of the case below, including the bench trial. He now has representation on appeal.

On August 12, 2009, the City moved for partial summary judgment on its maritime trespass claim. After considering Lozman's response, the district court granted the City's motion, finding that the Defendant was a "vessel" for purposes of federal admiralty jurisdiction. The district court also found that the Defendant was trespassing on the marina as of April 1, 2009. Lozman had received notice of the Defendant's failure to comply with the marina rules and regulations in early March 2009, and the notice expressly terminated the City's consent as of April 1, 2009. The Defendant, however, remained at the marina until its arrest on April 20, 2009. The district court concluded that the Defendant vessel remained at the marina after the City terminated consent.

On November 23 and 24, 2009, the district court held a two-day bench trial on the issues of damages for the trespass claim, and liability and damages for the maritime lien for necessaries claim. On January 6, 2010, the district court entered its findings of fact and conclusions of law, and issued an order of final judgment in the City's favor. The district court found that the Defendant's account was delinquent as of April 20, 2009 in the amount of $3,039.88. The court credited the City marina's ledger and the testimony of the City's forensic accountant in determining the amount owed. The court found no real harm resulting from the trespass, awarding the City nominal damages of $1.

On February 25, 2010, the entry of final judgment was amended to include $3,053.26 in prejudgment interest plus custodial fees. The district court also ordered the U.S. Marshal to release the Defendant and execute its sale in satisfaction of the judgment. Lozman filed an emergency motion to stay the sale and to stay enforcement of the district court's final judgment in this Court, which was denied on March 3, 2010. The City purchased the Defendant in a Bill of Sale executed on March 4, 2010. This timely appeal of both the district court's partial summary judgment and final judgment orders followed.

II.

The standard of review for a district court's grant of summary judgment is well settled. "This court reviews a district court's grant of summary judgment de novo, applying the same legal standards used by the district court." Krutzig v. Pulte Home Corp., 602 F.3d 1231, 1234 (11th Cir. 2010). "Summary judgment is appropriate where, viewing the movant's evidence and all factual inferences arising from it in the light most favorable to the nonmoving party, there is no genuine issue of any material fact, and the moving party is entitled to judgment as a matter of law." Id.; see also Celotex Corp v. Catrett, 477 U.S. 317, 322, 106 S. Ct. 2548, 91 L. Ed. 2d 265 (1986). As for the district court's entry of final judgment after a bench trial, "[w]e review a district court's factual findings when sitting without a jury in admiralty under the clearly erroneous standard. We review the district court's conclusions of law de novo." Sea Byte, Inc. v. Hudson Marine Mgmt. Servs., Inc., 565 F.3d 1293, 1298 (11th Cir. 2009) (quoting Venus Lines Agency, Inc. v. CVG Int'l Am., Inc., 234 F.3d 1225, 1228 (11th Cir. 2000)). "A finding of fact is clearly erroneous when the entirety of the evidence leads the reviewing court to a definite and firm conviction that a mistake has been committed." Id. (quoting Dresdner Bank AG v. M/V Olympia Voyager, 446 F.3d 1377, 1380 (11th Cir. 2006)).

Lozman first claims that the district court incorrectly concluded on summary judgment that the Defendant was a "vessel" subject to federal admiralty jurisdiction. He further says that the City did not have a maritime lien because the Defendant did not owe the City money for dockage, but rather the City owed Lozman. Lozman also asserts that the City improperly instituted this admiralty action in retaliation against him for the exercise of his First Amendment rights in opposing the City's development plan for its marina, and that the district court erred in finding that Lozman had failed to establish such a defense. Finally, Lozman argues that his March 2007 success in resisting an eviction attempt by the City in state court precludes the City, under the doctrines of judicial and collateral estoppel, from bringing a federal maritime claim against him in May 2009, and that the district court erred in declining to apply either estoppel doctrine. We consider each claim in turn.

A.

The United States Constitution extends the judicial power of the United States "to all Cases of admiralty or maritime Jurisdiction." U.S. Const. art. III, § 2, cl. 1. Under that clause, Congress has granted federal district courts exclusive original jurisdiction over "[a]ny civil case of admiralty or maritime jurisdiction." 28 U.S.C. § 1333(1). This is an in rem case against the Defendant for the maritime tort of trespass and for the enforcement of a maritime lien for necessaries. A "mandatory prerequisite" to the district court's admiralty jurisdiction over the Defendant, and to the attachment of a maritime lien, is that the Defendant be a "vessel" under federal law.[6] Crimson Yachts v. Betty Lyn II Motor Yacht, 603 F.3d 864, 872 (11th Cir. 2010). We review the district court's conclusion that the Defendant was a "vessel" de novo. Bunge Corp. v. Freeport Marine Repair, Inc., 240 F.3d 919, 922 (11th Cir. 2001).

6 Lozman spends considerable ink describing Florida state law and the difference under Florida law between a "floating residential structure" and a "vessel." Lozman claims that the Defendant is a "floating residential structure," not a "vessel," as the terms are defined under Florida law. These arguments miss the point. Federal law governs the existence of admiralty jurisdiction, and the term "vessel" is specifically defined in the United States Code. Accordingly, for purposes of federal admiralty jurisdiction, any differences among the definitions of vessel under the laws of various states or between state and federal law must yield to the federal definition and the required uniformity of federal maritime law. See Stewart v. Dutra Constr. Co., 543 U.S. 481, 490, 125 S. Ct. 1118, 160 L. Ed. 2d 932 (2005) ("[1 U.S.C.] § 3 continues to supply the default definition of 'vessel' throughout the U.S. Code . . . ."); S. Pac. Co. v. Jensen, 244 U.S. 205, 215-16, 37 S. Ct. 524, 61 L. Ed. 1086 (1917).

The determination of whether the Defendant is a "vessel" is dictated by binding precedent. Both this Court and the former Fifth Circuit in binding precedent have employed a broad definition of vessel pursuant to 1 U.S.C. § 3. Section 3 provides, in full: "The word 'vessel' includes every description of watercraft or other artificial contrivance used, or capable of being used, as a means of transportation on water." 1 U.S.C. § 3 (emphasis added). We have unambiguously said that the primary inquiry in determining whether a craft is a vessel is whether the craft was "rendered practically incapable of transportation or movement." Bd. of Comm'rs of the Orleans Levee Dist. v. M/V Belle of Orleans, 535 F.3d 1299, 1312 (11th Cir. 2008) (quoting Stewart, 543 U.S. at 494). In so doing, we have echoed the Supreme Court's pronouncement in Stewart, 543 U.S. 481, 125 S. Ct. 1118, 160 L. Ed. 2d 932, that the determination of whether a craft is a "vessel" focuses on "whether the watercraft's use 'as a means of transportation on water' is a practical possibility or merely a theoretical one." Id. at 496. We therefore look at the capability of the craft, "not its present use or station." Belle of Orleans, 535 F.3d at 1310.

Our cases provide further context for this broad definition. In Pleason v. Gulfport Shipbuilding Corp., 221 F.2d 621 (5th Cir. 1955), the Carol Ann, a salvage and repair vessel built for the Navy, had been declared surplus and was subsequently sold and re-sold to private parties. Id. at 622. One of the vessel's owners decided to scrap the vessel, and at the time the vessel was brought in for certain repairs, she was in the following condition: "her propellers and propeller shafts had been removed; she had no crew; none of her machinery was in operation; she had no light, heat, or power in operation; her main engines had been completely removed; all of her steering apparatus, with the exception of the rudder, had been removed and sold; her superstructure and masts were intact; her navigation lights were in place, though not operable; [and] her compartmentation, including cargo holds, was intact." Id. at 622-23. After these repairs were performed, the Carol Ann was moored to a dock by cables, and she received telephone and electrical service through connections to sources on land. Id. at 623. Although the Carol Ann was almost completely gutted, except for her superstructure, the former Fifth Circuit[7] held that she was a vessel.

Id. The Court, as it had done in the past, "saw fit to emphasize the words 'capable of being used' in discussing Section 3 of Title 1." Id. The Carol Ann was afloat and capable of being towed, had a deck, cabins, and superstructure, and therefore "was capable of being used as a means of transportation under tow" despite having "no steering mechanism" and "no motive power of its own." Id.

7 In Bonner v. City of Prichard, 661 F.2d 1206, 1209 (11th Cir. 1981) (en banc), we adopted as binding precedent all decisions of the former Fifth Circuit handed down prior to the close of business on September 30, 1981.

The case of Miami River Boat Yard, Inc. v. 60' Houseboat, Serial No. SC-40-2860-3-62, 390 F.2d 596 (5th Cir. 1968) is equally instructive. There, a panel of the former Fifth Circuit concluded that a houseboat with no motive power of her own that was used as a residence in a marina was still a vessel. Id. at 597. The undisputed facts showed that the defendant houseboat had "made the rather considerable maritime voyage to libelant's shipyard in Miami . . . with the expectation that she would be towed away." Id. The Court noted that a houseboat "affords a water-borne place to live with the added advantage of at least some maritime mobility." Id. Accordingly, "[t]hat she has no motive power and must, as would the most lowly of dumb barges, be towed does not deprive her of the status of a vessel." Id.

More recently, in 2008, we had occasion in Belle of Orleans to consider whether a riverboat casino that was moored to a dock by steel cables and had electrical, computer, and phone cables attached to a shore side source was a vessel. 535 F.3d at 1304. We held that it was. A panel of this Court reaffirmed that Pleason was still good law and that it "addressed precisely the legal issue we face in the instant case." Id. at 1306. We also found the riverboat at issue to be factually indistinguishable from the vessel in Pleason, with the exception that the riverboat had a working engine and other machinery and therefore motive power of its own. Id. at 1307. That distinction, of course, led us further toward the conclusion that the riverboat was capable of maritime transport and was, therefore, a vessel, but we did not depart from the Pleason analysis. Id.

We distinguished both legally and factually the Fifth Circuit's opinion in Pavone v. Mississippi Riverboat Amusement Corp., 52 F.3d 560

(5th Cir. 1995), on which Lozman now relies, where the court held that a floating casino that was semi-permanently and indefinitely moored to the shore was not a vessel because it was "removed from navigation" and "was constructed to be used primarily as a work platform." Id. at 570. We rejected the reasoning of the Fifth and Seventh[8] Circuits, both of which "focus on the intent of the shipowner rather than whether the boat has been 'rendered practically incapable of transportation or movement.'" Belle of Orleans, 535 F.3d at 1311 (quoting Stewart, 543 U.S. at 494). Again we observed that "[t]he owner's intentions with regard to a boat are analogous to the boat's 'purpose,' and Stewart clearly rejected any definition of 'vessel' that relies on such a purpose." Id. at 1311 (citing Stewart, 543 U.S. at 497 ("Under [1 U.S.C.] § 3, a 'vessel' is any watercraft practically capable of maritime transportation, regardless of its primary purpose . . . .") (footnote omitted)). Moreover, we noted that "such a test is incompatible with the Supreme Court's focus on providing uniformity within admiralty jurisdiction," id. (citing Doe v. Celebrity Cruises, Inc., 394 F.3d 891, 902 (11th Cir. 2004)), because "state law can change" and "an owner's intentions may change in ways never anticipated," id. at 1311-12.

8 See Tagliere v. Harrah's Ill. Corp., 445 F.3d 1012 (7th Cir. 2006).

A panel of this Court reiterated the analysis employed in Belle of Orleans and the enduring vitality of Pleason and 60' Houseboat still again in Crimson Yachts, 603 F.3d 864. After reviewing the purpose and history of maritime liens and prior precedent interpreting the term "vessel," the Court noted that a "case-by-case approach is often necessary to determine whether admiralty jurisdiction applies to novel or unusual situations." Id. at 875 (internal quotation marks omitted). We ultimately held that the Betty Lyn II, a yacht that had been drydocked, removed from the water with cranes, and temporarily disabled for extensive repairs, was still a vessel. Id. We stated that "[t]he BETTY LYN II need merely be capable of transportation on water to be a vessel. The law does not require that she be able to self-propel." Id. (citing Belle of Orleans, 535 F.3d at 1307; 60' Houseboat, 390 F.2d at 597). Although the yacht was on dry land for repairs, it retained the status of vessel because it still "could be towed upon 24 hours notice." Id.

Lozman's efforts to distinguish Pleason and the line of precedent that followed are unavailing. Aside from his discussion of Florida law, which is of no moment in defining the term "vessel" for purposes of federal admiralty jurisdiction, Lozman raises three somewhat interrelated arguments in an effort to avoid controlling precedent. First, he argues that the Defendant was not practically capable of transportation over water, even by tow. The record disputes Lozman's characterization. The Defendant in this case is virtually indistinguishable from the vessels in the aforementioned cases in terms of its capacity for maritime transport. Like the vessel in Pleason, the Defendant was moored to a dock by cables, received power from land, and had no motive power or steering of its own. Moreover, the Defendant was towed several times over considerable distances: first, from the place of purchase near Fort Myers to North Bay Village; next, among several marinas in North Bay Village; then, from North Bay Village down to the City; and finally, after its arrest, from the City to Miami.

Lozman claims, nevertheless, without any evidentiary support in the record, that each of the three times the Defendant was moved over 250 feet it sustained serious damage and that it would have sunk two out of the three times if immediate underwater repairs had not been performed. But absent a shred of evidence, and in light of the contradictory evidence of the actual voyages made by the Defendant under tow, this assertion alone cannot preclude a determination that the Defendant was practically capable of maritime transportation. In addition, as the district court recognized, in Belle of Orleans, the claimant raised a similar concern that moving the vessel would damage it, and we stated that "the BELLE OF ORLEANS was capable of moving over water, albeit to her detriment, and was capable of being transported under tow. As such, we hold that the BELLE OF ORLEANS is a 'vessel' for purposes of admiralty jurisdiction." 535 F.3d at 1312 (emphasis added).

Second, Lozman argues, again without any record support, that the Defendant was constructed using methods and materials appropriate for houses on land and, accordingly, that the Defendant is not a vessel. Thus, Lozman asserts that the Defendant is a "floating shack, built out of plywood with only 1/16" of fiberglass surrounding its unraked hull, without proper cleats for towing,[9] no bilge pumps, no navigation aids, no lifeboats and other lifesaving equipment, no propulsion, [and] no steering." In essence, Lozman claims that the Defendant "was designed as a residence that just happened to float." But the Defendant's design, however unusual or unorthodox, is of little moment. We clearly stated in Belle of Orleans that the status of "vessel" does not depend in any way on either the purpose for which the craft was constructed or its intended use. 535 F.3d at 1311.

> 9 Lozman's own brief and the evidence presented at trial appear to contradict this point. Before he even arrived in the City, and thus before the attachment of a maritime lien and the district court's exercise of its admiralty jurisdiction over the Defendant, Lozman had a repairperson fit the Defendant with four towing bitts prior to its approximately-seventy mile tow from North Bay Village to the City marina.

Lozman also uses these claims about the Defendant's construction to again suggest that the Defendant was not practically capable of moving over water, even by tow. But that argument, too, is contradicted by the record. The fact that the Defendant was an unusually designed craft is relevant only to the extent that the design prevents it from having any practical capacity for transportation over water, and the record is clear that the Defendant had this practical capacity. See Burks v. Am. River Transp. Co., 679 F.2d 69, 75 (5th Cir. Unit A 1982) ("No doubt the three men in a tub would also fit within our definition [of "vessel"], and one probably could make a convincing case for Jonah inside the whale."); McCarthy v. The Bark Peking, 716 F.2d 130, 134 (2d Cir. 1983) ("[V]irtually any capacity for use as seagoing transportation -- perhaps even the hypothetically plausible possibility has sufficed to lend the dignity of 'vessel' status to a host of seemingly unlikely craft.").

Finally, Lozman argues that the Defendant did not have a Hull Identification Number ("HIN") and could not obtain Coast Guard certification, both of which are required for legal navigability, and that therefore it cannot be considered a vessel. This argument misapprehends the relevant inquiry. As we recognized in Belle of Orleans, legal navigability is not the test for vessel status. 535 F.3d at

1311-12 ("[I]f legal navigability is the test for vessel status, any ship with an expired Coast Guard certification becomes a non-vessel . . . . Such a result is clearly not what the Supreme Court intended [in Stewart]."). Lozman claims the Defendant is distinguishable from the hypothetical vessel in Belle of Orleans because the Defendant could never obtain a Coast Guard certification in the first place. But in distinguishing this Court's hypothetical illustration of a principle, he fails to dispute -- nor could he dispute -- the principle itself; namely, that we do not consider legal navigability at all in determining whether a craft is a vessel, but rather only the craft's practical capacity for maritime transport.

In short, based on long precedent, the Defendant is a "vessel" under 1 U.S.C. § 3. Like the vessels in Pleason and 60' Houseboat, the Defendant was practically capable of transportation over water by means of a tow, despite having no motive or steering power of its own. The district court did not err in concluding that it had federal admiralty jurisdiction over the Defendant.

B.

Under 46 U.S.C. § 31342, a "person providing necessaries to a vessel" has a maritime lien on the vessel that may be enforced by means of an in rem civil action against the vessel. 46 U.S.C. § 31342(a). We have held that dockage, which was undisputedly provided by the City marina to the Defendant, constitutes "necessaries" for purposes of maritime law. Belle of Orleans, 535 F.3d at 1314 (citing Inbesa Am., Inc. v. M/V Anglia, 134 F.3d 1035, 1037-38 (11th Cir. 1998)).

Lozman does not dispute the legal standard for a maritime lien, but rather argues that the City has failed to prove that a maritime lien accrued in this case because he allegedly did not owe any money to the marina. The proper balance of Lozman's dockage account with the marina is a question of fact and was the primary issue in the two-day bench trial before the district court. Accordingly, we review the district court's factual determinations for clear error. Myers v. Cent. Fla. Invs., Inc., 592 F.3d 1201, 1211 (11th Cir. 2010). A "court will not disturb a district court's findings of fact under the clearly erroneous standard unless it is left 'with the definite and firm conviction that a mistake has been made' after making all credibility choices in favor of the fact-finder's choice, in light of the record as a whole." Meek v. Metro. Dade Cnty., 985 F.2d 1471, 1481 (11th Cir. 1993), abrogated on other grounds by Dillard v. Chilton Cnty. Comm'n, 495 F.3d 1324 (11th Cir. 2007) (per curiam) (quoting Maddox v. Claytor, 764 F.2d 1539, 1545 (11th Cir. 1985)). An appellate court may not reverse a district court's finding that is plausible in light of the entire record even if "convinced that had it been sitting as the trier of fact, it would have weighed the evidence differently." Anderson v. City of Bessemer City, 470 U.S. 564, 574, 105 S. Ct. 1504, 84 L. Ed. 2d 518 (1985).

Based primarily on the marina's records and the in-court testimony of marina director Edwin Legue, forensic accountant Glenn Troast, and Lozman himself, the district court found that Lozman owed the marina "$805.78 for unpaid dockage" and "$608.60 for unpaid late fees" as of March 31, 2009, and "$1624.50 in dockage at the transient rate for [the] period from April 2, 2009 to April 20, 2009, inclusive," for a total of $3,038.88.

Lozman makes several arguments in response, all of which invite us to reconsider the well-grounded factual findings of the district court. First, Lozman claims that one of his checks was not properly credited to his account. Second, Lozman asserts that he was erroneously charged late fees. Third, Lozman contends that he is entitled to a prorated dockage fee for the month of March 2006, because he paid for the full month but did not dock the Defendant at the marina until on or around March 17. Finally, Lozman claims that the marina owes him a credit for fifteen months of spotty or non-existent electrical service. We consider each claim in turn.

First, Lozman says that his September 2008 dockage fee check, #1157, was cashed by the City but was not properly credited to his account. As evidence, Lozman claims that his marina billing statement dated April 1, 2009, did not show a credit for this check. But the district court did not rely on the April 1, 2009 billing statement in computing the amount owed. Instead, the evidence upon which the district court relied was the marina's ledger card for Lozman's account, and the testimony of the City's forensic accountant, Glenn Troast, which was based on a review of that ledger. And the ledger has an entry for the amount of check #1157 on the date it was sent, September 9, 2008. The district court therefore found that check #1157, in addition to the other checks Lozman claimed were not properly credited to his account, were properly accounted for in the ledger.

Lozman further claims that the marina accounting staff intentionally held three of his checks for up to three months before depositing them. Presumably, Lozman is suggesting that the City's actions led him to unfairly incur late fees. At trial, however, forensic accountant Troast testified that Lozman was credited for any late fees that were assessed against him while those checks were being held. Indeed, the ledger shows that, on July 9, 2008, shortly after the City deposited the three checks in question, Lozman's account was credited $473.11 for past late fees.[10] At all events, we can find no clear error in the district court's factfinding.

> 10 Lozman also received substantial credits on other occasions. Thus, for example, the forensic accountant testified at trial that, in August 2007, the marina forgave a full month of unpaid dockage fees for July 2007, effectively crediting Lozman's account the unpaid amount.

Lozman's next claim is that he is entitled to a prorated dockage fee for March 2006, his first month at the marina. It is undisputed that Lozman paid the monthly fee in full and that he arrived at the marina on or around March 17, 2006. But those two undisputed facts alone do not lead to the conclusion that Lozman was entitled to pay a prorated dockage fee. Nothing in the Agreement itself addresses the issue of prorated monthly payments, and nothing in the record suggests that Lozman ever demanded a credit or proration of his March 2006 payment before this case began. Without more, the district court did not commit clear error by declining to find that the City owed Lozman a prorated portion of his March 2006 dockage fee.

Finally, Lozman asserts that he was owed "15 months electric, $750.00, for one outlet he paid for that never worked and that he did not use." Although Lozman claims that his electricity did not work for two years, the record lacks any evidence -- not even a single electrical bill -- to support this claim. In addition, it is undisputed that the City credited Lozman $450 for nine months of electrical service on July 9, 2008, because of alleged service interruptions.

At the end of the day, nothing in the record indicates that we may second-guess the district court's weighing of the evidence. We are not persuaded that the district court erred in its factfinding, and neither are we left, therefore, "with the definite and firm conviction that a mistake has been made." Maddox, 764 F.2d at 1545. The district court's factual findings regarding the amount Lozman owed under the City's maritime lien for necessaries were not clearly erroneous.

C.

Lozman claims next that the City's federal admiralty complaint against the Defendant "was simply part of an ongoing retaliation by the CITY against LOZMAN for his success (with the support of then Governor Bush and then Attorney General Crist) in stopping the CITY from using eminent domain to take thousands of homes and businesses, along with the CITY marina, to be given to a private developer in a 2.4 billion dollar redevelopment deal," as well as for his success in the state court eviction case.

In order to successfully advance a First Amendment retaliation defense, Lozman must show (1) that his conduct was constitutionally protected; and (2) that his conduct "was a substantial or motivating factor in" the City's decision to arrest the Defendant. Cuban Museum of Arts & Culture, Inc. v. City of Miami, 766 F. Supp. 1121, 1125 (S.D. Fla. 1991) (citing Mt. Healthy City Sch. Dist. Bd. of Educ. v. Doyle, 429 U.S. 274, 287, 97 S. Ct. 568, 50 L. Ed. 2d 471 (1977)); see also Gattis v. Brice, 136 F.3d 724, 726 (11th Cir. 1998) ("To succeed in a section 1983 suit based on a claim of retaliation for speech, the plaintiff must show that his speech was a substantial or motivating factor in the allegedly retaliatory decision." (internal quotation marks omitted)). If Lozman makes this showing, the burden then shifts to the City to show "by a preponderance of the evidence" that the action against the Defendant would have occurred "even in the absence of the protected conduct." Mt. Healthy, 429 U.S. at 287; see also Cuban Museum, 766 F. Supp. at 1125.

The district court concluded on summary judgment that Lozman had failed to show that his 2006 opposition to the marina redevelopment plan was a substantial or motivating factor in the City's decision to bring this case. The court, therefore, did not reach the question of whether Lozman's conduct was constitutionally protected or whether the City could show by a preponderance of the evidence that the arrest of the Defendant would have occurred even in the absence of Lozman's conduct. The district court noted that, while the timing of the City resolution mandating compliance with revised marina rules and regulations -- which occurred three months after Lozman's victory in the state court eviction case -- was "enough to raise eyebrows," it was still not enough, absent any firm evidence, to show that Lozman's speech was a substantial or motivating factor in the City's decision to implement those rules and to arrest the Defendant. The district court further found that the evidence submitted by Lozman -- much of which was inadmissible, and which consisted primarily of (1) the minutes from a City Council meeting held approximately one year before the decision to change the rules was made, and (2) newspaper articles asserting that the rules changes were effectuated as a personal vendetta against Lozman -- suggested at most an ongoing feud between Lozman and the City, but did "not establish a connection between Mr. Lozman's protected conduct and the specific action at issue here: the changing of the marina rules and their enforcement against the Defendant vessel."

The district court's conclusions were sound. On appeal, Lozman argues that what "is enough to raise eyebrows" -- here, the timing of the rules changes -- is circumstantial evidence sufficient to preclude summary judgment. We are unpersuaded. It is certainly true that "[w]here the circumstantial evidence and reasonable inferences drawn therefrom create a genuine issue of material fact for trial, summary judgment is improper." Chapman v. Am. Cyanamid Corp., 861 F.2d 1515, 1518-19 (11th Cir. 1988). "However, an inference based on speculation and conjecture is not reasonable." Id. at 1518. As noted by the City, "circumstantial evidence must do more than simply 'raise some eyebrows'; it must be sufficient to raise a jury question." Lozman has presented no evidence in the record to support his retaliation claims beyond the timing of the rules changes. And that timing is hardly enough to raise a genuine issue of material fact.

Indeed, the evidence that is in the record overwhelmingly contradicts Lozman's claims. To begin with, the new marina rules did not apply solely to the Defendant. Rather, the Defendant was one of seventeen vessels that were not in compliance with the new rules, and, on April 1, 2009, was the only non-compliant vessel remaining at the marina. Thus, there is no evidence to suggest that the Defendant was specifically targeted. The City's stated goals behind the revisions to the marina rules were "to become more fully compliant with state and federal laws and to better insulate the City from financial loss and liability exposure." Lozman marshals no evidence to dispute any of this.

Perhaps most significantly, the causal link between the March 2, 2007 state court eviction verdict in Lozman's favor and the June 20, 2007 rules changes is highly attenuated, if not wholly implausible. Notably, between those two events there was a new City Council election, which completely changed the composition of the City Council. As Lozman himself testified at the bench trial: "[T]he elections in Riviera Beach are in March. So the March, 2007, election all new people came in. And the feeling around town was they came in -- that my win and the eminent domain defeat had a lot to do with it." Indeed, Lozman supported the campaigns of two of the new council members elected in 2007, who then turned around and signed the unanimous City Council resolution authorizing the marina's new rules and regulations.

The district court did not err in granting summary judgment to the City on Lozman's affirmative defense of retaliation. Like the district court, we need not reach the questions of whether Lozman's speech was constitutionally protected and whether the City's rules changes and arrest of the Defendant would have occurred in the absence of Lozman's speech.

III.

Lozman's final argument is that the City was judicially estopped from bringing a federal maritime claim against the Defendant in light of the City's argument in state court that Lozman's dockage agreement with the marina gave rise to a nonresidential tenancy subject to Florida law. Lozman's argument is without merit. Judicial estoppel is "designed to prevent parties from making a mockery of justice by inconsistent pleadings." McKinnon v. Blue Cross & Blue Shield of

Ala., 935 F.2d 1187, 1192 (11th Cir. 1991). While judicial estoppel "cannot be reduced to a precise formula or test," Zedner v. United States, 547 U.S. 489, 504, 126 S. Ct. 1976, 164 L. Ed. 2d 749 (2006), three factors typically inform the inquiry: (1) whether there is a clear inconsistency between the earlier position and the later position; (2) a party's success in convincing a court of the earlier position, so that judicial acceptance of the inconsistent later position would create the perception that either the earlier or later court was misled; and (3) whether the inconsistent later position would unfairly prejudice the opposing party if not estopped. Jaffe v. Bank of Am., N.A., 395 F. App'x 583, 587 (11th Cir. 2010) (per curiam) (unpublished); see also Zedner, 547 U.S. at 504.

The first factor is crucial; without inconsistency there is no basis for judicial estoppel and no reason even to reach the other two factors. See Zedner, 547 U.S. at 506. Lozman does not even begin to show how there could be a "clear inconsistency" between the City's earlier position that a dockage agreement between him and the City is governed by state landlord-tenant law and the City's current position that the Defendant is a vessel subject to federal admiralty jurisdiction. Because there is no clear inconsistency here, the district court correctly concluded that the City was not estopped from bringing its action in admiralty against the Defendant.

Lozman makes a second estoppel argument, which is equally unpersuasive. Specifically, Lozman asserts that, because the state court ruled that the City's 2006 eviction attempt was improper retaliation, under the doctrine of collateral estoppel, the district court was required to rule that the City's admiralty action was also improper retaliation against him for the exercise of his First Amendment rights. An element of collateral estoppel is that "the issue at stake must be identical to the one alleged in the prior litigation." Greenblatt v. Drexel Burnham Lambert, Inc., 763 F.2d 1352, 1360 (11th Cir. 1985).[11] Moreover, "[t]he application of collateral estoppel is committed to the sound discretion of the district court," id., and, accordingly, we review the district court's decision whether or not to apply collateral estoppel for abuse of discretion. Dailide v. U.S. Att'y Gen., 387 F.3d 1335, 1341 (11th Cir. 2004).

11 "There are several prerequisites to the application of collateral estoppel: (1) the issue at stake must be identical to the one alleged in the prior litigation; (2) the issue must have been actually litigated in the prior litigation; and (3) the determination of the issue in the prior litigation must have been a critical and necessary part of the judgment in that earlier action." Greenblatt, 763 F.2d at 1360 (citing DeWeese v. Town of Palm Beach, 688 F.2d 731, 733 (11th Cir. 1982)).

The district court could not have abused its discretion in declining to apply collateral estoppel, because the issues at stake here are significantly different from those in dispute in the state court proceeding. In this case, the issues before the district court were whether the Defendant was a vessel, whether the Defendant was trespassing, and whether the City held a maritime lien for necessaries on the Defendant (and the amount owed under that lien). None of these issues were previously litigated. Lozman contends that the "identical" issue at stake is whether the City retaliated against him "for the exercise of his First Amendment rights, which issue was resolved in his favor in the state court action." But this statement of the issue is misleading. The factual predicate for the retaliation claim, as we have discussed, has wholly changed since the 2007 state court verdict in Lozman's favor. There is a new City Council, which passed a unanimous resolution revising the marina rules and regulations, and this is an in rem action against the Defendant based in large part on Lozman's failure to comply with those rules and regulations (and on Lozman's failure to pay dockage fees). The City's earlier 2006 eviction attempt -- the purported reasons for which were Lozman's failure to muzzle his small dog and his use of unapproved repairpersons -- is not identical or even similar -- factually or legally -- to the City's 2009 admiralty action. The district court was not required to give any credence to the state court proceedings in this case, and did not abuse its discretion in declining to apply collateral estoppel.

The district court's orders of partial summary judgment and final judgment in favor of the City are AFFIRMED.

LARRY D. SMITH, Plaintiff,

v.

MICHAEL J. ASTRUE,
Commissioner of Social Security,
Defendant.

1:10-cv-01527 GSA

UNITED STATES DISTRICT COURT
FOR THE EASTERN DISTRICT OF
CALIFORNIA

November 3, 2011

For Larry D. Smith, Plaintiff: Denise Bourgeois Haley, Steven Gilbert Rosales, LEAD ATTORNEYS, Law Offices of Lawrence D. Rohlfing, Santa Fe Springs, CA.

For Commissioner of Social Security, Defendant: Shea Lita Bond, LEAD ATTORNEY, Office of the General Counsel, Social Security Administration, San Francisco, CA; Benjamin E. Hall, ss, United States Attorney, Fresno, CA.

Gary S. Austin, UNITED STATES MAGISTRATE JUDGE.

ORDER REGARDING PLAINTIFF'S
SOCIAL SECURITY COMPLAINT

BACKGROUND

Plaintiff Larry D. Smith ("Plaintiff") seeks judicial review of a final decision of the Commissioner of Social Security ("Commissioner" or "Defendant") denying his application for disability insurance benefits pursuant to Title II of the Social Security Act. The matter is currently before the Court on the parties' briefs, which were submitted, without oral argument, to the Honorable Gary S. Austin, United States Magistrate Judge. [1]

---

1 The parties consented to the jurisdiction of the United States Magistrate Judge. (*See* Docs. 9 & 10.)

FACTS AND PRIOR PROCEEDINGS[2]

2 References to the Administrative Record will be designated as "AR," followed by the appropriate page number.

Plaintiff filed an application for disability insurance benefits in June 2006, alleging disability beginning November 1, 2005. AR 145-149. Plaintiff's application was denied initially and on reconsideration, and Plaintiff requested a hearing before an Administrative Law Judge ("ALJ"). AR 105-115. ALJ Michael J. Kopicki held a hearing on May 5, 2009, and issued an order denying benefits on July 22, 2009, finding Plaintiff was not disabled. AR 8-17, 121-124. On June 29, 2010, the Appeals Council denied review. AR 1-3.

Hearing Testimony

ALJ Kopicki held a hearing on May 9, 2009, in Fresno, California. Plaintiff appeared and testified; he was assisted by attorney Robert D. Hubbs. Vocational Expert ("VE") Kenneth Ferra also testified telephonically. AR 18-72.

Plaintiff was forty-nine years old at the time of the hearing. AR 25. He is six feet one inch tall, weighs 215 pounds and is left-handed. AR 25-26. Plaintiff lives with his parents, both of whom are retired and in their 70's. AR 24. He is presently separated from his wife. He has two boys in their 20's, one of whom is in prison. AR 26. Plaintiff does not have any source of income. He does receive food stamps. AR 24.

Beyond high school graduation, Plaintiff has attended community college courses for about two to three years. He earned six certificates from Shasta College in heavy-duty equipment repair. AR 25. Plaintiff also served in the Army and received an honorable discharge. AR 25.

In September 2005, Plaintiff began experiencing sharp pain in his right arm and thumb. Eventually, in November of that year, he underwent surgery on his neck. AR 27. He remained on his employer's payroll, despite being off work, until the following May. AR 27-28. Prior to having neck surgery, Plaintiff suffered from

170

painful headaches. AR 31. The surgery was successful; he no longer has headaches or popping in the neck. AR 32. He does feel pain in his shoulder socket on the right side, but believes that to be separate from the neck. AR 42-43.

When asked to identify his biggest present problem that does not permit him to work, Plaintiff indicated his lower back is the biggest problem. More particularly, a sharp stabbing pain in the lower back that travels into his right leg. AR 28. The more active Plaintiff is, the greater the pain. Pain medications take the edge off, but do not completely resolve the pain. AR 29. In the past, he has used a TENS unit to treat pain in his "whole back." AR 29-30. Plaintiff has been told that surgery on his back is not advisable "because the benefits are worse than the risks." AR 30. He was told this by a neurosurgeon in Martinez, whom also advised him to stop jogging and to limit "jolt[ing]" activities. AR 30-31.

Plaintiff is followed and treated for hepatitis. AR 32. He feels a constant ache on his right side. He has received Interferon treatments on two separate occasions. AR 32-34.

In 1986, Plaintiff broke his right ankle. He still feels a throbbing pain that sometimes shoots up the leg and down into the foot. The pain in his ankle affects his ability to work, because the more he uses it the more painful it becomes. AR 34.

In the past three years, Plaintiff has suffered three fractured ribs. Just two weeks prior to the hearing, Plaintiff fell and fractured a rib. AR 45. About four to five months prior to that occasion, while in Redding, Plaintiff fell off a step and landed on his back. AR 45-46. He attributes the falls to his ankle because it just gives out on him. AR 45-46.

Plaintiff has difficulty sleeping due to sleep apnea and insomnia. AR 35. He indicated he sleeps an average of eleven to fifteen hours a week. AR 40. Plaintiff has used Tylenol PM and Benadryl to help him fall sleep. AR 40. Because he doesn't get enough sleep, he is tired all the time. Nevertheless, he cannot nap during the day. AR 41-42. Plaintiff has a CPAP device as a result of the sleep apnea, but indicated it "irritates" him and causes him to awaken. AR 42. As a result of his fatigue, he is not alert, and is "a little spacey now and then." AR 42.

While he has been diagnosed with depression, Plaintiff does not take any medication related to his depression, nor does he attend therapy or counseling sessions. AR 35. He does take Alprazolam for anxiety. AR 35-36. He does not attend therapy or counseling due to a lack of transportation. AR 35. As a result of a driving under the influence conviction, Plaintiff's license was suspended. Thus, he must rely on his parents for transportation and does not wish to impose on them too often. AR 35.

When asked to describe a typical day, Plaintiff indicated he gets up around 5:00 or 6:00 a.m. He used to go to school, but does not attend any longer. He tries to help his dad in the back yard and help his mom around the house. AR 47. Specifically, when helping his dad in the backyard, Plaintiff will use a self-propelled lawn mower to mow about 350 to 400 square feet of lawn. He also waters the lawn. AR 47. Plaintiff cares for and feeds three dogs: a Labrador and two Dachshunds. AR 48. He will occasionally go grocery shopping with his parents. AR 48. When he helps his mother around the house, Plaintiff picks up after himself and will occasionally vacuum or perform whatever chore his mother asks him to do. AR 48. He watches about seven hours of television a day. AR 49. He does not read for pleasure much, other than an occasional magazine article. AR 50. Plaintiff uses his parents' computer to check email and surf the web. AR 51. He does not have any hobbies, nor does he belong to any clubs or organizations. AR 51. He does not attend church. AR 52. Plaintiff visits with friends when they pick him up. AR 51.

Plaintiff used to attend West Hills College in Lemoore, but the workload became overwhelming. He was taking over twelve units, including algebra and biology. AR 49-50. He dropped out and is not sure whether he will go back. AR 50-51. While he was attending school, about ninety percent of the classes he took were online classes. AR 51, 56. For a period of time, Plaintiff received extra help regarding study habits and memory training. AR 54-56.

When asked how far he can walk, Plaintiff indicated he can walk about three quarters of a mile before the throbbing and stabbing pain sets in. He can stand about three hours and can sit for about three hours. AR 52. He does not know how much weight he can lift. AR 52.

Plaintiff's work history for the previous fifteen years involves the following positions: long haul truck driver, maintenance mechanic, dispatcher, delivery driver, garbage collector and construction worker. Some of the work involved very heavy lifting. AR 57-63.

VE Kenneth Ferra indicated that Plaintiff's past relevant work was semi-skilled with an SVP [3] of four, varying in exertional levels to very heavy. AR 65.

    3 "SVP" refers to specific vocational preparation.

The VE was asked to consider a hypothetical worker of Plaintiff's age, education and work history, with the ability to lift twenty pounds occasionally and ten pounds frequently, who can stand or walk for six hours in an eight-hour workday and sit for six hours in an eight-hour workday, and whom can occasionally climb, stoop, kneel and crawl, with an additional limitation to simple, routine work. AR 65-66. VE Ferra indicated such an individual could not perform Plaintiff's past relevant work. AR 66. However, the individual is capable of performing the work of a cleaner, DOT [4] 323.687-014, with approximately 56,000 jobs available in California; a packing-line worker, DOT 753.687-038, with approximately 31,000 positions available in the state; and a sorter, DOT 539.687-186, with approximately 3,800 positions available. National figures are obtained by multiplying the state number by ten. AR 66.

    4 "DOT" refers to the Dictionary of Occupational Titles.

In a second hypothetical, the VE was asked to assume a hypothetical worker of Plaintiff's age, education and work history, with the ability to lift less than ten pounds either occasionally or frequently, who can stand or walk less than two hours in an eight-hour workday, who can sit for three hours in an eight-hour workday, and whom should never climb, balance, stoop, kneel, crouch or crawl, and whom should avoid moving machinery and extreme temperatures. AR 67. The VE indicated such an individual could not perform Plaintiff's past work, nor any other work in the national economy. AR 67.

Medical Record

The entire medical record was reviewed by the Court. AR 239-602. The medical evidence will be referenced below as necessary to this Court's decision.

ALJ's Findings

Using the Social Security Administration's five-step sequential evaluation process, the ALJ determined that Plaintiff did not meet the disability standard. AR 8-17.

More particularly, the ALJ found that Plaintiff had not engaged in substantial gainful activity since November 1, 2005. AR 10. Further, the ALJ identified the following severe impairments: degenerative disease of the cervical spine, status post fusion; degenerative disc disease of the lumbar spine; degenerative joint disease of the right ankle; sleep apnea; hepatitis C; and an adjustment disorder. AR 10. Nonetheless, the ALJ determined that the severity of the Plaintiff's impairment did not meet or exceed any of the listed impairments. AR 10-12.

Based on his review of the entire record, the ALJ determined that Plaintiff has the residual functional capacity ("RFC") to perform the full range of unskilled, light work. AR 12-16.

Next, the ALJ determined that Plaintiff could not perform his past relevant work. AR 16. Nevertheless, based upon Plaintiff's age, education, work experience and RFC, the ALJ determined there were jobs that existed in significant numbers in the national economy that Plaintiff could perform. Specifically, the ALJ found Plaintiff could perform the work of a cleaner, packager, and sorter. AR 16-17.

SCOPE OF REVIEW

Congress has provided a limited scope of judicial review of the Commissioner's decision to deny benefits under the Act. In reviewing findings of fact with respect to such determinations, this Court must determine whether the decision of the Commissioner is supported by substantial evidence. 42 U.S.C. § 405 (g). Substantial evidence means "more than a mere scintilla," *Richardson v. Perales*, 402 U.S. 389, 402, 91 S. Ct. 1420, 28 L. Ed. 2d 842 (1971), but less than a preponderance. *Sorenson v. Weinberger*, 514 F.2d 1112, 1119, n. 10 (9th Cir. 1975). It is "such relevant evidence as a reasonable mind might accept as adequate to support a conclusion." *Richardson*, 402 U.S. at 401. The record as a whole must be considered, weighing both the evidence that supports and the evidence that detracts from the Commissioner's conclusion. *Jones v. Heckler*, 760 F.2d 993, 995 (9th Cir. 1985). In weighing the evidence and making findings, the Commissioner must apply the proper legal standards. *E.g., Burkhart v. Bowen*, 856 F.2d 1335, 1338 (9th Cir. 1988). This Court must uphold the Commissioner's determination that the claimant is not disabled if the Secretary applied the proper legal standards, and if the Commissioner's findings are supported by substantial evidence. *See Sanchez v. Sec'y of Health and Human Serv.*, 812 F.2d 509, 510 (9th Cir. 1987).

REVIEW

In order to qualify for benefits, a claimant must establish that he is unable to engage in substantial gainful activity due to a medically determinable physical or mental impairment which has lasted or can be expected to last for a continuous period of not less than twelve months. 42 U.S.C. § 1382c (a)(3)(A). A claimant must show that he has a physical or mental impairment of such severity that he is not only unable to do her previous work, but cannot, considering his age, education, and work experience, engage in any other kind of substantial gainful work which exists in the national economy. *Quang Van Han v. Bowen*, 882 F.2d 1453, 1456 (9th Cir. 1989). The burden is on the claimant to establish disability. *Terry v. Sullivan*, 903 F.2d 1273, 1275 (9th Cir. 1990).

Here, Plaintiff argues that the ALJ's findings are not supported by substantial evidence and are not free of legal error because the ALJ failed to give specific and legitimate reasons for discounting the opinion of Plaintiff's treating physician, and erred when assessing Plaintiff's credibility. (Doc.14.)

175

DISCUSSION

The ALJ's Consideration of the Medical Opinion Evidence

Plaintiff argues that the ALJ erroneously rejected the opinion of his treating physician, Dr. Ney M. Aung. More specifically, he asserts the ALJ failed to provide specific and legitimate reasons for rejecting the expert's opinion. (Doc. 14 at 5-9.)

1. Applicable Legal Standards

Cases in this circuit distinguish among the opinions of three types of physicians: (1) those who treat the claimant (treating physicians); (2) those who examine but do not treat the claimant (examining physicians); and (3) those who neither examine nor treat the claimant (nonexamining physicians). As a general rule, more weight should be given to the opinion of a treating source than to the opinion of doctors who do not treat the claimant. *Winans v. Bowen*, 853 F.2d 643, 647 (9th Cir. 1987). At least where the treating doctor's opinion is not contradicted by another doctor, it may be rejected only for "clear and convincing" reasons. *Baxter v. Sullivan*, 923 F.2d 1391, 1396 (9th Cir. 1991). Even if the treating doctor's opinion is contradicted by another doctor, the Commissioner may not reject this opinion without providing "specific and legitimate reasons" supported by substantial evidence in the record for so doing. *Murray v. Heckler*, 722 F.2d 499, 502 (9th Cir. 1983).

The opinion of an examining physician is, in turn, entitled to greater weight than the opinion of a nonexamining physician. *Pitzer v. Sullivan*, 908 F.2d 502, 506 (9th Cir. 1990); *Gallant v. Heckler*, 753 F.2d 1450 (9th Cir. 1984). As is the case with the opinion of a treating physician, the Commissioner must provide "clear and convincing" reasons for rejecting the uncontradicted opinion of an examining physician. *Pitzer*, 908 F.2d at 506. And like the opinion of a treating doctor, the opinion of an examining doctor, even if contradicted by another doctor, can only be rejected for specific and legitimate reasons that are supported by substantial evidence in the record. *Andrews v. Shalala*, 53 F.3d 1035, 1043 (9th Cir. 1995).

The opinion of a nonexamining physician cannot, by itself, constitute substantial evidence that justifies the rejection of the opinion of either an examining physician or a treating physician. *Pitzer v. Sullivan,* 908 F.2d at 506 n.4; *Gallant v. Heckler,* 753 F.2d at 1456. In some cases, however, the ALJ can reject the opinion of a treating or examining physician, based in part on the testimony of a nonexamining medical advisor. *E.g., Magallanes v. Bowen,* 881 F.2d 747, 751-55 (9th Cir. 1989); *Andrews v. Shalala,* 53 F.3d at 1043; *Roberts v. Shalala,* 66 F.3d 179 (9th Cir. 1995). For example, in *Magallanes,* the Ninth Circuit explained that in rejecting the opinion of a treating physician, "the ALJ did not rely on [the nonexamining physician's] testimony alone to reject the opinions of Magallanes's treating physicians . . .." *Magallanes,* 881 F.2d at 752. Rather, there was an abundance of evidence that supported the ALJ's decision: the ALJ also relied on laboratory test results, on contrary reports from examining physicians, and on testimony from the claimant that conflicted with her treating physician's opinion. *Id.* at 751-52.

2. Summary of Relevant Medical Evidence

On or about November 19, 2006, orthopedic surgeon Philip Wirganowicz performed an orthopedic evaluation of Plaintiff, whose chief complaint was low back pain. The doctor reviewed various medical reports and took a medical history from Plaintiff. AR 324-325. Following examination of the cervical and lumbar spines, neck and back range of motion findings were all within normal limits, as were the range of motion findings in both the upper and lower extremities. AR 326-327. Station and gait were also within normal limits, as were the doctor's findings regarding Plaintiff's joints and pulses. AR 327. Neurologic findings were also normal. AR 327-328. Dr. Wirganowicz opined that Plaintiff was capable of lifting twenty-five pounds frequently and fifty pounds occasionally, and that he could sit, stand or walk for about six hours in an eight-hour workday with appropriate breaks. AR 328.

In a Physical Residual Functional Capacity Assessment dated January 25, 2007, reviewing consultant Dr. Irwin Weinreb found Plaintiff capable of lifting ten pounds frequently and twenty pounds occasionally, standing, walking and sitting for about six hours in an eight-hour workday, who can frequently balance and kneel, can occasionally climb ramps and stairs but should avoid ladders, ropes or scaffolds, and may occasionally stoop, crouch and crawl. AR 337-338. Dr. Weinreb found no manipulative, visual, communicative or environmental limitations. AR 339-343.

On or about March 13, 2007, internist Joseph M. Garfinkel completed an internal medicine evaluation of Plaintiff. The chief complaints were identified as right side pain, heart pain, low back pain and headaches. AR 344. Dr. Garfinkel took a history from Plaintiff and reviewed various medical records. AR 344-345. Upon examination, Dr. Garfinkel's findings regarding the head, neck, chest, lungs, cardiovascular system and abdomen were found to be normal. AR 345-347. No spasm was noted in the back, and range of motion findings were largely normal in both the lower and upper extremities. Strength was 5/5 in all extremities. AR 347. Gait was normal. AR 348. The doctor's impression included chronic back pain likely due to osteoarthritis, status post C6 surgery with residual symptoms, chest pain atypical for cardiac etiology, and a history of chronic headaches. AR 348. Dr. Garfinkel opined Plaintiff was capable of lifting and carrying twenty pounds occasionally and ten pounds frequently, could stand, walk and/or sit for six hours in an eight-hour workday, periodically alternating between standing and sitting every two hours, with the ability to occasionally climb, stoop, kneel or crouch. AR 348.

In a Physical Residual Functional Capacity Assessment prepared April 11, 2007, consultative reviewer M. L. Tambellini, M.D., found Plaintiff capable of lifting twenty-five pounds frequently and fifty pounds occasionally, standing or walking for six hours in an eight-hour workday, sitting for six hours in an eight-hour workday, without limitation regarding pushing or pulling. AR 359. The doctor found no postural, manipulative, visual, communicative or environmental limitations. AR 359-361.

On August 29, 2008, Plaintiff's treating physician, Dr. Aung, completed a Medical Source Statement - Physical wherein he opined that Plaintiff was capable of lifting and carrying, frequently or occasionally, less than ten pounds as a result of diagnoses regarding his right ankle and spine. The doctor also determined Plaintiff was capable of standing or walking less than two hours in an eight-hour work day for the same reasons. AR 493. Dr. Aung believed Plaintiff capable of sitting less than six hours in an eight-hour day, identifying three hours as Plaintiff's ability. Further, Plaintiff was to alternate sitting and standing every three hours. He was never to climb, balance, stoop, kneel, crouch or crawl. AR 494. Finally, Plaintiff was to avoid moving machinery and extreme temperatures. AR 494.

3. ALJ's Findings

Here, in relevant part, ALJ Kopicki found as follows:

> [I]n November 2006 Consultative orthopedist Dr. Wirganowicz diagnosed chronic low back pain and concluded that the claimant could perform the full range of medium work. The doctor's opinion is afforded some weight since at the time of the examination there was very little objective findings.
>
> In March 2007 Dr. Garfinkel performed a consultative internal medicine examination of the claimant, who complained of right side pain, heart pain, low back pain, and headaches. The claimant's physical examination was essentially within normal limits. Dr. Garfinkel diagnosed chronic back pain most likely osteoarthritis, status post C6 surgery with residual symptoms, right chest pain atypical for cardiac etiology, and a history of chronic headaches. The doctor concluded that the claimant could lift and carry 20 pounds occasionally and 10 pounds frequently; and stand or walk 6 hours and sit 6 hours in an 8-hour workday with alternating standing and sitting every 2 hours; and occasional climbing, stooping, kneeling or crouching. Dr. Garfinkel's medical opinion is given substantial weight as he had the opportunity of reviewing multiple medical records, plus he based his opinion both on clinical findings as well as the claimant's subjective complaints of pain.
>
> ....
>
> Dr. Aung completed a medical source statement (physical) in August 2008 indicating that the claimant had a less than sedentary residual functional capacity. Dr. Aung's opinion is given no weight as it is not supported by objective clinical evidence, is inconsistent with the claimant's activities of daily living and contrary to other more persuasive medical source opinions of record.
>
> ....
>
> The State agency medical consultants concluded that the claimant could perform work at the light level of exertion with occasional stooping, crouching and crawling. In April 2007 they completed

179

another residual functional capacity assessment indicating that the claimant can perform the full range of work at the medium level of exertion. However, I give substantial weight to the State agency medical consultants' opinion that the claimant can perform light work which is consistent with consultative examiner Dr. Garfinkel's opinion discussed above.

AR 14-15, internal quotations omitted.

4. Analysis

Here, ALJ Kopicki afforded no weight to Dr. Aung's opinion for specific and legitimate reasons after it was contradicted by both an examining physician and consultative reviewing physicians: (1) Dr. Aung's opinion was not supported by objective clinical evidence, (2) was inconsistent with Plaintiff's activities of daily living, and (3) was contrary to other medical source opinions.

A lack of supporting clinical findings is a valid reason for rejecting a treating physician's opinion. *Magallanes v. Bowen*, 881 F.2d 747, 751 (9th Cir. 1989). The consistency of a medical opinion with the record as a whole is also a relevant factor in evaluating a medical opinion. *Lingenfelter v. Astrue*, 504 F.3d 1028, 1042 (9th Cir. 20047); *Orn v. Astrue*, 495 F.3d 625, 631 (9th Cir. 2007). Additionally, a contrary opinion by an examining source can be a specific and legitimate reason for rejecting the opinion of a treating physician. Here, examining physician Dr. Garfinkel's opinion was clearly contrary to that of treating physician Dr. Aung. *See Tonapetyan v. Halter*, 242 F.3d 1144, 1149 (9th Cir. 2001); *Andrews v. Shalala*, 53 F.3d at 1041 ("Where the opinion of the claimant's treating physician is contradicted, and the opinion of a nontreating source is based on independent clinical findings that differ from those of the treating physician, the opinion of the nontreating source may itself be substantial evidence; it is then solely the province of the ALJ to resolve the conflict"). Dr. Garfinkel's findings are independent clinical findings, and thus are substantial evidence. *See Orn v. Astrue*, 495 F.3d at 632; *Miller v. Heckler*, 770 F.2d 845, 849 (9th Cir. 1985). Notably too, a treating physician's opinion is not conclusive as to a physical condition or the ultimate issue of disability. *Magallanes*, 881 F.2d at 751.

Dr. Aung treated Plaintiff from May 30, 2008, and thereafter for approximately three months until preparation of the medical source statement. As the Commissioner points out however, while the record as a whole contains information regarding Plaintiff's ankle joint degenerative disease and degenerative disc disease of the spine, Dr. Aung himself did not make those findings upon examination. Rather, treatment records from the Veteran's Administration during the relevant time period establish "that Plaintiff had a cyst containing sperm removed from his right testicle," was followed for psychiatric treatment, and medications were refilled. *See, e.g.* AR 495-602. Where a treating physician's conclusions about a claimant's functional limitations are not supported, the ALJ may reject that opinion. *Connett v. Barnhart*, 340 F.3d 871, 875 (9th Cir. 2003). Dr. Aung's statements about Plaintiff's functional limitations are not supported by this record.

Finally, Plaintiff's daily activities can be properly considered by the ALJ when assessing medical evidence. Ignoring whether or not Plaintiff continued to jog [5] at the time of the hearing, Plaintiff did testify that he used to attend college courses online, and is able to help his elderly parents with household chores, including mowing and watering the lawn, and vacuuming or performing whatever other household chores his mother might ask of him. AR 47-48. He cares for three dogs, and uses the computer for email and web surfing. AR 48, 50. Plaintiff also watches about seven hours of television a day. AR 49. He occasionally grocery shops and visits with friends. AR 48, 51. These activities certainly do not comport with Dr. Aung's physically-restrictive opinion, and these differences were properly considered. *See Rollins v. Massanari*, 261 F.3d 853, 856 (9th Cir. 2001).

> 5 This Court interpreted Plaintiff's testimony to be that he used to jog, but that he stopped doing so after being advised by a physician in Martinez to stop the activity. *See* AR 31.

The ALJ's Findings Regarding Plaintiff's Credibility

Next, Plaintiff complains that ALJ Kopicki erred when he found Plaintiff to be both sincere and less than credible. (Doc. 14 at 9-16.)

A two step analysis applies at the administrative level when considering a claimant's subjective symptom testimony. *Smolen v. Chater*, 80 F.3d 1273, 1281 (9th Cir. 1996). First, the claimant must produce objective medical evidence of an impairment that could reasonably be expected to produce some degree of the symptom or pain alleged. *Id.* at 1281-1282. If the claimant satisfies the first step and there is no evidence of malingering, the ALJ may reject the claimant's testimony regarding the severity of his symptoms only if he makes specific findings that include clear and convincing reasons for doing so. *Id.* at 1281. The ALJ must "state which testimony is not credible and what evidence suggests the complaints are not credible." *Mersman v. Halter*, 161 F.Supp.2d 1078, 1086 (N.D. Cal. 2001), quotations & citations omitted ("The lack of specific, clear, and convincing reasons why Plaintiff's testimony is not credible renders it impossible for [the] Court to determine whether the ALJ's conclusion is supported by substantial evidence"); Social Security Ruling ("SSR") 96-7p, 1996 SSR LEXIS 4 (ALJ's decision "must be sufficiently specific to make clear to the individual and to any subsequent reviewers the weight the adjudicator gave to the individual's statements and reasons for that weight").

An ALJ may consider many factors when assessing the claimant's credibility. *See Light v. Soc. Sec. Admin.*, 119 F.3d 789, 792 (9th Cir. 1997). The ALJ can consider the claimant's reputation for truthfulness, prior inconsistent statements concerning his symptoms, other testimony by the claimant that appears less than candid, unexplained or inadequately explained failure to seek treatment, failure to follow a prescribed course of treatment, claimant's daily activities, claimant's work record, or the observations of treating and examining physicians. *Smolen*, 80 F.3d at 1284; *Orn v. Astrue*, 495 F.3d at 638. "An ALJ is not 'required to believe every allegation of disabling pain' or other non-exertional impairment." *Orn v. Astrue*, 495 F.3d at 635.

The first step in assessing Plaintiff's subjective complaints is to determine whether Plaintiff's condition could reasonably be expected to produce the pain or other symptoms alleged. *Lingenfelter v. Astrue*, 504 F.3d at 1036. Here, the ALJ found that Plaintiff had the severe impairments of degenerative disease of the cervical spine status post fusion, degenerative disc disease of the lumbar spine, degenerative joint disease of the right ankle, sleep apnea, hepatitis C and an adjustment disorder. AR 10. This finding satisfied step one of the credibility analysis. *Smolen*, 80 F.3d at 1281-1282.

"Despite the inability to measure and describe it, pain can have real and severe debilitating effects; it is, without a doubt, capable of entirely precluding a claimant from working." *Fair v. Bowen*, 885 F.2d at 601. It is possible to suffer disabling pain even where the degree of pain is unsupported by objective medical findings. *Id.* "In order to disbelieve a claim of excess pain, an ALJ must make specific findings justifying that decision." *Id.* (citing *Magallanes v. Bowen*, 881 F.2d at 755). The findings must convincingly justify the ALJ's rejection of the plaintiff's excess pain testimony. *Id.* at 602. However, an ALJ cannot be required to believe every allegation of disabling pain. "This holds true even where the claimant introduces medical evidence showing that he has an ailment reasonably expected to produce some pain." *Id.* at 603.

Here, after summarizing Plaintiff's testimony and the medical record (AR 12-15), ALJ Kopicki made the following findings:

> In sum, the claimant lives at home and helps his elderly parents with daily activities. He presented at the hearing as a tanned, robust individual. He had an excellent response to neck surgery. He has Hepatitis C for which he underwent treatment in the past and currently is not sure whether he has any associated symptoms. He has pain and discomfort secondary to post traumatic changes in an ankle and degenerative changes in his lower back, yet can do yard work, jog, shops, pick up after himself, vacuum, look after his two dogs, read, and watch television. He no longer drives but that is because he was convicted of DUI. He retained the attention and concentration to take college classes, using the computer to study online. Again, he was a sincere witness but to the extent his allegations suggest an inability to perform unskilled light work they are considered no[t] fully credible.

AR 15.

The ALJ did not err. He provided clear and convincing reasons for rejecting Plaintiff's testimony as it related to Plaintiff inability to perform unskilled light work. ALJ Kopicki's reasons included his own observations during the hearing, Plaintiff's activities of daily living, and the objective medical evidence available. All of these considerations were proper. First, an ALJ may properly rely upon his observations made during the administrative hearing. *See Thomas v. Barnhart*, 278 F.3d 947, 960 (9th Cir. 2002); *Matney v. Sullivan*, 981 F.2d 1016, 1020 (9th Cir. 1992). Next, an ALJ can look to the activities of daily living as part of the credibility analysis. *See Orn v.*

Astrue, 495 F.3d at 638 (the ALJ may discount a claimant's credibility based on daily activities); *Burch v. Barnhart*, 400 F.3d 676, 680 (9th Cir. 2005); *Morgan v. Commissioner of Social Sec. Admin.*, 169 F.3d 595, 600 (9th Cir. 1999) (if a claimant is able to spend a substantial part of his day engaged in pursuits involving the performance of physical functions that are transferable to a work setting, a specific finding as to this fact may be sufficient to discredit a claimant's allegations); *Fair v. Bowen*, 885 F.2d at 603; *Thomas v. Barnhart*, 278 F.3d at 958-59. Lastly, an ALJ can consider how a claimant's allegations are inconsistent with the medical evidence. *See Stubbs-Danielson v. Astrue*, 539 F.3d 1169, 1175 (9th Cir. 2008); *Osenbrock v. Apfel*, 240 F.3d 1157, 1166 (9th Cir. 2001); *see also* 20 C.F.R. § 416.929 (objective medical evidence can be used in determining credibility; inconsistencies in evidence will support a rejection of credibility) & Social Security Ruling 96-7p, 1996 SSR LEXIS 4 (objective medical evidence is a useful indicator to assist in making a reasonable conclusion about credibility and the ability to function).

Moreover, Plaintiff's argument that because ALJ Kopicki found Plaintiff to be a sincere witness, he should also have found him to be credible, in not persuasive. Sincerity and credibility can be exclusive. Plaintiff can sincerely believe himself to be disabled, and yet, as pointed out by the ALJ here, there is evidence to the contrary in the form of medical records and Plaintiff's own abilities despite his severe impairments.

Finally, it is not the role of this Court to redetermine Plaintiff's credibility *de novo*. Although evidence supporting an ALJ's conclusions might also permit an interpretation more favorable to the claimant, if the ALJ's interpretation of evidence was rational, as here, the Court must uphold the ALJ's decision where the evidence is susceptible to more than one rational interpretation. *Burch v. Barnhart*, 400 F.3d at 680-81.

This Court finds that ALJ Kopicki's credibility findings justify his rejection of Plaintiff's pain testimony. *Fair v. Bowen*, 885 F.2d at 602. Therefore, his findings are supported by substantial evidence and are free of legal error.

CONCLUSION Based on the foregoing, the Court finds that the ALJ's decision is supported by substantial evidence in the record as a whole and is based on proper legal standards. Accordingly, this Court DENIES Plaintiff's appeal from the administrative decision of the Commissioner of Social Security. The Clerk of this Court is DIRECTED to enter judgment in favor of Defendant Michael J. Astrue, Commissioner of Social Security, and against Plaintiff, Larry D. Smith.

IT IS SO ORDERED.

Dated: November 3, 2011 /s/ Gary S. Austin, U.S. Magistrate Judge

SALVATORE DEGIORGIO, Petitioner,
v.
DANIEL FITZPATRICK, Respondent.

Case No. 08-CV-6551 (KMK) (LMS)
UNITED STATES DISTRICT COURT
FOR THE SOUTHERN DISTRICT OF
NEW YORK
March 12, 2013,

Salvatore DeGiorgio, Plaintiff, Pro se, Monticello, NY.

For Daniel Fitzpatrick, Defendant: Bonnie Mae Mitzner, LEAD ATTORNEY, The Sullivan County DA's Office, Monticello, NY.

KENNETH M. KARAS, UNITED STATES DISTRICT JUDGE.

ORDER ADOPTING REPORT AND RECOMMENDATION

KENNETH M. KARAS, District Judge:

Petitioner Savatore DeGiorgio filed a *pro se* petition for a writ of habeas corpus on July 23, 2008, pursuant to 28 U.S.C. § 2254, challenging his September 14, 2005 judgment of conviction in New York State County Court, Sullivan County. Petitioner was convicted of one count of Intimidating a Victim or Witness in the Third Degree (N.Y. Penal Law § 215.15(1)), one count of Aggravated Cruelty to Animals (N.Y. Agriculture and Markets Law § 353-a), one count of Aggravated Harassment in the Second Degree (N.Y. Penal Law § 240.30(1)), and one count of Criminal Contempt in the Second Degree (N.Y. Penal Law§ 215.50(3)). On November 3, 2005, Petitioner was sentenced to a determinate term of two (2) years in prison on the Aggravated Cruelty to Animals charge, an indeterminate term of one and one-third (1 1/3) to four (4) years in prison on the Intimidating a Witness charge, a determinate term of one (1) year on the Aggravated Harassment charge, and a determinate term of one (1) year on the Criminal Contempt charge. The sentences were to run concurrent with one another, except that the animal cruelty sentence was to run consecutive to the others.[1] (Sentencing Tr. 44.)

1 The Report and Recommendation states that the prison terms were all to be concurrent, (R&R 1), but this appears to be an error. The length of the sentence is immaterial to the outcome here.

The Court referred this case to Magistrate Judge Lisa Margaret Smith, pursuant to 28 U.S.C. § 636(b). (Dkt. No. 2.) Magistrate Judge Smith issued a Report and Recommendation ("R&R") concluding that the Court should deny the Petition. (Dkt. No. 14.) The R&R notified Petitioner of his right to file objections to the R&R, (R&R 16-17), but none were filed.

A district court reviewing a report and recommendation "may accept, reject, or modify, in whole or in part, the findings or recommendations made by the magistrate judge." 28 U.S.C. § 636(b)(1)(C); *see also Donahue v. Global Home Loans & Fin., Inc.*, No. 05-CV-8362, 2007 U.S. Dist. LEXIS 18605, 2007 WL 831816, at *1 (S.D.N.Y. Mar. 15, 2007). Under 28 U.S.C. § 636(b)(1) and Fed. R. Civ. P. 72(b), parties may submit objections to a magistrate judge's report and recommendation. The objections must be "specific" and "written," and they must be made "[w]ithin 14 days after being served with a copy of the recommended disposition," Fed. R. Civ. P. 72(b)(2); *see also* 28 U.S.C. § 636(b)(1)(C), plus an additional three days when service is made pursuant to Federal Rule of Civil Procedure 5(b)(2)(C)-(F), *see* Fed. R. Civ. P. 6(d).

"[W]here a party does not submit an objection, a district court need only satisfy itself that there is no clear error on the face of the record." *Donahue*, 2007 U.S. Dist. LEXIS 18605, 2007 WL 831816, at *1 (internal quotation marks omitted). In addition, a party's failure to object will waive that party's right to challenge the report and recommendation on appeal. *See FDIC v. Hillcrest Assocs.*, 66 F.3d 566, 569 (2d Cir. 1995) ("Our rule is that 'failure to object timely to a magistrate's report operates as a waiver of any further judicial review of the magistrate's decision.'" (quoting *Small v. Sec'y of Health & Human Servs.*, 892 F.2d 15, 16 (2d Cir. 1989))).

As noted, Petitioner has not filed objections to the R&R. Accordingly, the Court has reviewed the R&R under the clear error standard. In so doing, the Court has construed Petitioner's pro se pleadings liberally to raise the strongest arguments that they suggest. *See Erickson v. Pardus*, 551 U.S. 89, 94, 127 S. Ct. 2197, 167 L. Ed. 2d

1081 (2007) (per curiam); *Triestman v. Fed. Bureau of Prisons*, 470 F.3d 471, 474 (2d Cir. 2006) (per curiam). The Court finds no clear error in the R&R and therefore adopts its conclusions in their entirety.

Magistrate Judge Smith's R&R thoroughly addresses the single claim presented in the Petition -- a constitutional challenge to the sufficiency of the evidence under *Jackson v. Virginia*, 443 U.S. 307, 99 S. Ct. 2781, 61 L. Ed. 2d 560 (1979) -- and the Court can add little to the R&R's merits discussion. (R&R 11-16.) However, a few brief jurisdictional remarks are in order, as the Court has an independent and ongoing duty to assure itself that it has jurisdiction to render a decision. *See Coll. Standard Magazine v. Student Ass'n of State of Univ. of NY at Albany*, 610 F.3d 33, 35 (2d Cir. 2010) (Courts have "an independent obligation to consider the presence or absence of subject matter jurisdiction *sua sponte*." (internal quotation marks omitted)).

First, though the R&R does not directly address the question, the Court is satisfied that Petitioner meets the "in custody" requirement of 28 U.S.C. § 2254(a). That provision specifies that a federal court "shall entertain an application for a writ of habeas corpus in behalf of a person *in custody* pursuant to the judgment of a State court ...." 28 U.S.C. § 2254(a) (emphasis added). On June 24, 2008, when Petitioner filed the Petition here, he already had completed the prison term arising from these charges. (R&R 2.) However, he appears to have remained on parole until September 21, 2009. (*Id.*) The cases are clear that prisoners not incarcerated but instead living under a form of correctional supervision are nonetheless considered "in custody" for purposes of § 2254, and therefore the Court has jurisdiction to entertain this Petition. *See Scanio v. United States*, 37 F.3d 858, 860 (2d Cir. 1994) ("[A] petitioner under supervised release may be considered 'in custody'"); *Harvey v. City of New York.*, 435 F. Supp. 2d 175, 177 (E.D.N.Y. 2006) (same).

Second, as the R&R correctly notes, even if a court had initial jurisdiction to entertain a petition, it must assure itself that the case is not mooted by the expiration of a petitioner's entire state-imposed sentence. (R&R 8.) The governing law is that "[o]nce the convict's sentence has expired ... some concrete and continuing injury other than the now-ended incarceration or parole -- some 'collateral consequence' of the conviction -- must exist if the suit is to be maintained." *Spencer v. Kemna*, 523 U.S. 1, 7, 118 S. Ct. 978, 140 L. Ed. 2d 43 (1998).

Here, this requirement is met, even though Petitioner's whereabouts are unknown. While the R&R notes that Petitioner, an alien, had been facing removal proceedings as a result of his state convictions, (R&R 9), it appears to the Court that those proceedings have concluded and Petitioner has actually been removed from the country. A December 31, 2008 letter from Petitioner's immigration attorney apprised the Court that Petitioner was then facing removal proceedings, (Dkt. No. 13), and on September 30, 2009, the Board of Immigration Appeals affirmed an Immigration Judge's order that Petitioner be removed, *see In re DeGiorgio*, No. A012 381 134, 2009 WL 3250319 (B.I.A. Sept. 30, 2009). Since then, the Court has not received any correspondence from Petitioner or anyone in contact with him, and the Court's most recent mailing to Petitioner was marked return to sender. (Unnumbered Dkt. Entry of June 25, 2012.) Assuming Petitioner was removed sometime following the expiration of the immigration appeals process, there remains a live controversy. This is because the lifetime bar on reentry into the United States for aliens, like Petitioner, who have been convicted of an "aggravated felony" is a sufficiently concrete "collateral consequence" of a state conviction to maintain a petitioner's personal stake in the outcome. *See United States v. Hamdi*, 432 F.3d 115, 121 (2d Cir. 2005) (holding that a habeas petition from an alien who had been removed from the country "presented a live controversy because the writ, if granted, would remove a permanent bar on readmission and allow [a petitioner] to seek a purely discretionary form of relief from deportability."); *see also Mitchell v. People of N.Y.*, No. 03-CV-3303, 2007 U.S. Dist. LEXIS 85049, 2007 WL 3355550, at *5 (S.D.N.Y. Sept. 12, 2007), *adopted by* 2007 U.S. Dist. LEXIS 82560, 2007 WL 3340832 (same).

With the Court satisfied that it is appropriate to exercise jurisdiction over this Petition, the Court need not elaborate on the merits discussion in the R&R.[2] (R&R 11-17.) The Court finds no error, clear or otherwise, in the R&R's conclusion that the state appellate court's decision affirming Petitioner's conviction was neither "contrary to," nor "involved an unreasonable application of, clearly established

Federal law, as determined by the Supreme Court of the United States." *See* 28 U.S.C. § 2254(d).[3]

2 Although Petitioner's state appellate brief, which was appended to his habeas petition, raised the issue that his sentence was excessive, Petitioner did not argue to the state appellate court that the sentence in any way violated *federal* law, and so the R&R declined to entertain the excessive sentence argument on collateral review. (R&R 11 n.2.) This was proper because "the Second Circuit has broadly stated that '[n]o federal constitutional issue is presented where ... the sentence is within the range prescribed by state law.'" *Taylor v. Poole*, No. 07-CV-6318, 2009 U.S. Dist. LEXIS 76316, 2009 WL 2634724 (S.D.N.Y. Aug. 27, 2009) (quoting *White v. Keane*, 969 F.2d 1381, 1383 (2d Cir.1992) (per curiam) (alterations in original)). Petitioner, in his appellate brief, acknowledges that the sentences prescribed were all within the state statutory range. (State Appellate Br. 28 (noting that Petitioner was sentenced "to the maximum sentence possible on each count.")) Accordingly, even construing the prose pleading liberally, there is no federal issue presented, and therefore Petitioner is not entitled to habeas relief on this basis.

3 The Court wishes to make one minor correction to the R&R's factual description: the R&R says that the victimized dog was a Chihuahua, (R&R 14); actually, the dog was a **Dachshund**, *(see* Trial Tr. 27); *New York v. DeGiorgio*, 36 A.D.3d 1007, 827 N.Y.S.2d 342, 344 (App. Div. 2007). The minor error is entirely immaterial to the outcome.

Accordingly, it is hereby

ORDERED that the Report and Recommendation dated March 8, 2011, is ADOPTED in its entirety. It is further

ORDERED that the petition is dismissed with prejudice. It is further

ORDERED that because Petitioner has not made a substantial showing of the denial of a constitutional right, a certificate of appealability will not issue, *see* 28 U.S.C. § 2253(c)(2); *Lucidore v. N.Y. State Div. of Parole*, 209 F.3d 107, 111-12 (2d Cir. 2000), and the Court certifies, pursuant to 28 U.S.C. § 1915(a)(3), that any appeal from this Order would not be taken in good faith, and therefore in forma pauperis status is denied for the purpose of an appeal, *see Coppedge v. United States*, 369 U.S. 438, 444-45, 82 S. Ct. 917, 8 L. Ed. 2d 21 (1962). It is further

ORDERED that the Clerk of the Court is respectfully directed to enter a judgment in favor of Respondent and to close this case.

3

Dog shaped objects

papier mache, a Vienna Bronze and children's toys.

Wilson's Customs Clearanc, Inc. v. U.S.,
59 Cust. Ct. 36 (1967)

Blakley v. United States,
96-2 U.S. Tax Cas. (CCH) P50,693 (W.D. Tex.., 1996)

Imperial Toy Corp. v. Goffa Int'l Corp.,
988 F.Supp. 617, (E.D.N.Y., 1997)

WILSON'S CUSTOMS CLEARANCE, INC.
v.
UNITED STATES

Protests 65/19189 and 65/19211 against
the decision of the collector of customs at
the port of New York
UNITED STATES CUSTOMS COURT,
FIRST DIVISION
59 Cust. Ct. 36
July 19, 1967

Gurson L. Schweller for the plaintiff.

Carl Eardley, Acting Assistant Attorney General (*Glenn E. Harris* and *Andrew P. Vance*), for the defendant.

Before WATSON and BECKWORTH, Judges, and OLIVER, Senior Judge

OLIVER, Judge: The cases at bar which were consolidated at the time of trial relate to importations of articles invoiced as "papier mache dogs" or "papier mache ware." Duty was assessed at the rate of 35 per centum ad valorem under item 737.40 of the Tariff Schedules of the United States. Plaintiff claims that the imported articles are properly classifiable under item 256.75 of said tariff schedules at the rate of 8.5 per centum ad valorem as articles of papier mache. Various other claims mentioned in the protests were not pressed at trial or in the plaintiff's brief and are deemed abandoned. The official papers accompanying the protests were received into evidence without being marked.

The pertinent statutory provisions appear as follows:

Schedule 7, part 5, subpart E, headnotes 1 and 2:

1. The articles described in the provisions of this subpart (except parts) shall be classified in such provisions, whether or not such articles are more specifically provided for elsewhere in the tariff schedules, but the provisions of this subpart do not apply to --

* * *

2. For the purposes of the tariff schedules, a "toy" is any article chiefly used for the amusement of children or adults.

Item 737.40:

Toy figures of animate objects (except dolls):

Not having a spring mechanism:

* * *

Not stuffed:

* * *

Other   35% ad val.

Schedule 2, part 4, subpart D, headnote 1:

1. This subpart covers articles of pulp, of papier-mache, of paper, or of paperboard, not provided for elsewhere in this schedule or in schedule 7.

Item 256.mkd TArticles, of pulp, of papier-mache, of paper, or of paperboard, or of any combination thereof, not specially provided for:

* * *

Of papier-mache   8.5% ad val.

The imported merchandise as represented by plaintiff's exhibits 1 and 2 was accurately described in the Government's brief as follows:

Each exhibit consists of a dog-like figure, approximately 10 inches long, with a detachable head that is inserted into an opening in the neck portion of the body by means of a hook and an eye that are attached to the outside of the head and the inside of the neck respectively. There is a metal weight attached to the head, and a collar around the neck. Plastic eyes and nose are attached to the head of each figure. The exhibits have a suede-like finish, Plaintiff's Illustrative Exhibit 1 being black and gray, while Plaintiff's Illustrative Exhibit 2 is brown. When the head of the figure is subjected to a force acting against it the resulting movement, corresponding to the hook swinging through the eye, is that of a dog nodding its head.

Plaintiff's first witness was Mr. Theodore Royffe, owner and sole employee of Royffe Continenal, Inc., the actual importer in this case. [1] He testified that pursuant to negotiations with Korlis, Ltd., of Englewood, New Jersey, he went to Japan and arranged to have the instant merchandise manufactured. The entries involved cover three kinds of dogs, shepherd, **dachshund**, and cocker spaniel, and they are all produced by the same Japanese manufacturer. Exhibit 1 represents a shepherd and exhibit 2 a cocker spaniel.

> 1 At the outset of the trial, the Government moved and the court granted its motion to quash a subpoena duces tecum served the day before trial on the Regional Commissioner of Customs in New York to produce inter alia certain entry papers covering importations of similar items by a New Jersey importer.

The witness further stated that he sold the items exclusively to automotive stores or wholesalers who sell to automotive outlets, such as Rep Boys in Philadelphia, Western Tire in Chicago, E.J.B. Products in New York, and Korlis, Ltd., in New Jersey.He had seen this merchandise, and similar merchandise, used on the inside rear of automobiles, mounted on the bck shelf and plainly visible. He had never seen it used by a child and thought the presence of the hook to hold the head on, as well as the "toxic" nature of the material used, made it dangerous for youngsters.

On cross-examination, the witness testified that, besides papier mache, the items contained a weight of lead, some plastic, and cardboard.

Mr. Eric J. Browner of E.J.B. Products testified as plaintiff's second witness. He stated that his business was that of a general importer and that he had purchased items represented by exhibits 1 and 2 from Royffe Continental, Inc. He sold 120 dozen of them to Times Square Automotive which he characterized as a store dealing in supplies, gadgets, and accessories for automobiles. He also remembered selling them to two automotive jobbers, one in Providence and the other in Los Angeles. He had never sold them to toy stores. On many occasions, he had observed similar articles displayed in the rear of cars and he had never seen them any place else.

Plaintiff argues that the fact that these imports have been sold exclusively to automotive outlets and never to toy stores and that the witnesses Royffe and Browner observed them in use only as automobile ornaments is sufficient to show they are not articles chiefly used to amuse children or adults. The Government, on the other hand, argues that plaintiff's evidence is too limited to show the articles are not chiefly used by children, much less by adults, and that, in any event, plaintiff has failed to establish its claimed classification on the issue of chief value.

With the advent of the new Tariff Schedules of the United States, the definition of the term "toy" was changed to include articles used by adults. Under the definition appearing in paragraph 1513 of the Tariff Act of 1930, it was necessary to determine two things, namely, by whom is the article used and for what purpose. United States v. Calhoun, Robbins, & Co., 21 CCPA 167, T.D. 46495. Although the first of these two determinations is now eliminated, the second subsists. With respect to this second determination, it had always been held that not everything a child used would be a toy but that the character of amusement involved was that derived from an item which is essentially a plaything. United States v. Louis Wolf & Co., 26 CCPA 243, C.A.D. 23; F.F.G Harper Co. v. United States, 63 Treas. Dec. 948, T.D. 46423. It follows, therefore, that Congress has broadened the toy provision to include articles that may be described as essentially playthings for adults. Apropos of this is the following observation of Mr. Russell N. Shewmaker, Assistant General Counsel to the United States Tariff Commission, made during a hearing conducted by the Tariff Commission concerning the revised scope of the toy provision in the new schedules (1960 Tariff Classification Study, Explanatory and Background Materials, schedule, 7, page 682):

There is also another factor which I think is important here as we work with this provision. There has been in recent years a growth in the leisure time activities of adults. The adults are finding more and more time to play and to amuse themselves with various pursuits and, as Mr. Lerch said, they may be acting like a child sometimes when they are doing it, but nevertheless they are being amused. We were trying to help the tariff to go with the age.

In the recently decided case of Fred Bronner Corp. v. United States, 57 Cust. Ct. 428, C.D. 2832, we had occasion to review a significant line of cases distinguishing between a toy and articles of ornamentation, decoration, or display. The distinction exists regardless of the age of the users. In the instant case, the sole testimony offered is to the effect that these items, similar to those previously imported by others, have found but one use and that is as ornaments or objects of display for the rear window of automobiles. Such testimony, however, as pointed out by defendant, is limited to local observations in this city. Moreover, as merchants or executives commercially handling these items, the witnesses' testimony has limited effect since they mostly sell to other and distant distributors, and they did not disclose a very intimate knowledge of ultimate distribution and sale. Klipstein v. United States, 1 Ct. Cust. Appls. 122, T.D. 31120; F. B. Vandegrift & Co., Inc. v. United States, 56 Cust. Ct. 103, C.D. 2617.

Nevertheless, as is especially true in toy cases, the sample merchandise can offer potent evidence on the question of use, and when in harmony with the other evidence of record, can permit the drawing of inferences as to use nationally. Fred Bronner Corp., supra. There is precedent under the two previous tariff acts for viewing sample evidence as sufficiently persuasive to rebut the presumption of correctness on a toy classification and to shift the burden to the defendant. United States v. The Halle Bros. Co., 20 CCPA 219, T.D. 45995; United States v. Borgfeldt & Co., 13 Ct. Cust. Appls. 620, T.D. 41461.

We are inclined to the view that the present case presents one of those occasions where the sample merchandise itself supplies the necessary persuasiveness to carry the issue for the plaintiff, at least when the presumptive correctness of the collector's classification stands unsupported. The presence of a sharp and rather easily exposed hook renders the merchandise patently unusable by children of tender years. As for those over puberty, the articles represent essentially passive, uncomical, almost nonmanipulatable, yet finely finished replicas of well-known dog species. As such they are eminently suitable for purposes of display or ornamentation, no matter where that may be, and substantially incapable of functioning as objects of play or amusement in any normal or intelligent use. It is not a question of their appearing more suitable for one use than another as was the case in Fred Bronner Corp., supra, but of their offering mute testimony of their substantial incapability of use as classified. This type of potent evidence when in harmony with all other evidence presented satisfies the court that a shift in burden on this issue has taken place.

To discharge its two-fold burden in this classification case, it was for the plaintiff to show that the merchandise is properly dutiable as claimed, that is, as articles of papier mache under item 256.75. Rule 9(f)(i) of the General Headnotes and Rules of Interpretation preceding the new tariff schedules provides that the term "of" when used to relate a material to articles under a tariff provision means articles wholly or in chief value of that material. In conjunction with this, General Interpretative Rule 10(f) provides:

an article is in chief value of a material if such material exceeds in value each other single component material of the article:

Aside from the testimony of the importer that he had observed the manufacture of these articles in Japan, the record here is completely lacking in evidence on this issue of component material of chief value. Unlike the efficacy of the sample on the issue of use, the presence of a rather substantial amount of lead, as well as unknown amounts of nonpaper materials, renders it unsuitable as a competent source on this value issue. Compare John S. Connor, Inc. v. United States, 54 Cust. Ct. 213, C.D. 2536. In this situation, therefore, it was incumbent upon the plaintiff to show the costs of the different components used in producing these articles.

It is well settled that the proper method of determining the component material of chief value of an article is to ascertain the costs of the separate parts or component materials to the manufacturer at the time they are ready to be assembled or combined into the article. [Commercial Adolfo S. Pagan, Inc., et al. v. United States, 48 Cust. Ct. 210, 216, C.D. 2337, and cases cited therein.]

Having failed to offer the proofs required to sustain its claim, we have no alternative but to overrule plaintiff's protests without affirming the collector's classification. Judgment will issue accordingly.

LUCILLE CHRISTIE BLAKLEY and LUCILLE CHRISTIE BLAKLEY TRUST
v.
UNITED STATES OF AMERICA

NO. MO-94-CA-224-F
UNITED STATES DISTRICT COURT
FOR THE WESTERN DISTRICT OF TEXAS,
MIDLAND-ODESSA DIVISION
96-2 U.S. Tax Cas. (CCH) P50,693
September 12, 1996

For LUCILLE CHRISTIE BLAKLEY, plaintiff: Wiley France James, III, Mounce & Galatzan, El Paso, TX. Bernard Robert Given, II, Mounce & Galatzan, El Paso, TX.

For LUCILLE CHRISTIE BLAKLEY TRUST, plaintiff: Wiley France James, III, (See above). Bernard Robert Given, II, (See above).

For UNITED STATES, defendant: Louise P. Hytken, Department of Justice, Tax Division, Dallas, TX. Gregg D. Stevens, Dept. of Justice, Dallas, TX.

ROYAL FURGESON, UNITED STATES DISTRICT JUDGE

MEMORANDUM OPINION AND ORDER

1.0. Background

In this action, Plaintiffs Lucille Christie Blakley ("Mrs. Blakley") and the Lucille Christie Blakley Trust ("Trust") pursue a wrongful levy suit against the United States under 26 U.S.C. § 7426. Although Plaintiffs state several claims in their suit, their main action is for wrongful levy.

Plaintiffs filed suit after the United States seized personal property located at a residence, warehouse and office complex in Midland, Texas. It is the Government's position that the property belongs to David Porras ("Porras") against whom the Government has assessed federal income tax deficiencies in the amount of $ 36,677,296.45 for the years ended December 31, 1984; December 31, 1985; December 31, 1986; and December 31, 1987. Plaintiffs take the position that most of the seized property belongs to them, not to Porras. Mrs. Blakley is the mother of Porras and the beneficiary of the Trust. The trustee of the Trust is William Edmiston ("Edmiston"), a close personal friend of Mrs. Blakley and Porras and a long-time business associate of Porras.

In their suit, Plaintiffs set forth claims under theories involving (1) violations of constitutional rights, (2) conversion, (3) trespass, and (4) wrongful levy. They asked for an injunction requiring return of their property and prohibiting further seizure and for damages. After discovery and some preliminary hearings, the parties agreed to an early trial setting before the court.

Almost 4,000 items of personal property were seized in connection with this matter. Since it was not possible to bring all items into the courtroom for identification and discussion, most of the trial was conducted in a warehouse in Midland, Texas, where the United States stored the property. The process to view each item of property and to hear testimony about it took over four weeks, during the warmest days of the summer of 1995, in a facility where only a few small rooms were air-conditioned. The trial would have taken longer but the parties stipulated, in most instances, to divide equally property with an appraised value of under $ 50.00. Such a division was accomplished at time of trial and nothing further is necessitated for the court in that regard. After all testimony was completed, the court received briefs and heard oral arguments. The matter is now before the court for final decision. This Memorandum Opinion and Order constitutes the court's findings of fact and conclusions of law pursuant to Rule 52 of the Federal Rules of Civil Procedure.

2.0. Standard for Wrongful Levy

Before discussing the facts, the legal guidelines which govern a wrongful levy case should be set forth briefly. Under 26 U.S.C. § 7426, a third party (not the taxpayer) who claims an interest in property subjected to a tax levy can challenge the seizure in a "wrongful levy" action to recover the property. Here, Plaintiffs claim that they own most of the seized property. They argue that Porras, the delinquent taxpayer, has an interest only in a very small portion of the property. Consequently, they assert that most of the property should be returned to them.

To decide the matter, the court must undertake a three-step analysis. Initially, the Plaintiffs bear the burden to prove that they have some interest in the levied-upon property. *Morris v. United States*, 813 F.2d 343 (11th Cir. 1987); *Hill v. United States*, 844 F. Supp. 263 (W.D.N.C. 1993). Without any evidence of an interest in the property, the Plaintiffs have no standing to challenge the Government's levies and the case must be dismissed. *Comer Family Equity Trust v. United States*, 732 F. Supp. 755 (E.D. Mich. 1990).

The court has not found nor been cited to caselaw that provides a general analysis of the kind of proof that a plaintiff must produce to show "some" interest in the levied-upon property. Since the issue demands a detailed examination of the facts of each controversy, the cases concentrate on the specific, not the general. Reported cases indicate, however, that claims of "some" interest are normally buttressed by records and documents showing purchase, title, payment and the like. *See, e.g., Libutti v. United States*, 894 F. Supp. 589 (N.D. N.Y. 1995). Consequently, when a plaintiff's claims are completely unsubstantiated by records or documents, as here, then a dispute arises as to whether there is any showing of "some" interest. Such a dispute has arisen in this case. Under the circumstances, the court is of the opinion that it must make a thorough inquiry into the first step of the required analysis to determine if Plaintiffs can prove they have "some" interest in the property. Without documents or records to view, the court must thus judge the Plaintiffs' evidence solely upon the credibility of their witnesses.

If the Plaintiffs can meet this initial threshold and establish that they have an interest in the property, then the burden shifts to the Government to prove a nexus between the taxpayer and the property. *Flores v. United States*, 551 F.2d 1169 (9th Cir. 1977). Since the Government may levy only against property owned by the pertinent taxpayer, the property levied upon is wrongfully seized if it "does not, in whole or in part, belong to the taxpayer against whom the levy originated." *Arth v. United States*, 735 F.2d 1190, 1193 (9th Cir. 1984). The Government has the burden to establish by substantial evidence the nexus or connection between the taxpayer and the property. *Morris v. United States*, 813 F.2d at 345. If the Government meets its burden by showing a nexus between the taxpayer and the property, then Plaintiffs must finally demonstrate by a preponderance of the evidence that the taxpayer has no interest in the property. *Hill v. United States*, 844 F. Supp. at 274.

2.1. Overview

In considering this case, the court has centered its attention on the first step in the analysis of a wrongful levy claim: whether Plaintiffs have successfully proved "some" interest in the seized property. After lengthy deliberation, including an additional review of the excellent arguments and briefs submitted by counsel for Plaintiffs, the court has finally concluded that Plaintiffs have failed in their burden to show the requisite interest in any of the property. Although the details of the court's ruling are set forth below, the court observes that the basic reason for its decision rests upon the finding that the seized property has always been under the dominion and control of Porras, the delinquent taxpayer. It is he, not the Plaintiffs, who has had possession of and has exercised all indicia of ownership over the seized property, often with a major assist from Edmiston. Hence, Plaintiffs' claims of wrongful levy fail. From this overview, the court now turns to its factual and legal analysis.

2.2. Factual Introduction and Credibility Determinations

Mrs. Blakley, born in 1912, is a vigorous and engaging woman. She married twice before her marriage to her present husband, Mr. Blakley. She has never worked outside the home in any significant way. She has never been an interior decorator. She has never declared substantial income on her tax returns.

Porras is Mrs. Blakley's only child, born of her first marriage. His adult life has been spent in the interior decorating business. Porras and Edmiston met in 1974, began working together in the interior decorating business in 1977 and shortly thereafter began sharing living quarters at 28 Oaklawn Park in Midland, Texas. Edmiston still lives in the residence today. Porras, who lived there on and off until 1990, now lives in New Mexico. Like Porras, Edmiston has been assessed federal income tax deficiencies in substantial amounts.

The residence at 28 Oaklawn Park is a beautiful home and was beautifully decorated until the tax seizure. Government Exhibit 39, an article from the October 1977 issue of *Architectural Digest*, showcased the home in remarkable detail in both word and picture. Before the seizure, the residence was well-stocked with silver, china and crystal for use during the numerous, elaborate parties thrown by the two residents, according to Tom Simpson, an employee of Porras and Edmiston from June 1987 to May 1990. Simpson testified that much of the silver was either Gorham or Medallion, which Porras collected with a consuming interest. Dorothy Young, who also once worked for Porras, agreed that he collected fine silver. The residence included a Lalique table which Simpson took apart several times. The library was "loaded" with leather-bound books. Beautiful art hung on the walls. Porras particularly liked the French artist Eugene DeBlass. Bronzes, porcelains, obelisks and malachite furnishings were favorites of Porras, according to Simpson, and were generously placed throughout the residence. Simpson testified that Porras called everything in the residence "his stuff." [1]

1 It should be noted that Plaintiffs objected to the admissibility of any out-of-court statements by Porras on the grounds of hearsay. This evidentiary issue is discussed in Paragraph 2.2 of this Opinion and Order.

From the late 1970's through the middle of the 1980's, Porras was heavily involved in the Permian Basin oil boom. Before then, his interior decorating business was a successful one. After Midland and Odessa began to grow and prosper as oil prices increased dramatically, Porras borrowed millions of dollars to develop large office building projects in the two cities. According to Edmiston, Porras at one time during the period had a bank line of credit of $ 66,000,000.

Porras testified that for eight or nine years, until 1987 or 1988, he leased a Lear jet from GECC. Simpson testified that Porras also had two helicopters. For ground transportation, according to Simpson, Porras had in his possession at various times a Lamborghini, an Aston-Martin, a Jaguar, a Mercedes 560 SL, a Cadillac, a Bronco II, and a Wagonneer.

In 1979, Porras purchased a ranch called Pyramid Land and Cattle Company. Dedrick Baxter, an acquaintance of Porras and Edmiston, testified at trial that he attended cattle auctions at the ranch in 1984, 1985 and 1986 and was impressed with their extravagance. Elaborate bars and eating areas were arranged. Service was by crystal and china. Name entertainers performed. Fats Domino was scheduled for one performance, but some last-minute problem forced a cancellation. In the first auction he attended, Baxter saw Porras with a jeweled hat band.

Although Mrs. Blakley testified that she was a collector of art objects and fine furnishings, it is her son who has been the serious collector. Clear evidence of his appetite for collection comes from an article about a Dallas home he owned and decorated in the early part of the 1980's. The article, written by Lisa Ruffin, now Lisa Ruffin Harrison ("Ruffin"), appeared in the July/August 1981 issue of *Texas Homes*. On pages 101 and 103 of the article Ruffin noted:

> Porras is a great collector of everything: Chinese porcelain, sterling, rare books, crystal and glassware, acrylic and semi-precious metals and stones are only a conservative inventory of his ever-increasing cache. "I believe in lots of stuff," he laughs, indicating a crowded coffee table that would surely be a minimalist's nightmare, "lots of things to see and touch. With inflation, antiques are appreciating much faster than a savings account" he says, "and antique accessories are probably the best investment going. It's certainly nothing new; the Europeans have always put their money into things."

Although Porras disavowed the quotes attributable to him in the article, Ruffin testified at trial that she interviewed Porras for the article and that, to the best of her knowledge, the quotes were accurate. At no time did Porras ever contact her and deny the quotes or ask for any correction. Her testimony on the matter is credible; Porras's is not. Therefore, while Mrs. Blakley may have collected odds and ends during her life, the evidence clearly shows that her son was the one in the family who amassed a vast store of property over the years, either for appreciation in value, for personal accumulation or for business. He had both the desire and the means to do so.

Ruffin also testified that, based upon her interviews with Porras, she understood the Dallas home and all its contents belonged to him. Most of the furnishings, paintings and art objects shown in the pictures accompanying the article were seized by the Government in connection with this matter and were viewed by the court at trial. None of the items shown in the article were identified by Porras in his interview with Ruffin as belonging to Mrs. Blakley or the Trust. Indeed, from a reading of the article, it appears clear that Porras considered the contents of the home to belong to him.

The Trust, of which Mrs. Blakley is beneficiary, was started by her father. It was the subject of much controversy and litigation over the years. Finally, in 1988, as a part of a settlement of pending litigation, the Trust was re-formulated and Edmiston was appointed the Trustee. One of Edmiston's early decisions as Trustee was to cause the Trust to get into the business of interior decorating. The Trust operated both out of a warehouse leased by one of Porras's companies, not by the Trust, and out of an office leased by another of Porras's companies, not by the Trust, with a phone listing bearing Porras's name, not the Trust's. Much of the property seized by the Government came from the warehouse and the office. The rest of the furnishings and art objects seized by the Government came from the residence at Oaklawn. In 1991, Porras conveyed the residence to the Trust.

Edmiston has never kept an inventory of the interior decorating property owned by the Trust. He testified that no records exist to substantiate the Trust's ownership of any of its properties. In addition, there are no cost records relating to any of the Trust property. Edmiston has never caused financial statements to be prepared for the Trust. He has never filed tax returns for the Trust. No gain has ever been recorded in connection with the sale of any Trust property. Although Edmiston does not operate or manage the Trust in accordance with normal business or accounting procedures, neither Mrs. Blakley nor Porras object to his management. Instead, they take the position that Edmiston has improved the Trust results since taking charge. This position seems somewhat unusual since the "improved results" have not translated into additional income for Mrs. Blakley. Her joint U.S. Individual Income Tax Return (Form 1040) showed total income of $ 10,793 for 1988; $ 10,783 for 1989; $

9,482 for 1990; $ 596 for 1992; $ 1,255 for 1993; and $ 817 for 1994. The 1991 Return was not in evidence. *Government Exhibits 46 and 47.*

The lack of financial and accounting records for the Trust makes it impossible to determine whether the optimistic assessment of the performance of the Trust by Mrs. Blakley and Porras is valid; however, conventional business wisdom would cause a prudent observer to reject such an assessment. Still, Porras and Mrs. Blakley are supportive of Edmiston. Mrs. Blakley does not object to her diminishing reportable income. Nor does she question the decision by the Trust to compensate Porras and Edmiston for their services by paying their housing, transportation and per diem expenses on a periodic basis, rather than by paying them salaries or consulting fees.

Because of the nature of the management of the Trust by Porras and Edmiston, who together control the Trust's operation, either in name or in fact, there were suggestions at trial that the Trust was being conducted for an improper purpose. Dedrick Baxter testified that he sometimes dined with Porras and Edmiston at 28 Oaklawn Park. On one occasion, accompanied by his wife, he received advice from the two hosts to consider placing his property in Trust, as they had done. They explained that it was their way of insuring that their standard of living would never be compromised. Moreover, Simpson recounted that Porras said he could not hold anything in his name because of his problems with the Internal Revenue Service.

In this case, of course, the court is not required to make any judgments about Edmiston's fiduciary performance or Porras's role in that performance; the court is allowed, however, to examine the performance of both as it bears on the credibility of Edmiston on behalf of the Trust and on the credibility of Edmiston and Porras generally. In this regard, it is again worth repeating that it is contrary to normal protocols to do business without records. At trial, Porras and Edmiston failed to explain why they so consistently disregarded normal business practices. In addition to other matters, this lack of record-keeping severely eroded their credibility, especially in regard to claims on behalf of the Trust. At the same time, the court also observes that Mrs. Blakley had almost no records to support her claims of an interest in property. Although she did have cancelled checks, there were not enough to establish the widespread purchase of the volume of property claimed by her.

As the above discussion also indicates, much of the testimony of Mrs. Blakley, Porras and Edmiston was contradicted by other witnesses, all of whom were credible. In addition, Mrs. Blakley, Porras and Edmiston often contradicted each other, especially in regard to the particulars of property acquisition and ownership. There was ample room for contradiction with almost 4,000 items of property to identify, but the problem related less to sheer numbers and more to the tactic by Plaintiffs to claim as much property as possible, without regard to how sensible each individual claim was in relation to the facts. Such confusing, contradictory and inconsistent testimony substantially eroded the credibility of Mrs. Blakley, Porras and Edmiston. Their demeanor also caused credibility problems. For example, Mrs. Blakley was so obviously biased in favor of her son and so obviously hostile toward the Government that her testimony lost its balance. Her motivations are understandable, but they have caused the court in the end to reject almost all of her testimony.

2.2. Evidentiary Issue

Before addressing the property issues, the court will deal with a hearsay issue raised at trial. During the course of the proceedings, various witnesses testified about out-of-court statements by Porras. Plaintiffs objected because they took the position that Porras was not a party to the case and thus his statements were hearsay to them. The court admitted the testimony, reasoning that the statements by Porras were admissible because Porras had a community of interest with the Plaintiffs. Thus, his statements could be received as an admission of the Plaintiffs. It is true that the interest of Porras is completely aligned with the two Plaintiffs. The mutual goal for all three is to defeat the Government's levy. Based upon his status as the delinquent taxpayer, however, Porras cannot join the suit as a plaintiff because he has no standing to challenge the levy.

Although the court's reason for admitting Porras's statements would have been appropriate under common law, the reason is not appropriate under the Federal Rules of Evidence because the common law rule was not incorporated in the Federal Rules. Professor Graham explains the issue well in his treatise,

M. GRAHAM, FEDERAL PRACTICE AND PROCEDURE: EVIDENCE § 6719 (Interim Edition):

> At common law statements by a person in privity with a party were receivable in evidence as an admission of the party. An admission by one jointly interested was also receivable at common law against others similarly interested.

> Rule 801(d)(2) alters prior law by omitting any provision declaring either a statement by a person in privity with another or by one of persons jointly interested to be an admission by the other or others. Thus Rule 801(d)(2) in excluding such statements from the definition of admissions adopts the position advocated by Morgan and the Model Code of Evidence that considerations of privity and joint interest neither furnish criteria of credibility nor aid in the evaluation of testimony. Statements formerly treated as a separate category of admission will, however, frequently qualify as representative admissions, Rule 801(d)(2)(C), or as statements against interest, Rule 804(b)(3), or fall within another hearsay exception. Other such statements will meet the requirements of the other hearsay exceptions contained in Rules 803(24) and 804(b)(5).

Research after the trial unearthed Prof. Graham's excellent scholarship on this change made by the Federal Rules. The court still believes, however, that the statements of Porras were admissible, based upon Rule 803(24) rather than Rule 801(d)(2). Rule 803(24) states:

> The following are not excluded by the hearsay rule, even though the declarant is available as a witness:

> . . . .

> (24) Other exceptions. A statement not specifically covered by any of the foregoing exceptions but having equivalent circumstantial guarantees of trustworthiness, if the court determines that (A) the statement is offered as evidence of a material fact; (B) the statement is more probative on the point for which it is offered than any other evidence which the proponent can procure through reasonable efforts; and (C) the general purposes of these rules and the interests of justice will best be served by admission of the statement into evidence. However, a statement may not be admitted under this exception unless the proponent of it makes known to the adverse party sufficiently in advance off the trial or hearing to provide the adverse party with a fair opportunity to prepare to meet it, the

proponent's intention to offer the statement and the particulars of it, including the name and address of the declarant.

Prof. Graham observes that, as structured, "Rule 803(24) contains five express requirements," which are (1) equivalent trustworthiness, (2) necessity, (3) material fact, (4) satisfaction of purpose of Rules and (5) notice. *See id.* § 6775. The court has considered all five of these requirements; each has been met here.

The first is an equivalent circumstantial guarantee of trustworthiness. The trial testimony of Porras had little guarantee of trustworthiness. His out-of-court statements were especially important in evaluating the unusual positions taken by him and the two Plaintiffs in this case. The Government's witnesses, the persons recounting Porras's out-of-court statements, with the possible exception of Tom Simpson, had no reason to lie or obfuscate. Simpson has had past difficulties with the Internal Revenue Service and, at the time of trial, was trying to resolve them. His credibility was attacked by Plaintiffs. Yet, in the court's opinion, Simpson as well as all of the government's other witnesses appeared by their demeanor and consistent testimony to be credible and trustworthy. Their testimony about each statement made by Porras was believable because the statements were made under circumstances which were not suspect in any way. Moreover, the court allowed Porras, if he wanted, to be present during all testimony and to hear each witness. At times, he was present in court; at other times, he was not. He was also available to be a witness, did appear and testify as a witness and was available for full examination.

As a second matter, the introduction of the hearsay statements was necessary because they were more probative on the point for which offered than any other evidence which the Government could procure. A good example is Ruffin's testimony confirming her article about Porras's affinity for collecting things. Mrs. Blakley's testimony that she was the big collector in the family was not believable. Neither was Porras's denial of his appetite for collection. Based upon the totality of the facts, it only made sense that Porras, not Mrs. Blakley, was the serious collector in the family. Ruffin's confirming testimony was important to a full evaluation of the matter.

The third, fourth and fifth requirements of Rule 803(24) are also satisfied here, as this Opinion and Order illustrates in its applicable references to Porras's statements. Each statement was offered as proof of a material fact, so requirement three was met. In connection with requirement four, the general purposes of the Federal Rules of Evidence and the interests of justice were best served by the admission of each statement. Further in this regard, a trial is a search for the truth (Rule 102 of the Federal Rules of Evidence) and truth would have been a casualty in this case if Porras's testimony could not have been tested by his out-of-court statements. Finally, the fifth requirement of notice was met by the Government, in light of the Government's pretrial submission of its list of witnesses and in light of pretrial discovery. Because of Plaintiffs' lack of records, the Government worked diligently to "fill in the gaps" and Plaintiffs were well-aware of how the Government planned to proceed. Indeed, Plaintiffs did not complain about lack of notice in this regard and even filed a motion to strike Simpson's testimony.

2.300 Plaintiffs' Failure to Show Interest in the Seized Property

The court has already written that, as to the seized property, it finds that the Plaintiffs failed to show the requisite interest. To discuss the matter in some orderly fashion, the court now divides its analysis into categories of property. It should be noted that the claims of the Trust to an interest in the property are limited to the property discussed in the thirteenth category in Paragraph 2.313 below and listed in Appendix M. All other categories of property were claimed by Mrs. Blakley. In the order of presentation, the first category is "property belonging to others" (Appendix A); the second, "property not adequately identified or testified to" (Appendix B); the third, the "Sinclair property" (Appendix C); the fourth, "England-France purchases in 1981 (Appendix D); the fifth, "the Fur Coats" (Appendix E); the sixth, "Lalique furniture and furnishings" (Appendix F); the seventh, "books" (Appendix G); the eighth, "gifts" (Appendix H); the ninth, "jewelry" (Appendix I); the tenth, "coins" (Appendix J); the eleventh, "china, silver, crystal, flatware, glass, porcelain and pottery" (Appendix K); the twelfth, "property at 28 Oaklawn Park" (Appendix L); the thirteenth, "the Trust" (Appendix M); and the fourteenth, "Porras/Edmiston property" (Appendix N).

2.301 Property Belonging to Others

Plaintiffs stipulated by their testimony that 342 items seized by the Government belonged to others. This property, with a present value of $ 166,567.00, is listed at Appendix A. Plaintiffs agree that these items of property belong to someone else, not either to Mrs. Blakley or the Trust. Thus, neither she nor the Trust have an interest of any kind in the property. If those who allegedly have an interest in the property wish to make a claim, they are certainly entitled to do so. However, as between the Plaintiffs and the Government, the Plaintiffs cannot prevail by showing that someone else, not them, has an interest in the property. Without an interest, Plaintiffs have no claim.

2.302 Property Disavowed, Not Adequately Identified or Not Testified To

At trial, Mrs. Blakley presented the court with an affidavit entitled "Affidavit of Lucille Christie Blakley in Support of Proffer of Evidence Pursuant to Rule 43 of the Federal Rules of Civil Procedure." In the affidavit, she listed each item of property which she claimed to be hers. Approximately seventy percent (70%) of the property seized by the Government was on the list. At trial, Mrs. Blakley could not support the proffer. When she tried to validate her claims of ownership during her testimony, she was basically unable to do so. For example, in some instances, Mrs. Blakley listed property in her affidavit as belonging to her and then unequivocally disavowed any ownership during her courtroom testimony. Illustrations would be too numerous to mention, but two are Items # 1102 and # 1103, pieces of pottery. In addition, at no time during the trial did Mrs. Blakley or anyone else ever explain how she had the means or the wherewithal to acquire the millions of dollars of property set out in the affidavit. Under the circumstances, it is neither expedient nor necessary for the court to discuss further Mrs. Blakley's affidavit in the remainder of this Opinion and Order. The court should simply observe that the affidavit and list were contradicted too often to be accorded any weight whatsoever.

There were a substantial number of other instances where Mrs. Blakley testified (as opposed to listing by affidavit) that she had an interest in an item of property, but she did so with such hesitation or uncertainty that her own testimony was inadequate to show the interest, even when eventually she might declare the item to be hers. In other instances, Mrs. Blakley simply could not remember whether she had any interest in a particular item of property. Finally, there were also some items of property which were not the subject of any testimony. Therefore, as to these categories of property, including property disavowed, listed on Appendix B, totalling 1083 in number with a present value of $ 859,085.50, the court finds no interest was sufficiently shown.

Time and again, in trial, Mrs. Blakley would examine a particular item of property and then would state that "it's not mine." Such an admission ended further inquiry; no interest was shown. *See, e.g., Items # 1102 and # 1103.* At other times, she would state that "it looks like mine" or "I think it's mine" or "I believe it's mine" or "it may be mine" or "I have some like it" or "it's mine but I don't know how I got it, when I got it or where I got it" or "it's mine but I could be mistaken." *See, e.g., Items # 857, # 876, # 897, # 954, # 992, # 1054 and # 1442.* More often than not, this testimony would be given only after substantial hesitation or would be accompanied by testimony that Mrs. Blakley still "wasn't sure" about her interest in the property. *See, e.g., Item # 1031.* At other times, her claimed interest in property would be confusing, being clearly stated at one point and then disavowed at another, or directly contradicted by either Edmiston or Porras. *See, e.g., Item # 915.* This equivocal testimony is not adequate to establish the necessary interest in property that a plaintiff must show in a wrongful levy case.

There were also items of property where Mrs. Blakley's responses to questions of interest were either "I don't remember it" or "I never used it" or "I'm not familiar with it" or "I don't recognize it." *See, e.g., Items # 1048, # 1051, # 1975 and # 1976.* Again, this kind of testimony cannot create an interest in the seized property.

Finally, there were other items of property seized by the Government about which no testimony was offered by Plaintiffs, either by Mrs. Blakley on her own behalf or by Edmiston on behalf of the Trust. *See, e.g., Items # 885 and # 975* . Without any showing of interest, Plaintiffs cannot prevail.

The fact that Mrs. Blakley was unable to identify a substantial part of the property she originally claimed as hers in her pleadings and her proffer erodes her credibility in this matter. Throughout this kind of testimony, Mrs. Blakley often gave the clear appearance of someone striving to establish something that had no real basis in truth. Her overriding goal in all this testimony was obviously to help her son. [2]

2 The court has struggled with overlap in this case. There are instances throughout this opinion where the court rejects the Plaintiffs' claimed interest in an item of property for two or more reasons. For example, there were some specific items of Lalique glass in which Mrs. Blakley could not identify an interest. The court therefore rejected her claim under this Paragraph 2.302 of this Opinion and Order. At one point in her testimony, however, Mrs. Blakley made a general claim that all Lalique property was hers. That claim was rejected in Paragraph 2.306. Under the circumstances, a Lalique piece could be listed in Appendix B (2.202) and Appendix F (2.206). The court has tried to eliminate the overlap, although the large number of items makes it probable that one item may appear on more than one list.

2.303 The "Sinclair" Property

At trial Mrs. Blakley identified 133 items of property seized by the Government as belonging to her via her ex-husband Richard Sinclair. She married Sinclair in California in the 1960's. At some point in time, they separated and she moved back to Texas. Mrs. Blakley testified that, during the separation, Sinclair gave these 133 items to her for safekeeping. She further testified that Sinclair asked her to hold them until he notified her that he wanted them back. Later, before a divorce could be finalized and before some agreement about the property could be made, Sinclair died. Mrs. Blakley learned of his death after his funeral. Since no one ever asked for the property, she considered it hers.

On its face, this testimony is suspect. Experience teaches that, as a practical matter, one spouse separating from another in contemplation of divorce normally does not deliver property to the departing spouse for safekeeping. The testimony becomes even more suspect given the amount and value of the property. Appendix C shows the present estimated value of the 133 items to be $ 188,157.00. This is substantial in today's financial environment; if translated into 1960 figures, the total would be less but still substantial in relative terms.

Finally, if the items are examined separately, the incredulity of the testimony is accentuated. For instance, Mrs. Blakley testified that several large bronze pieces came from Sinclair. It would be highly unusual for such pieces to be casually given for safekeeping on a good faith understanding without any record to a soon-to-be-ex-spouse living over 1,000 miles away. Mrs. Blakley's testimony in this regard suffered further because one bronze piece, a man shooting an arrow (Item # 1035), that she testified came from Sinclair, was identified by Dorothy Young, an ex-Porras employee, as coming from Porras's showroom in Leland Ingram in Dallas.

The assessment of the testimony does not end here, however. During cross-examination, Mrs. Blakley acknowledged that she testified in an earlier deposition that little of the property seized by the Government came from Sinclair. In her deposition, given on February 27, 1995, on pages 18-21, she answered as follows:

> Q. Did you acquire any property from him (Sinclair) that was included in the property the IRS seized?
>
> A. No.
>
> . . .
>
> Q. You said none of the property. Any of the property that the IRS seized, did any of that property ever belong to Mr. Sinclair?
>
> A. Yes, some of the jewelry.
>
> . . .
>
> Q. What jewelry would that have been?
>
> A. It was a diamond ring, a nine-carat diamond ring, cuff links, gold chains.
>
> Q. Aside from that jewelry, would there have been anything else during the marriage to Mr. Sinclair that would be included in the property the IRS seized?
>
> A. I can't remember. I don't think so.

Mrs. Blakley's trial testimony varied widely from her deposition testimony on this point. Indeed, to change testimony so dramatically from February 1995 to the summer 1995 brings the subsequent testimony into serious question, especially when the subsequent testimony by itself is already flawed. Although, in her trial testimony, Mrs. Blakley did identify a diamond having come from Sinclair, that diamond listed in the inventory was five carats, not nine. Under all the circumstances, the court rejects any possibility that Mrs. Blakley could have an interest in the property shown in Appendix C.

2.304 England-France Purchases in 1981

Another example of Mrs. Blakley's lack of credibility relates to her testimony that she purchased 175 items for herself during trips to England and France in 1981. The present estimated value of those items is now $ 231,080. *See Appendix D*. Even adjusted for 1981 values, these purchases represent significant expenditures.

How Mrs. Blakley could have made these purchases is inexplicable. For her entire adult life, she has seldom worked. She has never developed any special job skills. Although she has long been the beneficiary of the Trust, it has never produced any substantial income for her. For example, in the Trust Statement for the fiscal year ending 2/29/80, the assets totalled $ 339,099.25 and the yearly income totalled $ 21,967.12 (*Government Exhibit 17*). In the Trust Statement for the fiscal year ending 2/28/82, the assets totalled $ 578,704.35 and the income totalled $ 21,572.44. (*Government Exhibit 18*). The sole reason for the increase in assets between the two years was an increase in the appraised value of the real estate in the Trust, 100.427 acres of land in Collin County, Texas. Still, the income for most years in the 1980's was around $ 20,000, not enough to finance a spending spree in England and France.

Moreover, Mrs. Blakley's husbands have never had a large corpus of funds from which she could draw. She has been married at least three times, but none of her husbands was shown to have showered her with money. Although Mrs. Blakley testified that Sinclair was wealthy, her entire testimony as to him has no corroborating support in the record and must be rejected. Further, no evidence was adduced to show that her present husband, Blakley, to whom she was married in 1973, is or has been wealthy in his own right.

Mrs. Blakley also testified that her father was wealthy, gave her money and bequeathed to her a substantial sum after his death in 1950. She did not present any documentation or other corroboration for this testimony but, as usual, simply asked the court to take her word for it. There are further problems with this testimony in light of the Inventory and Appraisement of her father's Estate approved on April 27, 1950, showing her father's community interest at death to be $ 25,736.97. (*Government's Exhibit 25, pp 11-13*) The court is not justified in accepting Mrs. Blakley's word on this matter.

Assuming that Mrs. Blakley actually went to England and France in 1981 to buy art and furnishings for herself, how or from whom did she get the funds? Based on the facts, only one reasonable source can be inferred: her son Porras. During the late 1970's and early 1980's, Porras had access to large sums of cash and the 1981 purchases would clearly have been within his means. Moreover, although Mrs. Blakley has considered herself a collector, the actual collector in the family has been Porras who parlayed his interest in things into a decorating business that, for a period of time, was very successful.

Finally, it is also extremely unclear why a woman approaching 70 years, even if she had the funds, would buy these 175 items for herself, when she had absolutely no obvious need for any of them and no place to store them. Why would she buy them and then deliver every single item to her son to be used in his home as furnishings or art or to be kept in his business as inventory? Under the circumstances, the best that can be said for Mrs. Blakley and her story is that she went on a pleasant trip across the Atlantic Ocean to buy things for her son and his business at his expense. If it were otherwise, the court would have expected to receive from her some evidence of bills of sale, shipping receipts or insurance documents substantiating the purchases. None was forthcoming. Her testimony on the 1981 purchases cannot thus be accepted as true. She failed to show the requisite interest in the property listed in Appendix D.

2.305 The Fur Coats

The Government seized 33 furs, with unknown value. Because some of the coats fit her, the court finds, without further analysis, the following items with the following descriptions belong to Mrs. Blakley and are thus awarded to her:

ITEM #	DESCRIPTION
3320	Yellow Thigh-Length
3323	Gray Thigh-Length
3328	Brown Jacket
3330	Brown Jacket
3332	Brown Full-Length
3334	Dark Brown Full-Length
3335	Black Full-Length
3339	Brown Jacket
3340	White Gray Jacket
3342	Brown Jacket

As to the rest of the furs, the court finds that no interest was shown as to Mrs. Blakley or the Trust and therefore all objections to the levy by the Government are denied. In fact, Kyle Perkins, who worked for Porras from May of 1981 to March of 1983, testified that Porras owned many furs, at least one of which was a gift from Edmiston. From the testimony and the court's examination of the furs listed on Appendix E, it is clear that Porras and, in one or two instances, Edmiston were owners of those furs. Therefore, Plaintiffs failed to show the requisite interest in the items described in Appendix E.

2.306 Lalique Furniture and Furnishings

As to the Lalique furniture and furnishings seized by the Government, Mrs. Blakley claimed in her testimony that all of it was hers. Porras testified that any Lalique purchases he made were for his customers, not for him. Both these statements lack credibility for several reasons.

Mrs. Blakley provided no information to explain how she obtained these glass pieces which are not inexpensive. She testified, for example, that in the 1980's she purchased a Lalique cyrus bowl with a present value of $ 3,000 (# 3182), a Lalique persepolis bowl with a present value of $ 5,000 (# 3183), 35 Lalique plates with a present value of $ 10,000 (# 3186), a Lalique vase with the present value of $ 3,600 (# 3194), and five Lalique ashtrays with a present value of $ 9,000 (# 3195). All Lalique pieces, numbering 44 with a present value of $ 93,455, are listed on Appendix F. These are expensive items and

Mrs. Blakley simply testified she bought them, without any further explanation. Her lack of substantial resources to purchase these items has already been chronicled in this Opinion and Order.

This problem of resources is further confirmed by a witness called by the Government, Dedrick Baxter, who testified that he met and then dealt with both Porras and Edmiston from 1984 to 1990. He recalled that both told him they were supporting their mothers and Mrs. Blakley's sister Mrs. Hayes. It makes sense that Porras was the main source of support for Mrs. Blakley in the 1980's, when he had access to substantial funds and when her Trust produced less than $ 2,000 per month, but it does not make sense that Porras would support his mother in such extravagance that she could buy, for herself, very expensive art and furnishings, like the Lalique pieces, almost on a whim.

There was more testimony raising credibility problems in connection with Mrs. Blakley's claim to ownership of the Lalique pieces. One government witness, Kyle Perkins, who worked for Porras between 1981 and 1983, testified that one Lalique table was kept at the Oaklawn Park home and that another was kept at the office, both the domain of Porras. Another government witness, Victor Peters, who was a manufacturer's representative for Lalique, testified that he sold and installed a Lalique table for Porras in 1985. He also testified that Porras showed him a collection of Lalique pieces at the Oaklawn Park home which Porras identified as his own. From this testimony, it is clear that the person possessing the Lalique pieces and holding them out as his own was Porras, never Mrs. Blakley. The credible testimony therefore is that the Lalique collection listed in Appendix F belonged to Porras and that neither Mrs. Blakley nor the Trust had any interest whatsoever in any of the items.

2.307 Books

Mrs. Blakley claimed an interest in the 490 leather-bound books which were seized from the Oaklawn Park residence. She testified that the books were purchased at various times in various places by various people. Although a substantial number of the books were stamped with Porras's initials, Mrs. Blakley said that his stamp was used because she did not have one.

Again, this testimony is not credible and flies in the face of reason, logic and the facts. Identification stamps for books are not expensive. It takes little effort to get such stamps. If she owned the books, she should have had her initials placed on them. She not only failed to put her "stamp" on the books, but she also failed to possess the books. Her testimony in this regard, as with so many things, is simply eroded by her efforts to "own" property which is so clearly not hers. The accumulated failure of such efforts damages all her testimony. The court rejects all claims by Mrs. Blakley of an interest in the 490 books listed in Appendix G.

2.308 Gifts

Mrs. Blakley claimed that she owned expensive pieces of art, shown in Appendix H, which were gifts from Porras or, in one or two instances, from Edmiston. She also claimed that Porras gave her a 1930 Model A Ford Replica with a present value of $ 7,500. At times, however, as to some of this art, she said she did not have an interest in it and then had to be corrected by either Edmiston or Porras that the art was in fact hers. Examples are Items # 848 and # 849 which she said she did not own but which Edmiston said she did own as a result of gifts from Porras.

At the time of the seizure, as with everything else, Mrs. Blakley did not possess any of these art objects (or the car either). No gift tax returns were ever prepared for these "gifts" and clearly, as to some, gift tax returns would have been required. Examples are three paintings by the French artist DeBlass: # 3153 with a present value of $ 90,000, # 3230 with a present value of $ 60,000 and # 3273 with a present value of $ 50,000. There was no evidence that "delivery" was ever even made of any gift.

The "gifts" are questionable for an additional reason. Why would a mother's only child and expected heir give valuable objects to her during her senior years which would cause her estate to be burdened with substantial taxes and which would possibly prevent him from realizing the very inheritance she would wish for him? The most devoted of sons would certainly find a more rational way to please his mother. Even the most devoted of mothers would not want gifts under such circumstances. Therefore, for all the reasons stated, the court rejects Mrs. Blakley's claims of interest as to the art objects listed on Appendix H (as well as to the Model A Ford Replica).

2.309 Jewelry

At trial, Mrs. Blakley claimed an interest in a substantial amount of the jewelry the Government had seized at the Oaklawn Park residence. She said much of it came to her from Mr. Sinclair, Mr. Blakley, Porras or her father. Porras and Edmiston, the past and present residents at Oaklawn, claimed an interest in a limited amount of the jewelry.

The claims do not fit with the independent evidence on the subject. For example, Stephan Magner from Nieman Marcus in Dallas testified that, in the late 1970's and early 1980's, his store sold about $ 1,500,000 worth of jewelry to Porras. For example, Magner identified a custom-made hat band of gold, diamonds and emeralds as a piece he sold to Porras for Porras to place on his straw hat (# 3077 with a present value of $ 30,000). Magner testified that the hat band cost between $ 40,000 and $ 50,000. Mrs. Blakley testified that Porras gave it to her. As was the usual custom of son and mother, no gift tax return was filed. No evidence was presented that Mrs. Blakley ever possessed the hat band, even from time to time. From what the court could glean, the hat band was bought by Porras for himself with no true intention to give it to his mother or anyone else.

Similarly, Magner testified that his store made two gold coin necklaces for Porras (# 3047 with a present value of $ 5,400 and # 3064 with a present value of $ 2,200), both of which Mrs. Blakley said were given to her by her son. The reason for the gifts remained unexplained throughout the trial. In addition, Magner also testified that his store mounted stones for three rings for Porras (# 3008, # 3010 and # 3018). Mrs. Blakley testified (1) that ring # 3008 was hers although she didn't remember the details of her acquisition, (2) that ring # 3010 came from New York, and (3) that ring # 3018 was not hers. Without any concern for consistency, Porras testified that he had these rings mounted for his mother.

Magner was a credible witness. His testimony established that Porras spent enormous amounts of money on jewelry. Magner did acknowledge that Porras gave jewelry to others, including very expensive watches to the pilots of his private airplanes, but he also confirmed that Porras was a significant collector of jewelry as well as coins and art. Although Porras testified to the contrary, his denials are at odds with independent, credible evidence. Mrs. Blakley and Porras are not believable in connection with their claims about who are the real owners of the jewelry. The court again rejects the claims of interest to another category of property, the jewelry, listed on Appendix I. [3]

3 Mrs. Blakley testified that much of the jewelry came from Mr. Sinclair, her previous, deceased husband. The court has already rejected her claims to the "Sinclair" property, listed in Appendix C. An effort has been made throughout this Opinion and Order to avoid duplication from Appendix to Appendix and such an effort was made between Appendix C and Appendix G, but the court cannot state with absolute certainty that it has achieved perfect separation in light of the large number of jewelry pieces which were seized.

2.310 Coins

Mrs. Blakley's claims of interest in the coins seized by the Government lack the same credibility that her above claims have lacked. As to one set of coins, she testified that she began collecting in the 1950's and 1960's although (1) she did not remember the name of the dealer who worked with her, (2) she did not know how to value coins and (3) she did not know anything about coins. It was merely something to do. As to another set of coins, she testified that she purchased them in the early 1970's through a New York coin dealer whom she did not remember. Another set of coins came from her father, who died over forty years ago.

This testimony flies in the face of all credible evidence. Mr. Magner testified that Porras was a coin collector. Mrs. Blakley admitted that she knew nothing about coins. The coins were under Porras's control in a much more real way than they were under her control. Further, no explanation was ever given about the whereabouts of Porras's collection, which apparently was missed in the thorough seizure effort by the Government, if indeed both Porras and Mrs. Blakley were to be believed. Finally, if Mrs. Blakley's father possessed coins at his death, his executor did not find them. They are not listed on the Inventory and Appraisement of the Estate and, based on the small size of the Estate, they could not have been valued under any miscellaneous listing.

It is clear to the court that the seized coins, listed on Appendix J, belonged to Porras and that Mrs. Blakley's claim to an interest in the coins must be rejected.

2.311 China, Silver, Crystal, Flatware, Glass, Porcelain and Pottery

Mrs. Blakley claimed that she owned a substantial amount of the china, silver, crystal, flatware, glass, porcelain and pottery seized by the Government. In almost every instance, she never used or possessed this property. As to the silver, for example, she had some checks showing that she had purchased some isolated items. She also testified that she inherited or received by gift some silver items which laid the foundation for further collection.

Her testimony, however, was contradicted by Tom Simpson, Porras's employee, who stated that Porras claimed the silver as his own. It was also contradicted by Dorothy Marie Young, who worked for Porras and Edmiston in Dallas from 1979 to 1985 and who testified that, while Mrs. Blakley collected dolls, Porras collected fine silver. Finally, it was contradicted by Karen McQuad, who is the property control manager for Christies in New York and who the Government called as a witness. She produced over one hundred pages of items, many involving beautiful silver pieces, which had been purchased by Porras between 1988 and 1990. *Government Exhibit 77*. Her firm could find no records that Mrs. Blakley had ever purchased anything from it.

There was also no showing that Mrs. Blakley had the means to collect or to store the silver or, for that matter, to collect or store the rest of the china, crystal, flatware, glass, porcelain and pottery in the great quantities that existed at the time of the seizure. On the contrary, the testimony of Simpson established that the real place of storage for and use of these items, especially the china, silver, crystal, flatware, glass and porcelain, was 28 Oaklawn Park, originally Porras's home and to this day Edmiston's residence. Furthermore, as to a substantial number of these items as with other items discussed in Paragraph 2.302, Mrs. Blakley's testimony was so ambivalent and equivocal that it did not amount to a claim at all. *See Appendix B*. For these reasons,

Mrs. Blakley's claimed interest in the property listed on Appendix K, with a present value of $ 378,943.50, is rejected and denied.

2.312 Property at 28 Oaklawn Park

Although much of the property seized at 28 Oaklawn Park has been addressed in other paragraphs, the property at Oaklawn Park which has not yet been addressed in this Opinion and Order is found to belong to Porras, not to Mrs. Blakley, regardless of her claims to the contrary. For example, in her Affidavit in Support of Plaintiffs' Original Petition and Sworn Application for Temporary Restraining Order and Preliminary Injunction dated November 12, 1994, Mrs. Blakley stated under oath that "all of the contents of the property located at 28 Oaklawn, Midland, Midland County, Texas are owned by me or the Lucille Christie Blakley Trust. . ." Given what the court heard and saw in the trial of this case, this claim must be rejected.

To begin with, the court is at a loss to understand how Mrs. Blakley could claim that "all of the contents" were either hers or the Trust's when, even accepting everything else the Plaintiffs have said as being true, it is still clear that "all of the contents" could not possibly have belonged to her or the Trust. Her own testimony, as well as that of Porras and Edmiston, contradicted her. The testimony of Dorothy Young, who once worked for Porras, also contradicted her. For example, Item # 1600, a bronze piece located at Oaklawn Park and therefore belonging to Mrs. Blakley based upon her affidavit, came from the inventory in Porras's Leland Ingram showroom in Dallas, according to Young. This is but one more example of why Mrs. Blakley's testimony, almost *in toto*, must be disregarded.

There are other reasons as well. Mrs. Blakley never lived at Oaklawn Park, although she did visit there occasionally. Until he conveyed the residence to the Trust (in a transaction which has questionable motivations), Porras held record title. After the conveyance, he still had full run of the home. There was no testimony that the conveyance of the residence caused any property to be moved or that the conveyance changed any title to any property in any way. Any claim of Mrs. Blakley to an interest in the Oaklawn property lacks credibility, conflicts with the believable evidence and must be rejected. *See Appendix L.*

2.313 Trust

On behalf of the Trust, Edmiston claimed an interest in 342 items of property with a present value of $ 144,281.00. *See Appendix M.* This property was allegedly owned by the Trust for its interior decorating business. The court rejects this claim as untenable because it is not supported by credible testimony.

Part of the legal arguments by both sides in this case related to whether the Trust was the alter ego or nominee of Porras. Was the Trust simply a front for Porras so that he could continue his decorating business outside the reach of the Internal Revenue Service? The court would have been required to reach the alter ego or nominee issue had the Trust presented credible evidence of its interest in the claimed property. The Trust failed, however, to do so.

One example will suffice to illustrate the failure. On behalf of the Trust, Edmiston claimed a painting by Christopher H. Shearer (# 2904). As to that item, Karen McQuad, the property control manager for Christies, testified that her firm sold it to Porras on May 31, 1990. *See Government Exhibit 77 (pp. 122-26).* McQuad testified to a substantial number of purchases by Porras between 1988 and 1990, the beginning years of the Trust, and not one purchase was in the name of the Trust. In fact, according to her, Christies had no record of any purchases by either Mrs. Blakley or the Trust at all. The Trust's claim to the Shearer painting, like its claims to all the property seized by the Government, was conveniently unsupported by records; Christie's records proved that, in one clear instance, the claim of an interest in the painting at issue had no validity.

The court does not take the position that an interest in property must be supported by records. However, when testimony is presented by witnesses with little credibility, then corroboration becomes essential. Moreover, as a practical matter in today's business world, records are critical to the sound operation of any enterprise. Records enable companies to establish lawful ownership, determine profits and losses, and generally to conduct affairs in a proper manner. This court has already noted its dismay over the lack of record-keeping by the Trust. Such a failure, being so out-of-the-ordinary, calls into further question every claim by Edmiston for the Trust. It is difficult for a fact-finder to give serious consideration to a claim when it conflicts with reason, logic and common sense. The presentation was not credible. It needed corroboration; none was forthcoming.

There are other reasons as well to reject the claims of the Trust. Edmiston, on the Trust's behalf, often claimed an interest in the same item of property to which Mrs. Blakley claimed an interest. It is not required that witnesses, to be believed, testify in court in perfect symmetry with one another. When, however, the testimony of witnesses comes into conflict too often under too many questionable circumstances, credibility suffers. Such is the testimony of Edmiston and Mrs. Blakley.

Before ending this discussion, one further comment is in order. At trial, Plaintiffs seemed to take the position that it was a foregone conclusion that the Trust had shown some interest in the property it claimed. After all, the Trust was in the interior decorating business. It needed property, the argument goes, to do its business. Moreover, since the Government pleaded and argued alter ego/nominee issues to the court, does it not follow that the Government conceded that some interest must have been shown by the Trust? As to the first argument, interior decorators do not need to have stores or showrooms to do their work. As to the second argument, while it is true that the alter ego/nominee issue was urged by the Government as a reason that the court should deny Plaintiffs' claims, the court does not believe that the Government's arguments can be construed as a concession or stipulation that the Trust successfully proved some interest in the seized property. It was, in fact, the Government who hotly contested the credibility of Plaintiffs' witnesses and who, in the end, convinced the court, through its own proof, that those witnesses could not be believed.

The Trust failed to present credible evidence of an interest in the property it claimed. Therefore, the court finds that the Trust failed to show an interest in the property listed in Appendix M and thus holds that all claims of the Trust are denied.

3.314 Porras/Edmiston Property

Porras and Edmiston admit to an interest in only 91 items of the almost 4,000 items seized by the Government. This amounts to basically two percent (2%) of the total seizure. The court has heard and seen many things in the trial of this case that have damaged the credibility of Porras and Edmiston, but the single fact that these two men admit to only a tiny interest in the seized property is perhaps most damaging of all.

For years, Porras has held himself out to be a consummate collector of art, fine furnishings, exquisite dinnerware, beautiful jewelry and expensive cars. Witness after witness called by the Government testified in detail to these facts. Yet, as Porras's story goes, after he fell into an argument with the tax collector, his entire estate essentially disappeared and, almost coincidentally, his mother and her Trust ended up with a treasure trove amounting to millions of dollars of property. The story and the facts simply do not fit together.

The court realizes that its findings and holdings in this matter are a rejection of most of what the Plaintiffs offered at trial. After much deliberation, however, the court is convinced that its rejection is justified. Plaintiffs came to trial with claims and evidence that were not credible and not believable; a clear example is the position by Porras and Edmiston that only two percent of the property seized in this matter belonged to them. Under all the circumstances, such a position is untenable. Their admission, of course, entitles the Government to the 89 items listed in Appendix N. It does much more, however; it reaffirms the court's credibility judgments.

3.0 Actions for Violations of Constitutional Rights, Conversion and Trespass

In addition to their action for wrongful levy, Plaintiffs have also sued for violations of constitutional rights, conversion and trespass.

3.1 Torts

Plaintiffs' tort actions for conversion and trespass are clearly barred by the doctrine of sovereign immunity. In order to sue the United States for torts, a plaintiff must comply with the Federal Tort Claims Act, 28 U.S.C. § 2671, unless the statute provides otherwise. The Federal Tort Claims Act does not waive sovereign immunity here because any "claim arising in respect of the assessment or collection of any tax" is expressly barred by 28 U.S.C. § 2680(c). Therefore, Plaintiffs' remedy in a suit for conversion and trespass in this matter had to comply with the requisites of the Federal Tort Claims Act.

Plaintiffs have not complied with the Act; accordingly, their suit for conversion and trespass is dismissed.

3.2 Constitutional Violations

Likewise, Plaintiffs' actions for constitutional deprivations under the Fourth and Fifth Amendments to the Constitution must fail. To begin with, it is clear that the Plaintiffs have already sought their sole relief in this matter under 26 U.S.C. § 7426.

The Fifth Circuit in *Baddour v. United States*, 802 F.2d 801 (5th Cir. 1986), has held that a person who is alleging a wrongful levy has the remedies provided in Section 7426 of the Internal Revenue Code as their sole remedy. The court stated that:

> [a] person alleging that his property has been wrongfully levied upon has an opportunity for full judicial consideration, in an adversary context of the validity of the levy. More than that the Constitution does not guarantee.

802 F.2d at 807. The Fifth Circuit further stated that
> ...creation of a damages remedy under circumstances where Congress has provided for corrections of tax collection errors could wreck havoc with the federal tax system.

802 F.2d at 807. In reaching this conclusion, the Fifth Circuit cited that Seventh Circuit's decision in *Cameron v. Internal Revenue Service*, 773 F.2d 126 (7th Cir. 1985), where the Seventh Circuit stated that a complaint for damages based upon an alleged constitutional tort may be dismissed for failure to state a claim either because (1) no constitutional source for the plaintiff's claim exists, or (2) Congress has created explicit remedies or (3) a court-created remedy would interfere with the effective functioning of government.

Although Plaintiffs argue otherwise in support of their position, the court believes that they misconstrue the authorities. For example, they cite *Terrapin Leasing, Ltd. v. United States*, 449 F. Supp. 7 (W.D. OK. 1978) to bolster their argument that they can sue the Government, but the case actually held that no cause of action exists against the United States for alleged constitutional violations due to the doctrine of sovereign immunity. The Supreme Court in *Bivens v. Six Unknown Agents of the Federal Bureau of Narcotics*, 403 U.S. 388, 29 L.

Ed. 2d 619, 91 S. Ct. 1999 (1971), also cited by Plaintiffs, held that agents of the federal government may be sued in their individual capacity for constitutional violations to the extent they exceed their scope of authority. The Plaintiffs' assertion that *Bivens* stands for the proposition that the United States may be sued for constitutional violations is therefore off target. *See also Davis v. Passman*, 442 U.S. 228, 60 L. Ed. 2d 846, 99 S. Ct. 2264 (1979) (holding that a lawsuit may be brought against an individual congressman charged with sexual discrimination under the Constitution); *Bolling v. Sharpe*, 347 U.S. 497, 98 L. Ed. 884, 74 S. Ct. 693 (1954) (holding that children of Washington D.C. cannot be denied admission to the public schools because of their race); *Carlson v. Green*, 446 U.S. 14, 64 L. Ed. 2d 15, 100 S. Ct. 1468 (1980) (holding against prison officials for constitutional violations resulting from the death of an inmate while in custody).

The Plaintiffs' reliance on *Rutherford v. United States*, 702 F.2d 580 (5th Cir. 1983) is also misplaced. In *Rutherford*, the Fifth Circuit remanded the case to the District Court so that it could determine whether an Internal Revenue Service agent in the case violated the taxpayers' constitutional rights by acting outside the scope of his authority. The case does not stand for the proposition that the United States may be sued for constitutional violations.

Another case cited by Plaintiffs, *Smith v. United States*, 458 F.2d 1231 (9th Cir. 1972), is also not on point. In *Smith*, the Internal Revenue Service seized a warehouse owned by a third-party to recover goods inside which were owned by the delinquent taxpayer. The Internal Revenue Service would not let the landlord into the property even though the landlord did not owe the Internal Revenue Service any taxes. The Court held that the Internal Revenue Service certainly had the right to seize the taxpayers' property, but that it had no right to lock the landlord out of his property.

In the case before this court, the Internal Revenue Service seized items in a warehouse that was owned by Midwestern Warehouses, Inc. and leased to HWD, a Porras controlled entity which is also deeply indebted to the Internal Revenue Service. At no time did the Government deny the landlord entry into the warehouse. Moreover, the Internal Revenue Service did not use the landlord's property for a storage facility without compensation. Instead, it leased a warehouse in Midland to store the items that were seized. Accordingly, the *Smith* case does not apply.

The Plaintiffs have brought this lawsuit against the United States of America. They have not sued any government employees in their individual capacity. Since Congress has provided the Plaintiffs with remedies pursuant to Section 7426 of the Internal Revenue Code, their constitutional claims fail.

3.21 The Fourth Amendment Allegations

Although the Plaintiffs conceded that the Government may obtain orders on an *ex parte* basis to effectuate the collection of its tax liabilities, they claim here that the Government still violated their Fourth Amendment rights. In support of their position, the Plaintiffs cite the case of *GM Leasing Corporation v. United States*, 429 U.S. 338, 50 L. Ed. 2d 530, 97 S. Ct. 619 (1977). However, *GM Leasing* stands for another proposition: it states that the Internal Revenue Service must apply to the court and obtain a writ of entry or warrant before it enters into a residence of a taxpayer. The Internal Revenue Service met the requirement set out in *GM Leasing*. It obtained a valid Writ of Entry from the United States Magistrate Judge prior to effectuating the seizure of the property of Porras and Edmiston.

The Plaintiffs further claim that the affidavit of Milton Patrick is defective and the Internal Revenue Service did not have probable cause and the writ should not have been issued. Patrick's affidavits are in evidence as Plaintiffs' Exhibit 12. The United States Magistrate Judge concluded, however, that the application to obtain the writ of entry was sufficient and this court agrees. The Magistrate Judge's determination will thus not be disturbed.

In *Phillips v. Commissioner*, 283 U.S. 589, 596-597, 75 L. Ed. 1289, 51 S. Ct. 608 (1931), the court rejected a constitutional challenge to the statutory system under which the taxes may be collected summarily without a pre-seizure judicial hearing. It was held that as long as there was an adequate opportunity for a post-seizure determination of the taxpayer's rights, the statute met the requirements of due process. *See Commissioner v. Shapiro*, 424 U.S. 614, 630-633, 47 L. Ed. 2d 278, 96 S. Ct. 1062 (1976).

The Internal Revenue Service did not violate the Fourth Amendment because it obtained a writ of entry prior to the seizure of Porras's and Edmiston's property. In the *Matter of Brown*, 84-2 U.S. Tax Cas. (CCH) P10,002 (D. Utah 1984), the District Court held that the standard for issuing an Internal Revenue Service writ of entry is not the same as a criminal warrant. Instead, the affidavit of the Internal Revenue Service must establish that the Government has the right to levy and seize assets of the taxpayer because the assessment has been made, the notice of assessment has been given, the Internal Revenue Service has demanded payment from the taxpayer and the taxes have still not been paid. Furthermore, the Government must establish there is probable cause to believe that there are assets which may be seized on the premises to be entered. *See also, In the Matter of Coppola*, 810 F. Supp. 429, 434 (E.D. N.Y. 1992), *aff'd*, 99 F.3d 402, 1995 WL 760573 (2d Cir. 1995). In *Coppola*, the District Court held that the Government only needed to demonstrate in its affidavits that there was probable cause that the place to be entered contained sizeable goods and that there was probable cause to connect the assets seized to the taxpayer. 810 F. Supp. at 434.

3.22 The Fifth Amendment Argument

It also appears that the Plaintiffs are complaining that they did not have the right to be heard prior to the seizure by the Internal Revenue Service. Since the Plaintiffs have an appropriate post-seizure remedy, a wrongful levy action pursuant to 26 U.S.C. § 7426, they do not have the right to be heard prior to the Internal Revenue Service seizure. In *The Matter of Carlson*, 580 F.2d 1365 (10th Cir. 1978), the court stated that:

> the policies favoring expeditious tax enforcement procedures are as compelling as the need to effect a speedy search of a suspect's premises. To allow a taxpayer to tie up the initial enforcement proceedings after he has been given notice of the jeopardy assessment most assuredly would subvert the statutory purpose of the jeopardy assessment provisions. By delaying enforcement a taxpayer could secrete or dissipate what assets he had left. The government's interests moreover cannot be adequately protected merely by sealing the safe deposit box. The government must be able to search the contents of the box to determine the value of what is there and to learn what other assets the taxpayer may have

elsewhere. We refuse to sanction the impeding of these investigatory functions and the concomitant frustration of the jeopardy assessment procedure which would result from intervention by the taxpayer in the pre-seizure enforcement proceedings.

580 F.2d at 1374.

In *United States v. Shriver*, 645 F.2d 221, 222 (4th Cir. 1981), the Court held that judges, in reviewing writs of entry affidavits, should simply determine whether the application and supporting affidavit showed probable cause to enter, search for, and levy upon personal property in aid of summary collection of assessed and unpaid taxes. The Court also held that the proceeding should not be converted into an adversary one or prolonged over a period of years while taxes presumptively due and owing remain uncollected.

Again, Plaintiffs attack the affidavit of Patrick. *See Plaintiffs' Exhibit 12*. However, his affidavit meets the requirements set forth in *Coppola* and *Brown*. The affidavit indicated that an assessment of income taxes had been made. Notice and demand upon Porras had been made and the taxpayer had refused to pay the tax. The affidavits show that there was probable cause to believe that property subject to the levy was in the place to be searched. For example, paragraph 7 of the affidavit to enter 28 Oaklawn Park provides in part that "A former employee has furnished us with information that would indicate that there are sufficient assets belonging to the taxpayer to warrant seizure action. Many of the assets are considered to be collectibles, i.e. paintings, bronzes, crystal, silver, antiques and jewelry." The affidavit showed the connection between Porras and the property by stating that the house at 28 Oaklawn Park was Porras's residence. Even if Porras was living in New Mexico at the time of the seizure, the Oaklawn house was certainly his residence whenever he was in Midland. Moreover, the proof at trial showed that the affidavit was accurate; the Government located virtually all of the type of items set forth in the affidavit at the house, warehouse, and office. Plaintiffs' Fifth Amendment argument therefore fails.

4.0. Summary

Based upon the findings and conclusions stated in this Memorandum Opinion and Order, it is hereby ORDERED, ADJUDGED AND

DECREED that Plaintiffs' Complaint seeking redress for wrongful levy, constitutional violations, conversion and trespass is dismissed.

It is further ORDERED, ADJUDGED AND DECREED that Plaintiffs' request for injunctive relief is denied.

It is further ORDERED, ADJUDGED AND DECREED that all costs are taxed against Plaintiffs.

It is further ORDERED, ADJUDGED AND DECREED that all pending motions are denied as moot.

SIGNED this 12th day of September, 1996.

ROYAL FURGESON

UNITED STATES DISTRICT JUDGE

JUDGMENT

This action came on for trial before the court. The issues were duly tried and heard. A decision was rendered in the court's Memorandum Opinion and Order, dismissing the Plaintiffs' claims, including their request for injunctive relief.

It is therefore ORDERED, ADJUDGED and DECREED that Plaintiffs Lucille Christie Blakley and Lucille Christie Blakley Trust take nothing and that their claims (including request for injunctive relief) be dismissed on the merits.

It is further ORDERED, ADJUDGED and DECREED that the Defendant United States of America recover of the Plaintiffs its costs of action.

It is further ORDERED, ADJUDGED and DECREED that all pending motions are denied as moot.

SIGNED this 12th day of September, 1996.

ROYAL FURGESON

UNITED STATES DISTRICT JUDGE

[Appendices omitted except Appendix D]
APPENDIX "A"
"Property Belonging To Others"
APPENDIX "B"

"Property Not Adequately Identified or Testified To"
APPENDIX "C"
"Sinclair Property"
APPENDIX "D"

"England-France Purchases in 1981"

ITEM NUMBER	DESCRIPTION	ESTIMATED VALUE
1	Antique Pine Secretary	1,000.00
12	47" Wood/Ormolu Plant Stand	750.00
16	Pine High Cabinet 2 Doors Over 2 Doors	1,800.00
21	Antique English Cabinet 6'H w/Bt Columns	1,750.00
63	Pine Shelf	150.00
70	Antique Pine Washstand with Marble Top	550.00
77	Pine Shelf	125.00
154	Rocking Horse - Possibly Pine	700.00
184	(3) Wooden Carved Girls - 51"T	3,750.00
195	Antique Pine Hutch	900.00
228	Victorian Armoire	1,000.00
267	Pine Chest of Drawers - 5 Drawers/3 Handles Missing	450.00
276	Large Pine Cabinet	1,200.00
277	Breakfront Cabinet	900.00
278	Pine Sideboard	900.00
285	(2) English Windsor Chairs	200.00
286	(2) English Windsor Chairs	200.00
287	(3) Cane Chairs-(12)Arm/(2) Sides w/Cane Seats	250.00
288	(6) Old Rush Seat Chairs	300.00
317	Hanging Pine Plate Rack (Repro)	250.00
339	Antique French Pine Buffet w/Glass Doors on Top	1,850.00
356	Large Pine Kitchen Table	675.00
508	# 508 + # 1534-French Ormolu Clock and Matching Pair	16,500.00
	Candelabras-Clock 28"H x 25"W-Signed on Dial	

ITEM NUMBER	DESCRIPTION	ESTIMATED VALUE
	F.Barbedienne, Paris	
584	French Table - 36" x 78"	600.00
786	High Back Pine Bench/Settle	1,200.00
789	Rosewood English Lap Desk Inlaid w/Brass	500.00
790	Box - English Palisander Wood Inlaid w/Brass	700.00
799	(4) Gilt Louis XVI Style Chairs w/Lyre Backs	800.00
817	(2) Black/Gold Candle Holders - Bronze Gilt	1,500.00
844	(2) New Carved Wood Standing Blackamoors	600.00
845	Large Pine Table w/4 Drawers (Work Table)	1,000.00
846	Carved Wood Console Table (Repro)	1,000.00
847	New Pedestal Base w/Faux Finish 22"x27"x6.5"H (Goes	50.00
	w/# 859)	
859	(2) Kneeling Wood Polychrome Blackamoors with Glass	1,500.00
	Top on Lucite Rest	
896	Antique Brass/Iron Clothes Rack	350.00
940	(2) Brass/Glass Display Cabinets-Doors Missing-$ 6000 if	3,500.00
	Doors are Found-incl/# 1684 (Shelf Brackets)	
980	Pine Partners Desk with Leather Inlay 5' x 8'	4,500.00
1000	Beveled Mirror in Pine Frame 55" x 79"	1,250.00
1021	Bronze of Winged Man 49"H	3,800.00
1022	(13) Pottery Umbrella Stand w/Walking Canes(300 + 1300)	1,600.00
1023	Bronze of Woman w/Wings - Gold Bronze Dore - Marble	1,500.00
	Base Signed Louis Moreau - 30"H	
1032	Bronze of Women Under Vail - E.Barrias	3,250.00
1033	Bronze of Boy w/Stick (La France) Dated Roma 1873 26"H	2,000.00
1036	Pr. of Bronze & Gilt Urns	5,000.00
1037	Pr. Green Marble Urns w/Bronze Dore Overlay	6,000.00

ITEM NUMBER	DESCRIPTION	ESTIMATED VALUE
1038	(2) Glass Containers	70.00
1097	Pottery Bowl W/# 1100	00.00
1099	Large Antique Jug	300.00
1100	Pitcher w/# 1097	200.00
1105	Old Bronze of Eagle w/Marble Base N/S	100.00
1106	Aluminum Monkey Sitting	40.00
1107	Bronze of Girl w/Ball on Wood Base (Old) N/S	175.00
1108	Bronze of Man on Onyx Base (Broken) Old N/S	250.00
1109	Antique Bronze Inkwell - Dog Head - N/S	200.00
1157	pr. Staffordshire Dogs (Repro)	150.00
1253	Camel W/Jockey - Vienna Bronze	150.00
1254	Vulture - Old Vienna Bronze	200.00
1267	Vienna Bronze Cat Rowing Boat	125.00
1268	Old Vienna Bronze Parrot - Small	125.00
1269	Old Vienna Bronze Small Parrot	125.00
1270	Old Vienna Bronze Small Parrot	100.00
1271	(2) Old Vienna Bronze Parrots	100.00
1287	Pr. Gilt and Bronze Candelabra w/Boys on Marble Base	300.00
1389	Old Vienna Bronze Squirrel in Tree-Match Holder	500.00
1390	Vienna Bronze Candlestick-Frog w/Dumbbell	500.00
1391	(2) Old Vienna Bronze Cats W/Instruments	300.00
1392	Old Vienna Bronze of a Blacksmith cat	250.00
1396	Old 10" Vienna Bronze Fox	600.00
1397	Old Vienna Bronze Bird	300.00
1402	(2) African Bronzes 2 1/2" of 2 People	60.00
1403	Old Vienna Bronze Cats on Date	125.00
1412	Old Vienna Bronze Snake	175.00
1414	Old Vienna Bronze Lizard	275.00
1420	Old Bronze Snail	250.00
1421	Bronze of Monkey	175.00

ITEM NUMBER	DESCRIPTION	ESTIMATED VALUE
1422	Spelter Dog	75.00
1426	Pair Bronze Candlesticks 5 1/2"H	175.00
1427	Bronze Bust of Boy 9"	100.00
1439	Bronze of Gun Rack w/Guns Civil War Style 10"H	275.00
1443	Candlestick - Tigereye - Corinthian Column 8" H	150.00
1447	Old Vienna Bronze Arab w/Rifle	275.00
1448	Old Unicorn Vienna Bronze	175.00
1457	Vienna Bronze Boy w/Cobra	425.00
1460	Vienna Bronze Peacock	650.00
1465	Vienna Bronze Cat	275.00
1466	Vienna Bronze Cats Holding Hands	225.00
1467	Vienna Bronze Cobbler on Blanket	475.00
1468	Vienna Bronze Pelican	250.00
1514	Large Pine Refectory Table (Old)	675.00
1515	Large 10' Pine Table (Repro)	775.00
1520	Old Stripped Pine Long Table	800.00
1643	30" Silver Plate and Gilt Candelabra - 3 Branch - Ornate	1,200.00
1649	Bronze of Mercury Sitting	350.00
1655	Clay Statue of Man	75.00
1684	(4) Brass Brackets for Display see # 940	00.00
1687	Old Vienna Bronze Lion on Stone Base	350.00
1700	Silver Plate and Parcel Gilt Epergne (3) Arms w/Crystal	3,500.00
	Bowls Supported by Camels with Crystal Vase at Top	
	Center - Includes # 2691, 2692	
1730	Old Vienna Bronze Basket w/Bird	375.00
1749	Old Vienna Bronze Dalmatian	150.00
1761	Old Silver Server w/Skating Boy 17" Long	800.00
1767	Pine Table - 10' Green Wash (Repro)	800.00

ITEM NUMBER	DESCRIPTION	ESTIMATED VALUE
1768	Oak Refectory Table 6'6"	550.00
1806	Bronze of Bust of Man	300.00
1813	Ink Well W/Deer Dated 1867, Sterling, English	1,200.00
1818	Vienna Bronze Arab Boy Sitting	350.00
1821	Vienna Bronze Cockatoo 10"	1,200.00
1825	Perfume Bottle - Silver/Green Rooster	175.00
1857	Unicorn-Chrome and Iron	125.00
1861	(3) Brass Planters	120.00
1884	Iron Shelf	150.00
1885	Chandelier - Iron - as is Glass Broken	300.00
1887	Vienna Bronze Tray	900.00
1905	Sconce	275.00
1918	Cherub Lamp	450.00
2198	Vienna Bronze 7" Lizard	575.00
2202	Vienna Bronze Dog	475.00
2228	Vienna Bronze Dog in Rocking Chair	225.00
2229	Oriental Carrying Chair	90.00
2230	Silver Oriental Rickshaw	90.00
2234	Vienna Bronze Dog	100.00
2236	Vienna Bronze of Arab in Tent	1,500.00
2265	Bronze of Boy Riding Iguana	200.00
2267	Bronze of Bighorn Sheet	75.00
2269	(2) Opium Bottles	105.00
2270	Opium Bottle - Malachite	150.00
2271	Vienna Bronze **Dachshund**	125.00
2309	Vienna Bronze Dog	275.00
2311	Vienna Bronze Deer	475.00
2312	Vienna Bronze Tiger on Marble Base	350.00
2313	Vienna Bronze Bird in Tree	500.00
2314	Vienna Bronze Boy Laying Down	450.00
2315	Vienna Bronze Tiger	750.00
2316	Bronze of 4 Kids in Shell - Gilt	600.00

ITEM NUMBER	DESCRIPTION	ESTIMATED VALUE
2317	Vienna Bronze Monkey w/Shell	450.00
2318	Vienna Bronze Dog	225.00
2319	Bronze of Dog	125.00
2320	Bronze of 2 Dogs Fighting Signed Chemin	600.00
2322	Bronze of Deer	125.00
2323	Vienna Bronze Dog	175.00
2324	(2) Bronze Ducks	100.00
2326	4" Vienna Bronze Owl	350.00
2328	Vienna Bronze Dogs in Canoe	400.00
2329	Statue of Man	75.00
2338	Sterling Inkwell	1,500.00
2357	Silver Pig	65.00
2377	Vienna Bronze Arab Writer	550.00
2378	Vienna Bronze Outstretched African	375.00
2389	Mirror W/Cherubs	125.00
2430	Tray - Base for # 2345	375.00
2436	Bronze of Basket	500.00
2594	Table - 10' Pine	900.00
2595	Table - 14' Pine	1,200.00
2616	Salt & Peppers - 21 Prs. - Animals - Most Sterling - 25.00	525.00
	Pair	
2667	Salt & Peppers - 12 Pairs, Sterling 3"H, 25.00 Pr.	300.00
2668	Sugar Shaker - Silver Plate, Ornate	100.00
2686	Table - 14' Pine	1,260.00
2709	(3) Glass Bowls	45.00
2805	Table - Pine 14'	1,350.00
2851	(2) African Bust Marble/Stone Inlaid w/Lapis Lazuli,	50,000.00
	Malachite and Other Semi-Precious Stones	
2909	96 pcs. English Silver Plate Knives, Forks, Spoons, 2	200.00
	Ladles, 1 Large Spoon, Plain	

ITEM NUMBER	DESCRIPTION	ESTIMATED VALUE
2910	12 Pieces Alvin Sterling "Bridal Rose" Teaspoons Book	420.00
	Value 35.00 Each	
2911	7 Pieces American Sterling Teaspoons Engraved Rose	140.00
	Pattern 9th Century 20.00 each	
2912	2 Pcs. - S.Kirk & Son Ornate Floral Patterns Serving Fork	100.00
	and Pick	
2913	12 Pcs. - Assembled Set, Coin and Sterling 6" Spoons	240.00
	(Similar to Gorham) "Tipt" Pattern	
2914	3 Pcs. - 61 Pcs. Silver Plate Knives, Fork, Spoons in	150.00
	Simple "Tipt" Pattern - English Sterling Fish Knife and	
	Fork	
2915	12 Misc. Silver Pcs. - 1 Large Sterling Serving Fork	240.00
	(125.00), 4 Small Sterling Spoons (40.00 Total), Sterling	
	Handle Meat Holder (30.00), Sterling Handle Cheese Cutter	
	(20.00), 5 Silver Plate Servers (25.00 Total)	
3187	Lalique "Vaguas" Vase 9 x 10.5	5,800.00
3189	Lalique Smokey Gray Colored 7:H Vase-3 Faces off	1,800.00
	Women	
3208	(2) Lalique Lighters - Lions	600.00
3216	(2) Lalique Lighters	400.00
3222	Lalique Vase "Narcisse" 10.75"H	2,190.00
3225	Lalique Table - La Fleur # 18 Top Damaged	40,000.00
3423	142 Pc. Set - Sterling Silver Shell Pattern Knives,	2,840.00

ITEM NUMBER	DESCRIPTION	ESTIMATED VALUE
	Forks,	
	Spoons, and 2 Lg. Ladles	
3424	(12) Knives-Silver/Bone English Sterling Blades Engraved	240.00
	Bone Handles 9"	
3472	111 Pc. Set-Silver Sterling English 1870 in Original Fitted	2,775.00
	Burl Walnut Container Setting for 12 Included 2 Lg.	
	Ladles, 2 Extra Lg. Serving Spoons, 12 Lg. Soup Spoons,	
	Fairly Plain Design and Heavy Quality	
175	TOTAL	231,080.00

IMPERIAL TOY CORPORATION,
Plaintiff,
-against-
GOFFA INTERNATIONAL CORPORATION,
Defendant.

97 CV 7072
UNITED STATES DISTRICT COURT
FOR THE EASTERN DISTRICT OF NEW YORK
988 F. Supp. 617
December 18, 1997

Barry I. Slotnick, Jacques M. Rimokh, of counsel, RICHARDS & O'NEIL, LLP, New York, New York.

For plaintiff: Charles W. Shifley, Marc S. Cooperman, Ronald C. Gorshe, Jr., of counsel, BANNER & WITCOFF, LTD., Chicago, IL.

For defendant: EDWARD S. HOCHMAN, ESQ., New York, New York.

Eugene H. Nickerson, U.S.D.J.

MEMORANDUM AND ORDER

NICKERSON, District Judge:

Plaintiff Imperial Toy Corporation (Imperial) brought this suit against defendant Goffa International Corporation (Goffa) claiming that Goffa has infringed its copyrights in ten plush animal toys in violation of 17 U.S.C. § 501 *et seq.* Plaintiff has moved for a preliminary injunction.

I

The moving papers show the following. Imperial is a designer and manufacturer of children's toys. In the spring of 1996 it began selling a line of plush stuffed animals called Friendly Pebble Pets, small toy animals with beanbag bodies covered in soft fabric. The line features a variety of animals, of which only the whale, penguin, turtle, lion, dolphin, toucan, lobster, frog, **dachshund** and goldfish are at issue in this case. These toys have enjoyed significant commercial success both nationally and in the New York area, and are sold at retail outlets such as Wal-Mart and K-Mart, and toy stores such as Kay-Bee Toys.

In July 1997 Imperial obtained a Goffa catalog sales sheet indicating that Goffa was marketing a line of plush toys called Bean Bag Friends. Imperial thereafter purchased the Goffa toys, and determined that they are similar in appearance to Friendly Pebble Pets.

Imperial mailed copyright applications for the ten Friendly Pebble Pets that are the subjects of this case on August 14, 1997. Nine of the ten toys were issued certificates of registration on October 31, 1997, and the tenth was registered on November 4, 1997.

Imperial filed suit in the Southern District of New York on November 4, 1997. The suit was voluntarily dismissed by Imperial because of improper venue, and was refiled in this Court on December 2, 1997. Imperial moved for a preliminary injunction on December 4, 1997.

II

To obtain a preliminary injunction, Imperial must demonstrate:

> (1) either a likelihood that [it] will succeed on the merits of [its] claim, or that the merits present serious questions for litigation and the balance of hardships tips decidedly toward the plaintiff; and (2) that without the injunction, [it] will likely suffer irreparable harm before the court can rule upon his claim.

Fisher-Price, Inc. v. Well-Made Toy Mfg. Corp., 25 F.3d 119, 122 (2d Cir. 1994).

A. *Likelihood of Success*

A plaintiff proves infringement by showing that: (1) he owns a valid copyright in the work; and (2) the defendant has copied protected elements of the plaintiff's work. *Fonar Corp. v. Domenick*, 105 F.3d 99,

103 (2d Cir.), *cert. denied*,   U.S.   , 139 L. Ed. 2d 191, 118 S. Ct. 265 (1997).

1. *Validity of the Copyright*

A certificate of copyright registration is prima facie evidence that the copyright is valid. 17 U.S.C. § 410(c); *Fonar Corp.*, 105 F.3d at 104. Imperial's registration of the ten Friendly Pebble Pets shifts to Goffa the burden of proving that the copyrights are invalid. *Fonar Corp.*, 105 F.3d at 104. The presumption of validity may be rebutted "where other evidence in the record casts doubt on the question." *Durham Indus., Inc. v. Tomy Corp.*, 630 F.2d 905, 908 (2d Cir. 1980). For example, proof that a work has been copied from a public domain source can rebut the presumption that a copyright of that work is valid. *See, e.g., Folio Impressions, Inc. v. Byer California*, 937 F.2d 759, 763 (2d Cir. 1991).

Goffa argues that Imperial does not hold a valid copyright on Friendly Pebble Pets. It accuses Imperial of registering products which it did not create, but it admits that it does know who did create the designs. Instead, Goffa has offered three different theories about who other than Imperial might have designed these toys.

First, Goffa speculates that the designs at issue have been in existence for decades, implying that the toys fall within in the public domain and cannot be copyrighted. But Goffa has not offered any toy actually existing in the public domain which Imperial may have copied. Mere conjecture is not sufficient to rebut the presumption of the validity of Imperial's copyright.

Goffa also alleges that Imperial has copied the Beanie Babies line of toys produced by Ty, Incorporated (Ty), which have been on the market since 1994. But Ty's Beanie Babies submitted to the Court on the hearing of the motion look quite different from Imperial's Friendly Pebble Pets and Goffa's Bean Bag Friends, which, as discussed hereafter, are for the most part virtually identical. For example, Ty's goldfish is an orange toy with black bead eyes and a puckered mouth. Imperial's version has a yellow body and a pinkish-red tail, face, and fins. Its eyes are larger than Ty's, are black and white, and bulge out of its head. It also has two yellow balls where its mouth would ordinarily be.

242

Goffa's version of the goldfish is identical to that of Imperial, down to the two strange yellow balls. The only difference is that the tail, face, and fins are a darker red than Imperial's toy. Because the Ty toy and the Imperial design are so easily distinguishable, the status of Ty's copyright has nothing to do with this case. Goffa's argument that Imperial has copied Ty is simply fatuous.

Imperial has offered an affidavit attesting that Friendly Pebble Pets were created by a Chinese entity called Shanghai Elcee, which assigned the rights to the toys to Imperial. The affidavits of Goffa's sales representatives respond that they do not believe that Shanghai Elcee--or any other Chinese factory, for that matter--had any role in originating the toys. But Goffa does not offer any evidence of who did design the toys, nor does it claim to have designed its own version of the toy.

The opinions of the Goffa sales representatives are not based on any first-hand knowledge, and consequently carry little (if any) weight. Imperial's evidence that it owns Shanghai Elcee's copyright is more credible than the unsubstantiated theory proffered by Goffa.

Goffa also seems to argue that because Shanghai Elcee is a Chinese entity, it cannot hold a copyright. This assertion is insupportable in the face of the United States copyright law, which gives copyright protection to all "original works of authorship fixed in any tangible medium of expression," with no reference to the nationality of the author of the work. 17 U.S.C. § 102(a); *see also Hasbro Bradley, Inc. v. Sparkle Toys, Inc.*, 780 F.2d 189, 192 (2d Cir. 1985) (holding that toys created in Japan are protected by the United State's copyright law even though they would not enjoy copyright protection under Japanese law).

Goffa's arguments are unconvincing and do not rebut the presumption of the validity of Imperial's copyright.

2. *Copying of Protected Elements*

To show copying in violation of the copyright law, Imperial must demonstrate that Goffa actually copied Imperial's work, and that elements of the copy are "substantially similar" to protected elements of the plaintiff's work. *Fisher-Price, Inc.*, 25 F.3d at 122--123.

A plaintiff can prove copying by showing that a defendant had access to its work, and that the works are similar enough to indicate that one copied the other. *Id.* Imperial has submitted evidence that the marketing of its Friendly Pebble Pets is sufficiently extensive to establish that Goffa had access to the toy. *See Conan Properties, Inc. v. Mattel, Inc.*, 712 F. Supp. 353, 360 (S.D.N.Y. 1989) ("Access may be inferred . . . if the plaintiff's work has been widely disseminated."). Moreover, access is also presumed when the two works are "strikingly similar." *Arnstein v. Porter*, 154 F.2d 464 (2d Cir. 1946). As discussed hereafter, Imperial's and Goffa's toys are in most respects practically identical. The only fair inference is that Goffa engaged in copying.

Once copying has been established, the court must determine whether there exists "a substantial similarity between protectible elements of the two works." *Fisher-Price, Inc.*, 25 F.3d at 123. The similarity between the toys must be measured by "whether an ordinary observer would overlook the dissimilarities between the artistic (protectible) aspects of the two works and would conclude that one was copied from the other." *Id.*

Comparing only the protectible elements of these toys, it is clear that all but one of Goffa's creations are substantially similar to the Friendly Pebble Pets. In fact, most of Goffa's toys do not vary one whit from Imperial's design. The toys do not merely share features characteristic of the animals that they represent; they contain identical, and in some instances bizarre, interpretations of those features.

a. *The Whale*

Imperial's whale is black with a white underbelly and white spots beside each eye. It has a thin red mouth. Its chin is level with its torso as if it is swimming straight ahead, but its eyes--which have white half-moons above a black iris with a white pupil--gaze downward. Goffa's whale contains these identical characteristics and no significantly different characteristics.

While the conventional black body, white underbelly, and whale-shaped tail presumably are characteristic of most whale dolls, the white spots beside the eye, red lips, position of the chin, and detailed eyeballs are protectible artistic expressions of a whale. A copy of Ty's Beanie Baby whale, submitted by Imperial on the motion, has none of these features but has black button eyes with no white part in them, a head that is angled downward, no white spots, and no lips at all.

b. *The Penguin*

Imperial's penguins have the following protectible characteristics: black button eyes; white patches around the eyes; feet shaped like half-moons that are sewed to the front seam of the body and are not stuffed with beanbag filler; a fat, blunt beak; and wings that curve toward their stomachs.

The only difference between the Imperial and Goffa penguins is that Goffa's doll's feet are red, while those of Imperial's doll are orange. This variation is so minimal that it is easy to miss at first glance. Ty's penguin possesses none of the above-described characteristics except for button eyes.

c. *The Turtle*

The two turtles present a more difficult question. They are similar in general contour, but the Goffa turtle has features not present in Imperial's turtle. Imperial's turtle is purple and yellow with half-moon feet that are unstuffed, a shell composed of twelve small trapezoids and one large hexagon, and only a suggestion of a mouth. Goffa's turtle is grey and beige, and has differently-shaped feet stuffed with beanbag filler. Its shell is outlined with a beige rim, and is composed of one hexagon and six trapezoids. The hexagon and trapezoids are of similar size. Goffa's turtle is slightly larger than Imperial's turtle, and has a thin, black smile on its face. The features which the turtle have in common--bald heads, small tails, shell-shaped bodies--are generic characteristics which would be common to any toy recognizable as a turtle. The Goffa turtle does not infringe the Imperial turtle.

d. *The Lion*

Goffa's and Imperial's lions have an identical body shape, including slightly curved thighs and blunted forepaws. Both share the following features. Their tails are unstuffed, and are tipped with a tiny bit of the same kind of fur that comprises their manes. The insides of their ears are white, but the outsides are the light tan color of the rest of their bodies. Their eyes and noses have the same dark plastic, and their mouths are an upside-down Y-shape stitched on in black thread.

The Goffa toy has a marginally smaller muzzle than the Imperial toy, and is slightly less well-stuffed. But these variations are so minimal that it is difficult to tell if they are caused by an alteration in the design, or are merely accidental variations that could occur among any mass-produced line of objects.

e. *The Dolphin*

Imperial's dolphin has a blue body with yellow patches around the eyes and a grey underbelly. Its chin thrusts forward as if it is staring straight ahead, and its muzzle is quite pronounced. Its tail looks more like that of a whale than a dolphin. Goffa's dolphin is identical in every way, except that the shade of blue of its body is slightly lighter than Imperial's dolphin.

Ty's dolphin shows that these artistic features are not necessary to the idea of a dolphin. Ty's dolphin contains none of the characteristics described here. Its body is an entirely different shape. In fact, it looks like a different kind of animal.

f. *The Toucan*

The toucans produced by both Imperial and Goffa are identical. Each has a black body, an orange chest, red patches around the eyes and red feet. The beak is composed of four orange fabric pieces, and is tipped in black. The tail looks as if it belonged to a beaver. The red crest is made of a single piece of felt cut in a wavy pattern. The waves of Imperial's crest are more pronounced that Goffa's, but in all other respects the toys are the same.

g. *The Lobster*

Imperial's lobster is bright orange, rather than the traditional red that one would expect a lobster to be. It has three red ribbons encircling its body. Its claws are larger than its six small legs, none of which are stuffed with beanbag filler. It has two black whiskers, one on each side of where its mouth should be.

Goffa's toy copies these features, including the fanciful orange color. The only difference between the brands is that Goffa's whiskers are comprised of two strands of black thread each instead of one, and the legs are slightly fatter. Otherwise, the lobsters are identical.

h. *The Frog*

Both frog dolls share the following characteristics: a green upper body, a white underbelly, a red smile with upturned corners, eyes that rise in peaks out of the head, and hands and feet with three points on them. Like all of the other toys at issue, with the exception of the turtle, the frogs seem clearly cut from the same pattern as the location of the seams on the bodies of the dolls indicates.

i. *The* **Dachshund**

Imperial's **dachshund** looks nothing like a real **dachshund**, because the body is not elongated and the feet are oversized. It has a wide-eyed stare, a black button nose, a little red tongue, and a knot tied in the end of its tail. Goffa's dog has the identical body shape, tongue, and knot in the tail. It is a slightly browner shade, and the eyes have white pupils that Imperial's dog lacks, but it is clearly cut from the same pattern as that of Imperial.

j. *The Goldfish*

Imperial's goldfish, already described above, has a yellow body and a pinkish-red tail, face, and fins. Its eyes bulge out of its head. It also has two yellow balls for a mouth, making the fish look diseased. Goffa's version is identical, down to the two strange yellow balls, but the tail, face, and fins are a darker red than Imperial's toy.

k. *Summary*

Because Goffa's toys employ the identical expressive elements and artistic touches of Imperial's whale, penguin, lion, dolphin, toucan, lobster, frog, **dachshund** and goldfish, a substantial similarity exists between Goffa's and Imperial's versions of these nine toys. The differences between these toys are so minor that most border on the invisible and are only apparent on very close inspection.

The two turtles have sufficient differences that the court cannot infer that Goffa copied from Imperial.

B. *Irreparable Harm*

To merit a preliminary injunction, Imperial also must show that it will suffer irreparable harm in the time before the court can rule on the merits of its claim. Irreparable harm is presumed once a prima facie showing of infringement has been made, unless the copyright holder unreasonably delays prosecuting his infringement claim. *Fisher-Price, Inc.*, 25 F.3d at 124. Imperial brought this suit within four months of learning of the existence of Goffa's toys. A four month delay, during which Imperial investigated the claim and registered its toys, is not unreasonable. *See id.* at 124 (finding that a six month delay was not unreasonable).

III

Goffa is preliminarily enjoined from importing, manufacturing, distributing, advertising, or selling its whale, penguin, lion, dolphin, toucan, lobster, frog, dachshund and goldfish toys. Imperial's request for an injunction against the manufacture and sale of Goffa's toy turtle is denied.

So ordered.

Dated: Brooklyn, New York

December 18, 1997

Eugene H. Nickerson, U.S.D.J.

4

Named Intellectual Property

The cases in this section are cases about inellectual
property law involving products named with dachshund.
Walt Disney case involving investment credits in the movie
"The Ugly Dachshund", *Ripple Junction* involves claims of
unfair competition for a t-shirt logo design, and *Embroidery
Library* is about a dachshund embrodery design.

Walt Disney Productions v. United States,
74-2 U.S. Tax Cas. (CCH) P9623 (C.D.CA., 1974)

Ripple Junction Design Co. v. Olaes Enters.,
2005 Copy. L. Rep. (CCH) P29,079 (S.D.OH Western Div, 2005)

Embroidery Library, Inc. v. Sublime Stitching, LLC,
Civil No. 09-2766 (JNE/AJB), (D.Minn, 2010)

Walt Disney Productions, Plaintiff
v.
United States of America, Defendant.

No. 73-2125-DWW
U.S. District Court, Central Dist. Calif.
34 A.F.T.R.2d (RIA) 5595
July 8, 1974

Findings of Fact and Conclusions of Law

WILLIAMS, District Judge: Following trial without a jury, the Court hereby makes the following findings of fact and conclusions of law as required by Rule 52(a) of the Federal Rules of Civil Procedure:

I. Findings of Fact

1. Plaintiff, Walt Disney Productions (hereinafter "Disney"), is a corporation duly organized and existing under the laws of the State of California with its principal offices in the City of Burbank, County of Los Angeles, State of California.

2. Disney's principal business activities since its organization have been the production and distribution of family entertainment motion picture films for exhibition in theatres, on television, and in homes, schools, and other places of non-theatrical entertainment, and the operation of the family amusement parks known as Disneyland and Walt Disney World.

3. As of its 1963 fiscal year, Disney had produced more than 250 motion picture film negatives.

4. During its fiscal years ended in 1963 through 1969 (which years, together with Disney's fiscal year ended in 1962 as it relates to an investment credit carry-back from 1964, are hereinafter the "fiscal years"), Disney completed production of, and placed in service, the negatives of motion picture films listed below (hereinafter the "investment credit negatives"), with respect to which it incurred the indicated production costs eligible for the investment credit:

(i) Investment Credit Negatives	(ii) Qualified Investment
Fiscal Year Ended Sept. 28, 1963	
Son of Flubber	$ 2,050,234
In Search Of The Castaways	527,035
Symposium On Popular Songs	82,207
Summer Magic	1,708,786
Savage Sam	1,653,822
The Yellowstone Cubs	235,866
Incredible Journey	875,653
Sword In The Stone	2,135,227
Little Dog Lost	131.718
Mooncussers	685,489
Johnny Shiloh	783,718
Man Is His Own Worst Enemy	179,518
Holiday Time At Disneyland	126,425
Greta, The Misfit Greyhound	58,633
Inside Outer Space	133,939
Three Tall Tales	158,491
The Silver Fox And Sam Davenport	87,974
Square Peg In A Round Hole	146,629
Sammy, The Way Out Seal	697,520
Hurricane Hannah	98,312
Fly With Von Drake	201,637
Total for year	$12,758,833
Fiscal Year Ended Oct 3, 1964	
Misadventure of Merlin Jones	$ 386,838
Three Lives Of Thomasina	1,213,660
A Tiger Walks	1,121,880
The Moon Spinners	2,433,842
Mary Poppins	4,363,772
Disneyland Goes To The World's Fair	297,790
Dr. Syn, Alias The Scarecrow (The Scarecrow Of	1,016,552
Romney Marshe)	
For The Love Of Willadean - Taste Of Melon	396,115

(i) Investment Credit Negatives	(ii) Qualified Investment
Legend Of Two Gypsy Dogs	155,461
Ballad Of Hector, Stowaway Dog	988,471
Mediterranean Cruise	345,563
Bristle Face	536,022
The Waltz King	895,053
Wahoo Bobcat	197,498
Truth About Mother Goose	193,262
In Shape With Von Drake	184,194
A Rag, A Bone, A Box Of Junk	64,772
Total for Year	$14,790,745
Fiscal Year Ended Oct. 2, 1965	
The Tatooed Police Horse	$ 170,562
Emil And The Detectives	967,987
Those Calloways	1,840,785
Country Coyote Goes Hollywood	255,283
The Monkey's Uncle	704,098
That Darn Cat	1,520,622
Tenderfoot	858,496
One Day At Teton Marsh	212,396
Disneyland 10th Anniversary	320,408
Ida, The Offbeat Eagle	262,312
Gallegher	799,885
An Otter In The Family	261,385
Kilroy	1,017,795
The Legend Of Young Dick Turpin	684,361
Further Adventures Of Gallegher	812,638
Total for year	$10,689,013
Fiscal Year Ended Oct. 1, 1966	
Winnie The Pooh And The Honey Tree	$ 159,243
The Ugly Dachshund	848,420
Lt. Robin Crusoe, U.S.N.	2,505,747
Run, Appaloosa, Run	193,720
Fighting Prince of Donegal	1,349,655
Follow Me Boys	2,108,489

(i) Investment Credit Negatives	(ii) Qualified Investment
Music For Everybody	327,324
Minado, The Wolverine	235,303
Ballerina	780,706
Run, Light Buck, Run	207,846
Concho, The Coyote Who Wasn't	188,823
Legend Of El Blanco	257,289
Total for year	$ 9,162,565
Fiscal Year Ended Sept. 30, 1967	
Adventures Of Bullwhip Griffin	$ 2,164,179
Monkeys Go Home	1,669,154
The Gnome-Mobile	2,626,824
The Legend Of The Boy And The Eagle	197,864
Jungle Book	3,907,005
Charlie, The Lonesome Cougar	591,842
101 Problems of Hercules	237,145
Gallegher Goes West	1,221,147
Ranger's Guide To Nature	304,265
Joker, The Amiable Ocelot	274,468
Disneyland Around The Seasons	173,210
Willie And The Yank	1,015,929
Boy Who Flew With Condors	215,029
Atta Girl, Kelly	1,044,868
Salute To Alaska	286,029
Not So Lonely Lighthouse Keeper	218,841
How The West Was Lost	255,616
Total for year	$16,403,415
Fiscal Year Ended Sept. 28, 1968	
The Happiest Millionaire	$ 3,614,628
Blackbeard's Ghost	2,248,303
Never A Dull Moment	1,901,608
The One And Only Family Band	3,038,874
Winnie The Pooh And The Blustery Day	683,135
The Horse In the Grey Flannel Suit	2,376,961
One Day On Beetle Rock	203,820
Boy Called Nuthin	710,718

(i) Investment Credit Negatives	(ii) Qualified Investment
Disneyland/From Pirates Of Carribbean	186,051
Way Down Cellar	562,606
Pablo And The Dancing Chihuahua	541,095
My Family Is A Menagerie	263,735
Young Loner	678,680
Wild Heart	$ 212,765
Ranger Of Brownstowne	302,308
Nature's Charter Tours	413,176
Boomerang, Dog Of Many Talents	765,777
Pacifically Peeking	474,972
Total for year	$19,179,212
Fiscal Year Ended Sept. 27, 1969	
The Love Bug	$ 3,104,954
Smith	1,418,334
Rascal	1,523,299
Hang Your Hat On The Wind	290,840
Brimstone, The Amish Horse	206,969
Treasure Of San Bosco Reef	733,351
Owl That Didn't Give A Hoot	309,072
Mickey Mouse Anniversary Show	177,879
Solomon, The Sea Turtle	256,657
Pancho, Fastest Paw In The West	345,221
Secrets Of Boyne Castle	1,096,742
Nature's Better Built Homes	350,577
Ride A Northbound Horse	661,241
Wild Geese Calling	295,388
My Dog The Thief	994,433
Total for year	$11,864,957

5. From the dates of their completion, Disney has at all times been the owner (a) of each investment credit negative produced initially for television exhibition, and (b) of 22 of the 41 investment credit negatives produced initially for theatrical exhibition. Disney has been the owner of an undivided interest of between 89 1/2 percent and 99 percent of the remaining 19 investment credit negatives produced initially for theatrical exhibition from the dates of their completion.

The portion of the 19 investment credit negatives not owned by Disney is owned by certain of its key creative employees. The production costs eligible for the investment credit as set forth in column (ii) of paragraph 4 above include only those costs attributable to Disney's ownership interest.

6. Negatives produced by Disney are used in its business only to make positive prints.

7. The prints are rented for exhibition in theatres, on television, and in homes, schools, and other places of non-theatrical entertainment.

8. After being used for a number of exhibitions, a print wears out and new prints must then be manufactured from the negative in order to continue exhibition of the film.

9. Besides normal wear, many prints are destroyed in whole or in part in the course of their use, and new prints must then be manufactured from the negative in order to continue exhibition of the film.

10. When not being used for the purpose of manufacturing positive prints, Disney's motion picture film negatives are stored in specially constructed fireproof and explosion-proof vaults under conditions of controlled temperature and humidity.

11. Disney's motion picture films, as contrasted to films produced by many other production companies, are based on stories and themes which have a broad and continued appeal both to adults and to children over many years and can be shown or reissued to entertain each generation as it reaches certain age levels.

12. Disney's experience through each of the fiscal years showed that most of its negatives had continued to earn income annually and that all of its negatives produced more than eight years previously earned income for at least eight years; that this income was derived from more than one type of commercial use; that many of its films produced for initial theatrical release had been shown on network television, often more than once, and syndicated on television abroad; that many of its films produced for initial showing on network television had been exhibited theatrically and syndicated on television abroad; that many films continued annually to be reissued theatrically and rerun on television, often several times; that many

films were exhibited in schools, homes, churches, and other places of non-theatrical entertainment; that footage from many films had been used in producing other films; that films produced for initial showing on black and white television sets originally had been produced in color in anticipation that they would be reshown years later when color television sets came into general use; and that Disney's negatives had been used repeatedly over periods of at least eight years to make new prints.

13. Domestic television syndication represents a substantial market for exploitation of the investment credit negatives once network contractual restrictions prohibiting such syndication terminate.

14. In reliance on their many years of experience in producing, distributing, reissuing and syndicating Disney's films, Disney's executives properly concluded in each year from 1963 through 1969 that the investment credit negatives placed in service in each of the fiscal years had a useful life in Disney's business of at least eight years as of the date when placed in service.

15. Each of the investment credit negatives is property upon which a deduction for depreciation under the income forecast method is allowable for income tax purposes and upon which depreciation has been allowed under such method.

16. In depreciating investment credit negatives under the income forecast method for each of the fiscal years, Disney was not required to estimate, and did not estimate, the useful life of the investment credit negatives in terms of years.

17. Each of the investment credit negatives had a useful life of at least eight years as of the date when placed in service.

18. Each of the investment credit negatives was located and used in the United States.

19. Disney timely filed its United States corporation income tax returns and its claims for refund with respect to the fiscal years.

20. Disney's claims for refund asserted a right to the investment credit equal to 7 percent of the production costs eligible for the investment credit, which as set forth in column (ii) of paragraph 4

above, totals $6,639,412. The credit for each of the fiscal years (taking into account the carry-back from 1964 to 1962) is as follows:

Fiscal Year	Qualified Investment	Investment Credit
1962		$ 170,466 *
1963	12,758,833	893,118
1964	14,790,745	864,886
1965	10,689,013	748,231
1966	9,162,565	641,380
1967	16,403,415	1,148,239
1968	19,179,212	1,342,545
1969	11,864,957	830,547
Total	$94,848,740	$6,639,412

* Carryback from 1964.

21. Disney has not received any credit or refund of all or any part of the credits referred to in its claims for refund, and at the time of filing the complaint in this suit, more than six months had passed since the date each such claim was filed.

22. Disney timely filed the complaint in this suit on September 7, 1973.

23. To the extent that any finding of fact is deemed a conclusion of law, it is to that extent hereby made a conclusion of law.

II. Conclusions of Law

1. The Court has jurisdiction of this civil action against the United States for recovery of an internal-revenue tax alleged to have been erroneously collected. Title 28, U.S.C., Section 1346(a) (1).

2. Venue is in the United States District Court for the Central District of California by virtue of Disney's principal place of business. Title 28, U.S.C., Section 1402(a) (2).

3. Each of the investment credit negatives constitutes "tangible personal property" for purposes of the investment credit. Title 26, U.S.C., Sections 38 and 46 through 48. Walt Disney Productions v. United States, 327 F. Supp. 189 (C.D. Cal. 1971); aff'd as modified, 480 F.2d 66 (9th Cir. 1973), cert. denied, 94 S. Ct. 1451 (1974).

4. Disney overpaid its federal income taxes for the fiscal years in an amount equal to 7 percent of the qualified investment (as indicated in column (ii) of paragraph 4 of part I above) incurred by it to produce the investment credit negatives.

5. Disney is entitled to a refund of federal income taxes erroneously collected from it by defendant with respect to the fiscal years in the amounts specified below, plus interest as allowed by law, together with the costs and disbursements of this suit for refund, and judgment shall be entered accordingly.

Fiscal Year Ended	Refund Due
1962	$ 170,466
1963	893,118
1964	864,886
1965	784,231
1966	641,380
1967	1,148,239
1968	1,342,545
1969	830,547
Total	$6,639,412

6. To the extent that any finding of fact is deemed a conclusion of law, it is to that extent hereby made a conclusion of law.

Ripple Junction Design Co.,
Plaintiff,
vs.
Olaes Enterprises, Inc., d/b/a ODM,
Defendant.

Case No. 1:05-CV-43
UNITED STATES DISTRICT COURT
FOR THE SOUTHERN DISTRICT OF OHIO,
WESTERN DIVISION
Copy. L. Rep. (CCH) P29,079
September 8, 2005

For Ripple Junction Design Co, Plaintiff: Alison Joy Bouffard, Cincinnati, OH; Jason M Cohen, Karen Kreider Gaunt, Keating Muething & Klekamp - 1, Cincinnati, OH.

For Olaes Enterprises Inc, doing business as ODM, Defendant: William Henry Blessing, Cincinnati, OH; Darren James Quinn, Del Mar, CA.

Sandra S. Beckwith, Chief Judge, United States District Court.

ORDER

This matter is before the Court on Defendant Olaes Enterprises, Inc.'s motion to dismiss, transfer or stay (Doc. No. 9). For the reasons set forth below, Defendant's motion to dismiss is GRANTED IN PART AND DENIED IN PART; Defendant's motion to transfer is MOOT; Defendant's motion to stay is MOOT.

I. *Background*

On January 24, 2005, Plaintiff Ripple Junction Design Co. ("Ripple Junction") filed a complaint asserting federal claims of trademark and copyright infringement against Defendant Olaes Enterprises, Inc. ("ODM"). The complaint also asserts a claim against ODM under the Lanham Act for false designation of origination and a state common law claim for unfair competition. Ripple Junction's claims relate to the following marks: "MY WIENER" "MY WIENER (with the image of a profile of a **Dachshund**)," and "I [SEE SYMBOL IN ORIGINAL] WIENER (with the image of a profile of a **Dachshund**)." Complaint P4. Ripple Junction has filed both trademark and copyright applications, but to date no action has been taken. *See id.; id.* P6. The complaint alleges that ODM has infringed its trademarks and copyrights by selling t-shirts that sometimes bear an image of a **Dachshund** and with the sayings "My Wiener is Happy," "My Wiener Likes You," or "Balanced Wiener." *Id.* P12.

The complaint discloses that Ripple Junction sent a cease and desist letter to ODM in September 2004, but an exchange of correspondence between the parties did not resolve the dispute. *Id.* PP12-16. Instead, in December 2004, ODM filed a complaint for a declaratory judgment of non-infringement against Ripple Junction in the United States District Court for the Southern District of California. However, Judge Benitez recently dismissed ODM's case in California as not being appropriate for declaratory relief on the grounds ODM was using its declaratory judgment as a means of forum shopping. Additionally, Judge Benitez ruled that the first-to-file rule did not apply because ODM was forum shopping. *See* Doc. No. 18.

On February 18, 2005, ODM filed a motion to dismiss, transfer, or stay this case. In its motion, ODM argued that this Court should stay this case or transfer it to the Southern District of California under the first-to-file rule. However, Judge Benitez's decision that the first-to-file rule does not apply and dismissing ODM's declaratory judgment action moots this aspect of ODM's motion. Alternatively, ODM argues that the Court should dismiss Ripple Junction's claims pursuant to Rule 12(b)(6) of the Federal Rules of Civil Procedure. ODM argues that the complaint insufficiently states a claim for trademark infringement because it fails to allege the exact word or graphic designations it claims as a trademark. ODM also argues that "wiener" cannot be registered as a trademark because it is a generic or common descriptive term. ODM moves to dismiss Ripple Junction's copyright infringement claims because, although it has filed applications for registration with the PTO, its applications have not yet been approved. Finally, ODM moves to dismiss Ripple Junction's claim for injunctive relief, which is pled as a separate cause of action, because injunctive relief is not a substantive cause of action.

II. *Rule 12(b)(6) Standard of Review*

A motion to dismiss pursuant to Rule 12(b)(6) operates to test the sufficiency of the complaint. In its consideration of a motion to dismiss under Rule 12(b)(6), the court is required to construe the complaint in the light most favorable to the Plaintiff and accept all well-pleaded factual allegations in the complaint as true. *Scheuer v. Rhodes,* 416 U.S. 232, 236, 94 S. Ct. 1683, 40 L. Ed. 2d 90 (1974) and *Roth Steel Products v. Sharon Steel Corp.,* 705 F.2d 134, 155 (6th Cir. 1983). A court, however, will not accept conclusions of law or unwarranted inferences which are presented as factual allegations. *Blackburn v. Fisk University,* 443 F.2d 121, 124 (6th Cir. 1974). A court will, though, accept all reasonable inferences that might be drawn from the complaint. *Fitzke v. Shappell,* 468 F.2d 1072, 1076-77 n.6 (6th Cir. 1972).

When considering the sufficiency of a complaint pursuant to a Rule 12(b)(6) motion, this Court recognizes that "a complaint should not be dismissed for failure to state a claim unless it appears beyond doubt that the Plaintiff can prove no set of facts in support of his claim which would entitle him to relief." *Conley v. Gibson,* 355 U.S. 41, 45-6, 78 S. Ct. 99, 2 L. Ed. 2d 80 (1957).

III. *Analysis*

A. *Trademark Infringement*

In order to prevail on a claim for trademark infringement, the plaintiff must establish: 1) ownership of a specific service mark in connection with specific services; 2) continuous use of the service mark; 3) establishment of secondary meaning if the mark is descriptive; and 4) a likelihood of confusion amongst consumers due to the contemporaneous use of the parties' service marks in connection with the parties' respective services. *Homeowners Group, Inc. v. Home Mktg Spec., Inc.,* 931 F.2d 1100, 1105 (6th Cir. 1991).

Contrary to ODM's motion, Ripple Junction's trademark infringement complaint satisfies each of these elements. The complaint alleges that Ripple Junction is the owner of the copyrights using "WIENER" and the image of a **Dachshund** in connection with selling clothing and novelty goods. Complaint P8. The complaint further alleges that Ripple Junction has been using these marks since August of 2003. *Id.* P5. The complaint alleges that customers will likely be confused by ODM's use of similar marks. Complaint PP22-23. Although ODM argues that "WIENER" is merely a generic or descriptive term, the complaint alleges that its marks are famous and "enable consumers to rely upon the WIENER name and **Dachshund** dog logo when purchasing clothing and/or novelty goods." Complaint PP10, 11. This last contention is sufficient to allege that Ripple Junction's trademarks have acquired secondary meaning. *See Champions Golf Club, Inc. v. The Champions Golf Club, Inc.,* 78 F.3d 1111, 1117 (6th Cir. 1996) ("To acquire a secondary meaning in the minds of the buying public, an article of merchandise when shown to a prospective customer must prompt the affirmation, 'That is the article I want because I know its source,' and not the negative inquiry as to 'Who makes that article?'"). Therefore, the complaint meets all of the requirements to state a claim for trademark infringement. Finally, the Court notes that Ripple Junction's marks are entitled to protection under the Lanham Act even if they are unregistered. *Two Pesos, Inc. v. Taco Cabana, Inc.,* 505 U.S. 763, 767-68, 112 S. Ct. 2753, 120 L. Ed. 2d 615 (1992).

Accordingly, ODM's motion to dismiss Ripple Junction's Lanham Act trademark infringement claims is not well-taken and is DENIED.

B. *Copyright Infringement*

ODM moves to dismiss Ripple Junction's claims for copyright infringement because the Copyright Office has not approved its applications for copyrights. Ripple Junction argues that the filing of its applications with the Copyright Office is sufficient to confer standing to sue ODM for copyright infringement. It is well-established that registration is a prerequisite to filing suit for copyright infringement. *Murray Hill Pub., Inc. v. ABC Comm., Inc.*, 264 F.3d 622, 630 (6th Cir. 2001). In this case, the complaint demonstrates that Ripple Junction has filed applications to register its copyrights, but that the Copyright Office has taken no action on its applications. The question presented is whether a plaintiff satisfies the condition precedent by merely filing an application for registration or whether the Copyright Office must approve the application and issue a certificate of registration before the plaintiff can maintain a lawsuit for copyright infringement.

There is a split of authority on whether an application for registration satisfies the condition precedent. *See Apple Barrel Prod., Inc. v. Beard*, 730 F.2d 384, 386 (5th Cir. 1984) (in order to establish standing, plaintiff only need show payment of fee, deposit of work in question, and receipt by the Copyright Office of the registration application); *Iconbazaar, L.L.C. v. America Online, Inc.*, 308 F. Supp.2d 630, 633 (M.D.N.C. 2004) (same) (collecting cases identifying split of authority); *La Resolana Architects, PA v. Clay Realtors Angel Fire*, 416 F.3d 1195, 1200-01 (10th Cir. 2005) ("Only upon registration or refusal to register is a copyright holder entitled to sue for copyright infringement under § 411."); *Marshall & Swift v. BS & A Software*, 871 F. Supp. 952, 957-58 (W.D.Mich. 1994) (application for copyright registration insufficient to satisfy condition precedent; plaintiff must obtain certificate of registration before filing suit); *Loree Rodkin Mgmt. Corp. v. Ross-Simons, Inc.*, 315 F. Supp. 2d 1053, 1054-56 (C.D.Cal. 2004) (same).

The Sixth Circuit has not specifically addressed whether the registrant's application for a copyright satisfies the condition precedent necessary to filing an action for copyright infringement. As a matter of straightforward statutory construction, this Court agrees with those courts, in particular the court in *Rodkin Mmgt.*, who have decided that a district court does not have subject matter jurisdiction over a copyright infringement action until the Copyright Office issues a certificate of registration to the applicant, or the Copyright Office refuses the application. In other words, merely filing an application for registration is insufficient to satisfy the condition precedent to filing an infringement suit.

Section 411(a) of the Copyright Act provides in relevant part:

Except for an action brought for a violation of the rights of the author under section 106A(a), and subject to the provisions of subsection (b), no action for infringement of the copyright in any United States work shall be instituted until preregistration or registration of the copyright claim has been made in accordance with this title. In any case, however, where the deposit, application, and fee required for registration have been delivered to the Copyright Office in proper form and registration has been refused, the applicant is entitled to institute an action for infringement if notice thereof, with a copy of the complaint, is served on the Register of Copyrights.

17 U.S.C. § 411(a). [1] This section makes clear that an infringement suit may not instituted until registration of the copyright is completed. In turn, § 410(a) states that:

When, after examination, the Register of Copyrights determines that, in accordance with the provisions of this title, the material deposited constitutes copyrightable subject matter and that the other legal and formal requirements of this title have been met, the Register shall register the claim and issue to the applicant a certificate of registration under the seal of the Copyright Office.

17 U.S.C. § 410(a). Section 410(a) shows that a claim is not registered until the Copyright Office determines that the material under submission is copyrightable and the other formal requirements of the Act have been met. Read together, § 411(a) and § 410(a) show that "registration" means that the Copyright Office has determined that the copyright claim has been approved and that an infringement suit may not be instituted until registration has been completed. Had Congress wished to authorize the filing of infringement suits upon an application to register a copyright it could have easily said so. The Court notes that § 409 is entitled "Application for Copyright Registration" and sets forth the information and materials the applicant is required to file with Copyright Office to obtain registration. Thus, Congress clearly wanted to differentiate the application process from the registration process.

1 "Preregistration" suggests an application process. "Preregistration," however, is a term of art under the Copyright Act which applies to a class of works determined by the Register of Copyrights to have a history of infringement prior to authorized commercial distribution. 17 U.S.C. §

408(f). Although other classes of works may be eligible for preregistration, it appears that Congress enacted the preregistration provisions to protect producers of motion pictures and sound recordings from pre-distribution infringement. Preregistration is not a substitute for registration, however, and Ripple Junction does not otherwise contend that the preregistration provisions apply here. *See generally* 70 Fed. Reg. 42286-01 (July 22, 2005).

The Court also notes that § 411(a) provides that an infringement suit may be initiated after the application for registration is refused. If a party could file an infringement suit merely upon filing his application for registration, there would be no need to include a provision stating that a suit can be maintained after the application is refused. A party could simply file suit when he filed his application for registration and it would make no difference whether the application was granted or refused in terms of satisfying the condition precedent. The Court must interpret a statute to give effect to each clause, sentence, and word so that none is rendered superfluous or surplusage. *United States v. Perry*, 360 F.3d 519, 537 (6th Cir. 2004). An interpretation of § 411(a) that allows filing an infringement suit upon application for registration would read out of the statute the provision that a suit can be filed after the application is refused. Finally, the Court observes that by specifically stating that an infringement suit may be instituted after registration is completed, or the application is refused, but omitting that suit can be instituted upon application for registration, Congress intended for the Copyright Office to have the first opportunity to review the merits of the claimed copyright.

For the reasons stated, the Court concludes that the condition precedent to filing an infringement suit established by § 411(a) is not satisfied by the filing of an application for registration. Rather, in order to bring an infringement action on a copyright, the Copyright Office must have either registered the copyright or refused the application. In this case, the complaint demonstrates that Ripple Junction has filed applications to register its copyrights, but they have not been registered by the Copyright Office. Nor has the Copyright Office refused Ripple Junction's applications. Consequently, Ripple Junction has not met the condition precedent to filing an infringement suit and the Court does not have jurisdiction over its copyright infringement claims. Accordingly, ODM's motion to dismiss Ripple Junction's copyright infringement claims is well-taken and is GRANTED. Count Three of the complaint is DISMISSED WITHOUT PREJUDICE.

C. *Miscellaneous*

ODM moves to dismiss Ripple Junction's claim for injunctive relief because it is a form of relief rather than a cause of action. The Court notes and appreciates the technical accuracy of the distinction identified by ODM. Nevertheless, the Lanham Act authorizes a district court to award injunctive relief to the plaintiff. *Frisch's Restaurants, Inc. v. Elby's Big Boy of Steubenville, Inc.*, 670 F.2d 642, 647 (6th Cir. 1982). Dismissing Ripple Junction's claim for injunctive relief because it is captioned as a cause of action rather than a claim for relief elevates form over substance. Accordingly, ODM's motion to dismiss Ripple Junction's claim for injunctive relief is not well-taken and is DENIED.

Finally, ODM argues that Ripple Junction's unfair competition claims should be dismissed to the extent they coincide with rights provided under the Copyright Act. Ripple Junction responds that its unfair competition claims arise only under the Lanham Act, not under the Copyright Act. This argument overlooks, however, Count Five of the complaint, which states in pertinent part, "The acts complained of in Counts One through Four constitute unfair competition under the common law of the State of Ohio, and under the federal unfair competition laws. " Complaint P39.

The Court agrees with ODM that Ripple Junction's state law unfair competition claims are preempted to the extent they are based on ODM's alleged infringement of its copyrights. *See ATC Dist. Group, Inc. v. Whatever It Takes Trans. & Parts, Inc.*, 402 F.3d 700, 713-14 (6th Cir. 2005). Therefore, to that extent, ODM's motion to dismiss is well-taken and is GRANTED. On the other hand, state law unfair competition claims are not preempted by federal law and in fact parallel Lanham Act claims for trademark infringement and false designation of origin. *Interactive Prods. Corp. v. a2z Mobile Office Solutions, Inc.*, 326 F.3d 687, 694 (6th Cir. 2003). Therefore, to the extent Ripple Junction's common law unfair competition claims parallel the

Lanham Act, ODM's motion to dismiss is not well-taken and is DENIED.

Conclusion

In conclusion, ODM's motion to dismiss, transfer, or stay is GRANTED IN PART, DENIED IN PART, and MOOT IN PART. To the extent that ODM moves to transfer or stay this case under the first-to-file rule, the motion is MOOT. ODM's motion is well-taken and is GRANTED to the extent it seeks dismissal of Ripple Junction's federal copyright claims and state unfair competition claims which are based on copyright infringement. Ripple Junction's federal copyright claims are DISMISSED WITHOUT PREJUDICE. Ripple Junction's state law unfair competition claims based on copyright infringement are preempted, and therefore, are DISMISSED WITH PREJUDICE. ODM's motion to dismiss Ripple Junction's federal Lanham Act claims, parallel state law unfair competition claims, and claim for injunctive relief is not well-taken and is DENIED.

IT IS SO ORDERED

Date September 8, 2005

Sandra S. Beckwith, Chief Judge

United States District Court

**Embroidery Library, Inc.,
Plaintiff/Counterdefendant,
v.
Sublime Stitching, LLC, and Jenny
Hart, Defendants/Counterclaimants.**

Civil No. 09-2766 (JNE/AJB)
UNITED STATES DISTRICT COURT
FOR THE DISTRICT OF MINNESOTA
January 20, 2010

For Embroidery Library, Inc., a Minnesota Corporation, Plaintiff, Counter Defendant: Courtland C Merrill, Mary L Knoblauch, Richard T Ostlund, Anthony Ostlund Baer & Louwagie PA, Mpls, MN.

For Sublime Stitching, LLC, a Texas Limited Liability Company, Jenny Hart, an individual, Defendants, Counter Claimants: Karl E Robinson, Hellmuth & Johnson, PLLC, Eden Prairie, MN.

JOAN N. ERICKSEN, United States District Judge.

ORDER

This case is before the Court on the motion of Embroidery Library, Inc., to dismiss certain of Sublime Stitching, LLC, and Jenny Hart's counterclaims. For the reasons set forth below, the Court grants in part the motion and grants Sublime Stitching and Jenny Hart (collectively, Defendants) leave to amend their Counterclaim.

I. BACKGROUND

Embroidery Library is a Minnesota corporation that sells embroidery designs over the Internet. In May 2008, Embroidery Library began selling contemporary embroidery designs over the Internet through its Urban Threads website. Hart is the sole member of Sublime Stitching, a Texas limited liability company that sells embroidery designs over the Internet.

Embroidery Library filed suit against Defendants in state court asserting claims for defamation/libel per se, tortious interference with business relations, unfair competition, and violation of the Minnesota Deceptive Trade Practices Act (MDTPA), Minn. Stat. § 325D.44 (2008). After removing on the basis of diversity jurisdiction, Defendants answered and asserted counterclaims for copyright infringement under the Copyright Act, 17 U.S.C. §§ 101-1332 (2006); unfair competition and false advertising in violation of the Lanham Act, 15 U.S.C. §§ 1051-1141n (2006); common law unfair competition; violation of the MDTPA; and tortious interference with business relations.

With respect to their non-copyright counterclaims, Defendants allege that Embroidery Library, through statements made by one of its employees on its Urban Threads website, misrepresented Urban Threads as "an independent design ('indie') company that is not affiliated with any other company, including [Embroidery Library]." Defendants also allege that certain statements misrepresent Urban Threads as the "first and/or only one in the field of contemporary, alternative embroidery patterns."

Instead of answering the Counterclaim, Embroidery Library filed a motion to dismiss. Specifically, Embroidery Library seeks dismissal of the non-copyright counterclaims and portions of the copyright counterclaim.

II. DISCUSSION

The parties agree that Defendants' averments of misrepresentation are analyzed under Rule 9(b) of the Federal Rules of Civil Procedure, which requires particularity in pleading. To satisfy Rule 9(b), the pleading "must specifically allege the 'circumstances constituting fraud,' including 'such matters as the time, place and contents of false representations, as well as the identity of the person making the misrepresentation and what was obtained or given up thereby.'" *Abels v. Farmers Commodities Corp.*, 259 F.3d 910, 920 (8th Cir. 2001) (citation omitted). Rule 9(b) must be interpreted "in harmony with the principles of notice pleading." *Id.*

Under the notice pleading standard set forth in Rule 8, a complaint need not contain "detailed factual allegations," but more is required than "an unadorned, the-defendant-unlawfully-harmed-me accusation." *Ashcroft v. Iqbal,* 129 S. Ct. 1937, 1949, 173 L. Ed. 2d 868 (2009). "A pleading that offers 'labels and conclusions' or 'a formulaic recitation of the elements of a cause of action will not do.' Nor does a complaint suffice if it tenders 'naked assertion[s]' devoid of 'further factual enhancement.'" *Id.* (quoting *Bell Atl. Corp. v. Twombly,* 550 U.S. 544, 555, 127 S. Ct. 1955, 167 L. Ed. 2d 929 (2007) (citation omitted)). Only a complaint that states a plausible claim for relief survives a motion to dismiss. *Id.* at 1949-50.

A. Copyright claim

Embroidery Library contends that Defendants cannot recover statutory damages and attorney fees for six of the seven asserted copyrights. The Copyright Act provides that "[n]o award of statutory damages or of attorney's fees . . . shall be made for . . . any infringement of copyright commenced after first publication of the work and before the effective date of its registration, unless such registration is made within three months after the first publication of the work." 17 U.S.C. § 412(2).

In April 2009, Sublime Stitching filed a lawsuit in the Western District of Texas alleging that Embroidery Library infringed the same copyrights Defendants assert here. [1] Consequently, the date the alleged infringement of those copyrights began is no later than April 2009. The copyright registrations attached to Defendants' Counterclaim indicate that six of the seven copyrights were registered in May 2009, after the alleged infringement began and more than three months after the dates of first publication of the works. [2] Accordingly, § 412(2) precludes Defendants from recovering statutory damages or attorney fees for the alleged infringement of those six copyrights. [3] The Court dismisses Defendants' counterclaim for copyright infringement insofar as it seeks statutory damages and attorney fees for infringement of those six copyrights.

---

1 Sublime Stitching did not serve the summons and complaint on Embroidery Library, and dismissed the Texas lawsuit without prejudice on August 27, 2009.

2 The six works are "Spaced Out," "Monkey Love," "Darling **Dachshunds**," "Vital Organs," "Sexy Librarians and Secretaries," and "Winterland" embroidery pattern sheets. Their registrations indicate that they were first published in February 2003, April 2005, February 2003, July 2008, July 2008, and November 2005, respectively.

3 Defendants do not dispute the dates of first publication, registration, or infringement of these six works, instead contending that Embroidery Library's motion is premature because damages are determined at the end of an action. Defendants cite no authority indicating that dismissal based on § 412(2) is improper on a motion to dismiss, and courts have granted Rule 12(b)(6) motions under such circumstances. *See, e.g., Ez-Tixz, Inc. v. Hit-Tix, Inc.,* 919 F. Supp. 728, 736 (S.D.N.Y. 1996) (gathering cases).

B. Lanham Act claims

Defendants assert counterclaims under section 43(a) of the Lanham Act, which provides in relevant part:

> (1) Any person who, *on or in connection with any goods or services,* or any container for goods, uses in commerce any word, term, name, symbol, or device, or any combination thereof, or any false designation of origin, false or misleading description of fact, or false or misleading representation of fact, which--
>
> > (A) is likely to cause confusion, or to cause mistake, or to deceive as to the affiliation, connection, or association of such person with another person, or as to the origin, sponsorship, or approval of his or her goods, services, or commercial activities by another person, or
> >
> > (B) in commercial advertising or promotion, misrepresents the nature, characteristics, qualities, or geographic origin of his or her or another person's *goods, services, or commercial activities,* shall be liable in a civil action by any person who believes that he or she is or is likely to be damaged by such act.

15 U.S.C. § 1125(a)(1) (2006) (emphases added).

Embroidery Library argues that statements about Urban Threads' corporate status are not "in connection with" goods or services as required by § 1125(a)(1). This argument conflates the "in connection with" requirement of § 1125(a)(1) with the "goods, services, or commercial activities" requirement of § 1125(a)(1)(B), and reads the "commercial activities" language out of § 1125(a)(1)(B). *See Windsor on the River Assoc., Ltd. v. Balcor Real Estate Fin., Inc.,* 7 F.3d 127, 130 (8th Cir. 1993) ("Accordingly, 'we must avoid statutory interpretation that renders any section superfluous and does not give effect to all of the words used by Congress.'" (quoting *In re Oxborrow,* 913 F.2d 751, 754 (9th Cir. 1990))). Moreover, several of the cases Embroidery Library cites to support this argument are unpersuasive because they involve an earlier version of the Lanham Act which required the false representation to be affixed to the defendant's goods and did not prohibit misrepresentation of another's "commercial activities." *See Proctor & Gamble v. Haugen,* 222 F.3d 1262, 1268, 1271-72 (10th Cir. 2000) ("However, the [1988 Amendments to the Lanham Act] also overruled aspects of existing law, most significantly by covering trade libel or product disparagement (i.e., misrepresentations about the plaintiff's goods and services) and by permitting actions based on misrepresentations about commercial activities as well as goods and services."). The other cited cases were not decided based on the "in connection with" requirement or are neither binding authority nor persuasive. The Court concludes that under a plain reading of § 1125(a)(1), the alleged statements, which were made on the Urban Threads website for selling embroidery patterns, were "in connection with" goods, namely, embroidery patterns.

Embroidery Library also maintains that the alleged misrepresentations do not relate to Urban Threads' "commercial activities" within the meaning of § 1125(a)(1)(B). Defendants respond that Urban Threads' affiliation with Embroidery Library constitutes a "commercial activity" and, despite their assertion of Lanham Act counterclaims only under § 1125(a)(1)(B), contend that the alleged misrepresentations state a claim under § 1125(a)(1)(A) (prohibiting statements likely to cause confusion, mistake, or deception as to the affiliation, connection, or association of a person with another person). In addition, Defendants seek leave to amend their Counterclaim.

The Court questions whether Urban Threads' affiliation with Embroidery Library constitutes a "commercial activity" within the meaning of the Lanham Act. *See Interfood Holding, B.V. v. Rice,* 607 F. Supp. 2d 1059, 1061-63 (E.D. Mo. 2009) ("Allegedly false statements such as these, about the founding of, officers of, and control of various corporate entities, are not the sorts of statements about goods, services, or even commercial activities which are within the scope of the Lanham Act's prohibition."). However, the Court declines to decide this issue at this time because, for the reasons stated below, the Court grants Defendants leave to amend their Counterclaim.

Embroidery Library filed its Complaint and Motion to Dismiss Counterclaims before December 1, 2009, which is the effective date of the 2009 amendments to the Federal Rules of Civil Procedure. The 2009 amendments shall "govern in all proceedings thereafter commenced and, insofar as just and practicable, all proceedings then pending." Under the unique facts and circumstances of this case, the Court concludes that amendment of Defendants' Counterclaim is governed by the previous Rule 15, which permitted amendment of a pleading once as a matter of course before the party is served with a responsive pleading. *See* Fed. R. Civ. P. 15 cmt. to 2009 amendments ("Former Rule 15(a) addressed amendment of a pleading to which a responsive pleading is required by distinguishing between the means used to challenge the pleading. . . . Serving a motion attacking the pleading did not terminate the right to amend, because a motion is not a 'pleading' as defined in Rule 7."). Since Embroidery Library filed a motion to dismiss rather than a responsive pleading, Defendants may amend their Counterclaim once as a matter of course. [4] *See id.* The Scheduling Order in this matter sets a deadline for amendment of the pleadings of February 1, 2010. Consequently, Defendants shall file and serve an Amended Counterclaim on or before February 1, 2010. Should Defendants fail to do so, the Court will consider the remainder of Embroidery Library's motion after that date. [5]

[4] Under the 2009 amendments, if the pleading is one to which a responsive pleading is required, Rule 15 permits amendment of the pleading once as a matter of course "21 days after service of a responsive pleading or 21 days

after service of a motion under Rule 12(b), (e), or (f), whichever is earlier."
Fed. R. Civ. P. 15(a)(1)(B).

5 Embroidery Library also contends that dismissal of the Lanham Act
counterclaims is warranted because they contain nothing more than
conclusory allegations and the alleged statements are puffery. In addition,
Embroidery Library maintains that dismissal of the Lanham Act
counterclaims requires dismissal of the other non-copyright counterclaims.
In light of the Court's decision to grant Defendants leave to amend their
Counterclaim, the Court does not reach these arguments.

III. CONCLUSION

Based on the files, records, and proceedings herein, and for the
reasons stated above, IT IS ORDERED THAT:

> 1. Embroidery Library's Motion to Dismiss Counterclaims [Docket
> No. 5] is GRANTED insofar as it seeks dismissal of Defendants'
> counterclaim for statutory damages and attorney fees for
> infringement of Sublime Stitching's copyright in its "Spaced Out,"
> "Monkey Love," "Darling Dachshunds," "Vital
> Organs," "Sexy Librarians and Secretaries," and "Winterland"
> embroidery pattern sheets.

> 2. Defendants shall file and serve an Amended Counterclaim on or
> before February 1, 2010.

Dated: January 20, 2010

/s/ Joan N. Ericksen

JOAN N. ERICKSEN

United States District Judge

5
Of dachsunds and spaniels

In Re Schilling is a case that relates to the rejection of a design patent for a drinking glass design. In dissent, Judge Rich would reverse that rejection, writing that the new cups and the prior art:

> look no more alike than a dachshund looks like a spaniel -
> though both are dogs and have heads, tails, four feet, fur,
> and facial features, as well as certain similar lines.

In *Tiara Engle*, the the Plaintiffs argument requires the court to parse the meaning of the word "including" in a statute about medical examinations. Judge Mollway explains:

> Plaintiffs' position is that the word "including" introduces
> subsets ... the same way that one could refer to "dogs,
> including collies, cocker spaniels, and dachshunds."
> "Including," by Plaintiffs' reading, means "having as
> members," with each member being a full-fledged ... as a
> collie is, by itself, a dog.

In re Schilling,
421 F.2d 747 (C.C.P.A., 1970)

Engle v. Liberty Mut. Fire Ins. Co.,
402 F. Supp. 2d 1157 (D.HI 2005)

IN RE PAUL K. SCHILLING

No. 8250
United States Court of
Customs and Patent Appeals
421 F.2d 747
February 26, 1970

Charles O'Connell, attorney of record, for appellant.

Joseph Schimmel for the Commissioner of Patents. *Raymond E. Martin,* of counsel.

Before RICH, ALMOND, BALDWIN, LANE, Associate Judges, and MCMANUS, Judge, sitting by designation.

ALMOND, Judge, delivered the opinion of the court:

This appeal is from the decision of the Patent Office Board of Appeals, adhered to on reconsideration, affirming the rejection of appellant's application [1] for a design patent on a tumbler.

1 Serial No. D85,502 filed May 28, 1965.

The claim reads: "The ornamental design for a Tumbler, as shown." The drawing shows the following configuration:

[Graphic omitted. See illustration in original.]

Appellant tells us that his tumbler is primarily a plastic receptacle designed as a disposable drinking glass, originally designed for air line use. An important feature, appellant says, is superior stackability.

The references relied on below are:

Harrison	2,982,440	May 2, 1961

Plastics, March 1955, page 69, cup in Fig. 3.

Harrison discloses a plastic food container which may be shipped in stacked or nested relation. Prior to placing material in the container for canning, the container bottom is concave upward. At the end of the canning, as the container cools inward pressure results in moving the bottom upward, resulting in an article as shown in Fig. 2 below.

[Graphic omitted. See illustration in original.]

Plastics discloses a plastic cup having a handle. The design details are apparent from Fig. 3 of the reference:

[Graphic omitted. See illustration in original.]

The examiner rejected the claim as unpatentable over Harrison in view of Plastics under 35 USC 103. It was his view that it would be obvious to a worker of ordinary skill in the art to form the container body of Harrison "in the shorter height and curved sidewalls configuration suggested by the body of the 'Plastics' cup." Such modification, he thought, would result in an appearance over which the claimed design presented no patentable or unobvious ornamental distinction.

In affirming, the board made the following analysis:

Both appellant's tumbler and the plastic container disclosed in Harrison, the primary reference, have a relatively large diameter upper end and a substantially smaller diameter lower end. In vertical contour the walls of appellant's tumbler are constantly curved, the major upper portion of the walls being convexly curved and the lower end portion being slightly concavely curved, whereas in Harrison the walls in vertical contour are straight from top to bottom. Both appellant's tumbler and the Harrison container * * * have similarly upwardly domed bottom walls.

The Plastics publication discloses * * * a plastic cup, which has a relatively large diameter upper end and a substantially smaller lower end. In vertical contour the walls of the cup in the Plastics publication are curved similarly to the walls of appellant's tumbler.

Our comparison of appellant's tumbler with the container disclosed in the Harrison patent discloses that appellant's tumbler differs in appearance from the Harrison container in the curved contour of the side walls. However, since the Plastics publication discloses a cup with side walls having a curved contour similar to the contour of the side walls of appellant's tumbler, it is our opinion that to provide the container in Harrison with side walls having a curved contour such as disclosed in the cup in the Plastics publication would involve merely the obvious combination of old design shapes of containers brigning about the expected appearance and, hence, unpatentable over the cited references. In re Garbo, 48 CCPA 845; * * * 287 F.2d 192; 129 USPQ 72 * * *.

Acknowledging that there is similarity "between the structures and the references and the design which has been developed by the applicant" and that the "previous devices could be used for the same" purpose, appellant argues that the previous devices are not of the same design, nor, it is contended, is "the idea of combining a frustoconical container with a rounded bodied cup * * * within the usual province of the designer." Specifically, appellant contends that his tumbler has a convex outer surface which curves but slightly, with a relatively large radius of curvature and a lower portion reversely curved on a shorter radius but with a continuous curve rather than a small radius fillet between the tumbler portions. In the Plastics structure, appellant argues, the body of the cup curves inwardly to practically the top of the foot portion of the cup, and the rim extends almost cylindrically to its bottom edge, with a small radius of curvature or fillet connecting the rounded body of the cup to the foot portion. No one looking at the structure and the tapered glass of Harrison, it is alleged, would devise appellant's particular form of outline.

Appellant further contends that the board erred in failing to follow In re Laverne, 53 CCPA 1158, 356 F.2d 1003, 148 USPQ 674 (1966). In that case, this court noted the practical difficulty of ascertaining, in the field of design, who under 35 USC 103 is a "person having ordinary skill in the art." There the court felt that "what we have to do is to determine obviousness to the ordinary intelligent man. The test is inherently a visual test, for the design is nothing more than appearance, and the appearance is that of the article as a whole." The court then found that the claimed design had a "distinctly different appearance" from the design of the single prior art reference relied upon for a rejection under 35 USC 103.

[1] We are unable to perceive that the board erred in the manner alleged. The board's decision set forth an analysis in support of the opinion that the design in question is obvious. Nothing thus appears

to be contrary to the view expressed in Laverne, supra. Nor are we persuaded by appellant's additional allegation of commercial success and considerable argument of functional superiority of his design. As noted by the examiner, no evidence of commercial success has been presented in support of that allegation. Nor does the alleged superior stackability of the tumbler lend patentable weight to the design. In In re Garbo, 48 CCPA 845, 287 F.2d 192, 129 USPQ 72 (1961), it is stated:

* * * [A] design may embody functional features and still be patentable, but in order to attain this legal status * * *, the design must have an unobvious appearance distinct from that dictated solely by functional considerations.

Having carefully considered the references and appellant's arguments, we find ourselves in agreement with the board's analysis, supra.Appellant has not presented us with any detailed analysis of the differences between the claimed design and the design of the references that would lead us to conclude that the net result of such differences add up to an appearance "distinctly different" from the appearance of Harrison as modified by Plastics. We think that the principle stated in In re Lamb, 48 CCPA 817, 286 F.2d 610, 128 USPQ 539 (1961), has application to the situation here presented:

When considering the patentability of a design it is the appearance as a whole which must be considered, and the mere fact that there are differences over the prior art structures is not alone sufficient to justify a holding that the design is patentable.

The decision of the board is, therefore, affirmed.

Judges Baldwin and McManus concur in the result.

DISSENT

RICH, Judge, dissenting.

The majority decision is, in my opinion, wrong since it fails to follow the reasoning of the unanimous opinion in In re Laverne, 53 CCPA 1158, 356 F.2d 1003, 148 USPQ 674 (1966), while acknowledging it as a viable precedent.

The references here are not half as good as was the single reference in Laverne. The majority opinion makes it perfectly clear by illustrations how far afield the references here are, when applying a test of whether a claimed design looks like a prior art design to the ordinary intelligent man, the test we there found appropriate, under 35 USC 103, in design cases. Schilling's Fig. 2 compared with Harrison's Fig. 2, both reproduced in the opinion, speak louder than a thousand words. There is no resemblance in overall, design-as-a-whole appearance. Similarly, applicant's tumbler looks no more like the "Plastics" tea or coffee cup than most old-fashioned glasses (in the contemporary beverage sense) look like most coffee cups. They look no more alike than a **dachshund** looks like a spaniel - though both are dogs and have heads, tails, four feet, fur, and facial features, as well as certain similar lines.

What the examiner here was doing was hindsight redesigning, or new designing, to reconstruct Schilling's design out of elements he could find in prior art objects, after analyzing appellant's design. The board did likewise. If this is a permissible ground of rejection, then we had better forget about trying to make design patents work as an incentive to new design, as the statute intended, and get on with the enactment of a better law. [1] But while we have the design patent law we should try to make it serve its intended purpose, a purpose Congress has had in mind since it first legislated on designs in 1842.

1 See "Report of the President's Patent Commission" (1966), Recommendation IV-1, "All provisions in the patent statute for design patents shal be deleted, and another form of protection provided."

The Garbo case, cited in the board's opinion and by the majority, has no relevance here, as can be seen from the paragraph quoted therefrom by the majority. The opinion went off on functionality as well as obviousness. There was nothing "ornamental" about the so-called design in that case, though he found that issue was not before us. It was an arrangement of driver training units and a cinema screen and projector in a trailer, a functionally obvious arrangement.

There was no particular need for appellant here to present us with any "detailed analysis of the differences between the claimed design and the design of the references." They are more apparent from mere observation - and much more striking - than were the differences in Laverne. The trouble here is that the design has been talked to death. Apparently no one is willing to contemplate them. But ornamental designs are entirely a matter of appearance and cannot be verbalized.I fail to see how more verbalization by the appellant could have furthered his cause.

I find here, beyond question, even more clearly than in Laverne, the "distinctly different appearance" we there referred to. I agree with In re Lamb but find the majority has disregarded the "appearance as a whole which must be considered." The Lamb case was distinguished in Laverne where it was pointed out that the same design was involved as was shown in the reference, merely modified. It was a design for a knife handle having finger-grip depressions. The application showed it for a steak knife. The reference was Lamb's own patent on the same generic handle design for a carving knife, which he had merely scaled down. The case has no relevance as a precedent. The quotation from its opinion is definitely out of context.

See the analysis of Laverne in IDEA, Vol. 13, No. 2 (Fall 1969), p. 495.

I would reverse.

TIARA ENGLE and
PORTNER ORTHOPEDIC REHABILITATION,
INCORPORATED, Plaintiffs,
vs.
LIBERTY MUTUAL FIRE
INSURANCE COMPANY, et al.,
Defendants.

Civ. No. 04-00256 SOM/BMK
UNITED STATES DISTRICT COURT FOR
THE DISTRICT OF HAWAII
402 F. Supp. 2d 1157
July 11, 2005

For Plaintiffs: Harvey M. Demetrakopoulos, argued Roy K.S. Chang, appeared, but did not argue Shim & Chang, Honolulu, HI.

For Defendants: R. John Seibert, argued McCorriston Miller Mukai MacKinnon LLP, Honolulu, HI.

SUSAN OKI MOLLWAY, UNITED STATES DISTRICT JUDGE.

ORDER GRANTING DEFENDANT LIBERTY MUTUAL FIRE INSURANCE COMPANY'S MOTION FOR PARTIAL JUDGMENT ON THE PLEADINGS; ORDER GRANTING LIBERTY MUTUAL'S MOTION FOR PARTIAL SUMMARY JUDGMENT

I. *INTRODUCTION.*

What does it mean to be included? Much of this insurance coverage dispute turns on how one dissects the unassuming word "including" as it is used in a Hawaii insurance statute. Plaintiffs, an insured and her treatment provider, say the word "including" introduces examples, so that a reference to an independent medical examination ("IME") as "including" a record review means that a record review is a kind of IME. Defendant Liberty Mutual Fire Insurance Company, by contrast, says that "including" introduces component parts, so that the record review is included in the IME, but is not itself an IME.

This exercise in lexicography is the subject of a motion for partial summary judgment brought by Liberty Mutual and of a counter-motion brought by Plaintiffs Tiara Engle and Portner Orthopedic Rehabilitation, Incorporated. The court grants Liberty Mutual's motion for partial summary judgment and denies Plaintiffs' counter-motion.

Liberty Mutual also moves for judgment on the pleadings as to certain other claims. That motion is unopposed and is granted.

II. BACKGROUND.

On May 2, 2003, Engle was a passenger in a car that was involved in an accident. The car was insured by Liberty Mutual, and Engle sought benefits under the "Personal Injury Protection" provisions of Liberty Mutual's policy. Liberty Mutual paid Engle's bills for emergency room treatment on the day of the accident and for later massage and chiropractic treatment at Portner Orthopedic through August 2003.

On November 10, 2003, Liberty Mutual asked Dr. Clifford Lau, an orthopedist, to perform a "record review" of Engle's medical condition and to opine on, among other things, whether Engle required future treatment. In retaining Dr. Lau, Liberty Mutual cautioned Dr. Lau that his charges for completing the assignment could not exceed the fee limits for IMEs set forth in Haw. Rev. Stat. § 431:10C-308.5(b).

Based on his review of Engle's medical records, Dr. Lau opined that further treatment was not necessary. Liberty Mutual then issued a "Denial of Claim" letter to Engle, stating that Liberty Mutual would no longer pay for Engle's treatments. Engle continued to receive treatments, and Portner continued to bill Liberty Mutual for these treatments.

On March 8, 2004, Plaintiffs filed suit in the First Circuit Court of the State of Hawaii. Their Complaint alleged tortious breach of contract, as well as violations of Haw. Rev. Stat. §§ 431:13-103(a)(11), 431:10C-308.5(b), and Haw. Rev. Stat. Ch. 480. Plaintiffs sought general damages, special damages, "other economic and non-economic damages," punitive damages, treble damages, prejudgment interest, costs, and reasonable attorney's fees.

On April 21, 2004, Liberty Mutual removed that case to this court. In its Notice of Removal, Liberty Mutual stated that "the amount in controversy is greater than $ 75,000.00, exclusive of interest and costs."

III. *STANDARD OF REVIEW.*

Rule 12(c) of the Federal Rules of Civil Procedure states:

> After the pleadings are closed but within such time as not to delay the trial, any party may move for judgment on the pleadings. If, on a motion for judgment on the pleadings, matters outside the pleadings are presented to and not excluded by the court, the motion shall be treated as one for summary judgment and disposed of as provided in Rule 56, and all parties shall be given reasonable opportunity to present all material made pertinent to such a motion by Rule 56.

The standard governing a Rule 12(c) motion for judgment on the pleadings is essentially the same as that governing a Rule 12(b)(6) motion. The motion will not be granted if, accepting as true all material allegations contained in the nonmoving party's pleadings, the moving party is entitled to judgment as a matter of law. *Lake Tahoe Watercraft Recreation Ass'n v. Tahoe Reg'l Planning Agency*, 24 F. Supp. 2d 1062, 1066 (E.D Cal. 1998). For a Rule 12(c) motion, the allegations of the nonmoving party must be accepted as true, while the allegations of the moving party that have been denied are assumed to be false. *Hal Roach Studios, Inc. v. Richard Feiner & Co., Inc.*, 896 F.2d 1542, 1550 (9th Cir. 1989). Judgment on the pleadings is proper when the moving party clearly establishes on the face of the pleadings that no material issue of fact remains to be resolved and that it is entitled to judgment as a matter of law. *Id.* However, judgment on the pleadings is improper when the district court goes beyond the pleadings to resolve an issue; such a proceeding must properly be treated as a motion for summary judgment. *Id.*

Summary judgment shall be granted when

> the pleadings, depositions, answers to interrogatories and admissions on file, together with the affidavits, if any, show that there is no genuine issue as to any material fact and that the moving party is entitled to a judgment as a matter of law.

Fed. R. Civ. P. 56(c); *see also Addisu v. Fred Meyer, Inc.*, 198 F.3d 1130, 1134 (9th Cir. 2000). One of the principal purposes of summary judgment is to identify and dispose of factually unsupported claims and defenses. *Celotex Corp. v. Catrett*, 477 U.S. 317, 323-24, 106 S. Ct. 2548, 91 L. Ed. 2d 265 (1986).

Summary judgment must be granted against a party who fails to demonstrate facts to establish what will be an essential element at trial. *Id.* at 322. The burden initially lies with the moving party to identify for the court "the portions of the materials on file that it believes demonstrate the absence of any genuine issue of material fact. " *T.W. Elec. Serv., Inc. v. Pac. Elec. Contractors Ass'n*, 809 F.2d 626, 630 (9th Cir. 1987) (citing *Celotex Corp.*, 477 U.S. at 323). "When the moving party has carried its burden under Rule 56(c), its opponent must do more than simply show that there is some metaphysical doubt as to the material facts." *Matsushita Elec. Indus. Co., Ltd. v. Zenith Radio Corp.*, 475 U.S. 574, 586, 106 S. Ct. 1348, 89 L. Ed. 2d 538 (1986) (footnote omitted). The nonmoving party may not rely on the mere allegations in the pleadings and instead must set forth "specific facts showing that there is a genuine issue for trial." *Id.* At least some "'significant probative evidence tending to support the complaint'" must be produced. *Summers v. A. Teichert & Son, Inc.*, 127 F.3d 1150, 1152 (9th Cir. 1997) (quoting *Anderson v. Liberty Lobby, Inc.*, 477 U.S. 242, 252, 106 S. Ct. 2505, 91 L. Ed. 2d 202 (1986)). "If the factual context makes the non-moving party's claim implausible, that party must come forward with more persuasive evidence than would otherwise be necessary to show that there is a genuine issue for trial." *Cal. Architectural Bldg. Prods., Inc. v. Franciscan Ceramics, Inc.*, 818 F.2d 1466, 1468 (9th Cir. 1987) (citing *Matsushita*, 475 U.S. at 587).

However, when "direct evidence" produced by the moving party conflicts with "direct evidence" produced by the party opposing summary judgment, "the judge must assume the truth of the evidence set forth by the nonmoving party with respect to that fact." *T. W. Elec. Serv.*, 809 F.2d at 631. All evidence and inferences must be construed in the light most favorable to the nonmoving party. *Id.* Inferences may be drawn from underlying facts not in dispute, as well as from disputed facts that the judge is required to resolve in favor of the nonmoving party. *Id.*

IV. ANALYSIS.

A. This Court Has Jurisdiction In This Matter.

A district court has diversity jurisdiction over a case in which the plaintiff and defendant are not citizens of the same state and in which the amount in controversy exceeds $ 75,000, as measured at the time of removal. *See Sparta Surgical Corp. v. Nat'l Ass'n of Sec. Dealers, Inc.,* 159 F.3d 1209, 1213 (9th Cir. 1998). When, as here, a defendant requests removal from state court and the complaint does not allege an amount in controversy, the removing defendant must prove the amount in controversy by a preponderance of the evidence. *See Sanchez v. Monumental Life Ins. Co.,* 102 F.3d 398, 404 (9th Cir. 1996).

Although the Complaint did not state a specific damage amount, it clearly prayed for compensatory and punitive or treble damages, as well as attorney's fees. Liberty Mutual's Notice of Removal stated that "the amount in controversy is greater than $ 75,000.00." Plaintiffs do not present any evidence that, at the time of removal, a lesser amount was in controversy. [1] Having examined the record, the court concludes, by a preponderance of the evidence, that the amount in controversy requirement is satisfied in this case.

> 1 At the July 5, 2005, hearing on the present motions, Plaintiffs represented that, because many of the claims listed in the Complaint were not viable and were therefore the subject of a judgment on the pleadings, only a small damage claim and the possibility of punitive damages (plus interest, costs, and attorney's fees) remained in this case. The court, however, must measure the amount in controversy at the time of filing, not at the time of the hearing. Accordingly, Plaintiffs' statement does not affect this court's jurisdiction.

B. Liberty Mutual's Motion for Partial Judgment on The Pleadings is Granted.

Plaintiffs have brought claims under Haw. Rev. Stat. § 431:13 and Haw. Rev. Stat. Chapter 480, and for tortious breach of contract. Under Fed. R. Civ. P. 12(c), Liberty Mutual moves for judgment on the pleadings on these claims, arguing that there is no private right of action under Haw. Rev. Stat. § 431:13, that Plaintiffs have no standing to bring a claim under chapter 480, and that the Hawaii Supreme Court has eliminated the cause of action for tortious breach of contract. Plaintiffs do not oppose Liberty Mutual's motion for partial judgment on the pleadings. Accordingly, Liberty Mutual's motion for judgment on the pleadings is granted with respect to these claims.

C. Liberty Mutual Was Not Required to Follow the IME Procedures Set Forth in Haw. Rev. Stat. § 431:10C-308.5(b) for Dr. Lau's Record Review.

1. This Court, Sitting In Diversity, Follows State Law.

Federal courts sitting in diversity must apply substantive state law. *See Feldman v. Allstate Ins. Co.*, 322 F.3d 660, 666 (9th Cir. 2003). In this case, the court follows substantive Hawaii law. The court "must use its best judgment to predict how the Hawaii Supreme Court would decide the issue." *Burlington Ins. Co. v. Oceanic Design & Const., Inc.*, 383 F.3d 940, 944 (9th Cir. 2004). A federal district court may look to state trial court decisions as persuasive authority, but those decisions are not binding on the federal court. *See Spinner Corp. v. Princeville Dev. Corp.*, 849 F.2d 388, 390 (9th Cir. 1988); *see also King v. Order of United Commercial Travelers of America*, 333 U.S. 153, 161, 68 S. Ct. 488, 92 L. Ed. 608 (1948).

The court is aware that, on June 30, 2005, shortly before this court's hearing on July 5, 2005, Judge Bert I. Ayabe of the First Circuit Court of the State of Hawaii issued a minute order in *Sakoda v. AIG Hawaii Ins. Co, Inc.*, Civil No. 04-1-0436, interpreting the very provision at issue in this case. Judge Ayabe ruled that a record review was indeed an IME under state law. Under the rules articulated by the Ninth Circuit, Judge Ayabe's order is of persuasive value to this court, but is not binding authority.

2. A Record Review Is Not An Independent Medical Examination.

Having been informed of Judge Ayabe's ruling, this court, following the hearing on the present motions, restudied the IME issue. Notwithstanding the great respect this court has for Judge Ayabe, this court remains convinced that the Hawaii Supreme Court would not apply IME statutory requirements to a mere record review or to an opinion based only on a record review.

Section 431:10C-308.5(b) of the Hawaii Revised Statutes limits the charges that providers may receive for IMEs. The statute also imposes other requirements on IMEs and IME providers. The statute states, in relevant part:

> The charges and frequency of treatment for services specified in section 431:10C-103.5(a) . . . shall not exceed the charges and frequency of treatment permissible under the workers' compensation supplemental medical fee schedule. Charges for independent medical examinations, including record reviews, physical examinations, history taking, and reports, to be conducted by a licensed Hawaii provider unless the insured consents to an out-of-state provider, shall not exceed the charges permissible under the appropriate codes in the workers' compensation supplemental medical fee schedule.
>
> * * * *
>
> The independent medical examiner shall be selected by mutual agreement between the insurer and claimant; provided that if no agreement is reached, the selection may be submitted to the commissioner, arbitration or circuit court. The independent medical examiner shall be of the same specialty as the provider whose treatment is being reviewed, unless otherwise agreed by the insurer and claimant.

Haw. Rev. Stat. § 431:10C-308.5(b).

Plaintiffs contend that, because Dr. Lau was not selected by mutual agreement and because he did not have the same specialty as the provider whose treatment was being reviewed, Liberty Mutual violated Haw. Rev. Stat. § 431:10C-308.5. Liberty Mutual, by contrast, argues that Haw. Rev. Stat. § 431:10C-308.5 does not apply to record reviews conducted in the absence of physical examinations. The court agrees with Liberty Mutual and concludes that the IME provisions in Haw. Rev. Stat. § 431:10C-308.5(b) do not apply to a record review performed in isolation, without other accompanying procedures necessary to complete an IME, particularly an in-person examination.

With respect to statutory interpretation, the Hawaii Supreme Court has stated:

> When construing a statute, our foremost obligation is to ascertain and give effect to the intention of the legislature, which is to be obtained primarily from the language contained in the statute itself.

> And we must read statutory language in the context of the entire statute and construe it in a manner consistent with its purpose.

> When there is doubt, doubleness of meaning, or indistinctiveness or uncertainty of an expression used in a statute, an ambiguity exists. . .

> In construing an ambiguous statute, the meaning of the ambiguous words may be sought by examining the context, with which the ambiguous words, phrases and sentences may be compared, in order to ascertain their true meaning. Moreover, the courts may resort to extrinsic aids in determining legislative intent. One avenue is the use of legislative history as an interpretive tool.

Gray v. Administrative Director of the Court, 84 Haw. 138, 147, 931 P.2d 580, 589 (1997) (internal citations omitted).

a. *The Statute Does Not Equate a Record Review With an IME.*

This court's inquiry begins with the language of the statute. In construing the term "IME," the court gives the term its ordinary, natural meaning. *See Leocal v. Ashcroft,* 543 U.S. 1, 125 S. Ct. 377, 378, 160 L. Ed. 2d 271 (2004). Taken both in isolation and in the context of the statute, the term "IME" does not refer to a record review in the absence of an actual examination of the subject.

In its ordinary, natural meaning, the term "independent medical examination" refers to a procedure that includes an in-person examination. Numerous court orders, for example, use "IME" to refer to the "Physical and Mental Examination" procedures set forth in Haw. R. Civ. P. 35 and Fed. R. Civ. P. 35. *See Sice v. Oldcastle Glass, Inc.,* 2005 U.S. Dist. LEXIS 550, No. Civ. A.03-BB-114, 2005 WL 82148 at *3 (D. Colo. Jan. 10, 2005) (holding that a motion for "IME" met Fed. R. Civ. P. 35(a) requirements); *see also Liftee v. Boyer,* 108 Haw. 89, 117 P.3d 821, No. 23760, 2004 WL 2943127 (Haw. App. Dec. 21, 2004) (describing a physical examination as a "Rule 35 IME"); *Glover v. Grace Pacific Corp.,* 86 Haw. 154, 948 P.2d 575 (Haw. App. 1997) (motion for an "IME" involving an in-person examination could be filed pursuant to Haw. R. Civ. P. 35(a)). Physical and mental examinations performed pursuant to Haw. R. Civ. P. 35 and Fed. R. Civ. P. 35 necessarily involve in-person examinations. Both the Hawaii and the federal rules state that courts "may order the party to submit to a physical or mental examination . . . or to produce for examination the person" who is to be examined.

Courts routinely use the term "IME" to describe procedures in which in-person examinations were conducted. Plaintiffs cite no instance in which any court or other entity has used the term "IME" to refer to a mere record review.

Rejecting this judicial use of the term "IME," Plaintiffs focus on the portion of section 431:10C-308.5(b) that states, "Charges for independent medical examinations, including record reviews, physical examinations, history taking, and reports, to be conducted by a licensed Hawaii provider unless the insured consents to an out-of-state provider, shall not exceed the charges permissible under the appropriate codes in the worker's compensation supplemental medical fee schedule." This sentence is not labeled as a "definition" provision and instead relates to billing issues. Indeed, the statute has the title "Limitation on Charges," although it does include several requirements not directly tied to fees.

Plaintiffs say that the word "including" in the statutory language indicates that reviews, physical examinations, history takings, and reports are types of IME. That is, Plaintiffs' position is that the word "including" introduces subsets of IMEs, in much the same way that one could refer to "dogs, including collies, cocker spaniels, and **dachshunds**." "Including," by Plaintiffs' reading, means "having as members," with each member being a full-fledged IME, just as a collie is, by itself, a dog.

Under Plaintiffs' reading, even a mere history taking is an IME. Thus, according to Plaintiffs, any "licensed Hawaii provider" performing a history has to be in the same field as the doctor whose work is being reviewed and has to be approved by "mutual agreement." Plaintiffs further say that an out-of-state provider may be used only with the insured's consent.

Nothing in the statute suggests that Hawaii's legislature intended to impose the exceptional burdens that flow from Plaintiffs' interpretation. Insurers would no longer be able to use in-house providers at all. An out-of-state insurer would have to retain licensed Hawaii providers absent insureds' consent. Plaintiffs' statutory interpretation would give insureds veto power even if a doctor were limiting herself to performing only a ministerial history taking, not rendering opinions.

Plaintiffs dismiss this possibility, explaining that the statute applies only to "medical" reviews, that is, reviews that result in the rendition of opinions by doctors. The statute, however, speaks of history taking and record review by licensed Hawaii providers. It is not limited to history taking and record review involving "medical" review or physician opinions. Plaintiffs are therefore adding language to the statute without any basis and going far beyond interpretation.

The more natural reading of the statute is to interpret "including" as meaning "having as parts." While the word "including" may certainly be used to introduce examples in various contexts, reading it as meaning "having as parts" requires fewer somersaults and interpolations in the context of the statute in issue. Indeed, *Black's Law Dictionary* lists "to contain as a part of something" as the definition of "include." *Black's Law Dictionary* 777 (8th ed. 2004). If "including" means "having as parts," then the statute is referring to an IME made up of several parts such as history taking and record review, with history taking and record review not being IMEs on their own. In that event, "including" would be used much as it is used in the statement "I prepared a brief, including doing the research, consulting with the client, drafting, and assembling exhibits." None of the items after "including" is itself a finished brief. A more homey example involves a parent's instruction to a child not to play video games until the child has finished his homework, including math, science, and social studies. The child could not then play video games upon solving math problems, because math was only a part of the required homework, not an example, complete in itself, of the homework referred to by the parent.

b. *The Legislative History Indicates that Record Reviews are Not IMEs.*

Like the statutory language, the legislative history of Haw. Rev. Stat. § 431:10C-308.5(b) establishes that mere record reviews are not IMEs. The language concerning charges for record reviews, physical examinations, history taking, and reports that are included in IMEs was added in a 1998 amendment. The added language is shown by the following underlining:

> Charges for independent medical examinations, *including record reviews, physical examinations, history taking, and reports,* to be conducted by a licensed Hawaii provider unless the insured consents to an out-of-state provider, shall not exceed the charges permissible under the workers' compensation schedules for consultation for a complex medical problem.

1997 Haw. Sess. Laws 543.

The Conference Committee Report for the amendment notes that the changes to the statute closed a perceived loophole in the statute that allowed doctors to charge insurers separately for in-person examinations and record reviews:

> The bill incorporates measures designed to eliminate abuses and excessive charges associated with independent medical examinations (IMEs). The bill clarifies that the workers' compensation fee schedule charge allowable for IMEs may not be exceeded by submitting a separate charge for the report or other ancillary procedures incident to the conducting of an IME.

Conf. Com. Rep. No. 117 on H.B. 2823 (Haw. 1998).

The purpose of the 1998 amendments was to require that charges for an IME include charges for all parts of the IME, not just for the physical examination portion. Thus, the statutory restrictions on IME charges extended to any record review, history taking, or report that was part of the IME. The legislative history does not indicate that the amendment was intended to subject record reviews that are not part of IMEs to IME regulations. To the contrary, the Committee Report distinguishes between IMEs and parts of IMEs such as "the report or other ancillary procedures incident to the conducting of an IME."

Plaintiffs contend that the purpose of the statute was to regulate the IME process and to provide for fairness in an insurer's decisions. Because a record reviewer's recommendation that an insurer deny benefits has the same result as a doctor's decision to deny benefits following an IME, Plaintiffs argue that the same regulations should govern both procedures. A policy of achieving such fairness by regulating mere record reviews is not, however, suggested by the legislative history. Just as Plaintiffs' interpretation of the statutory language forced them to interpolate words, their policy analysis forces them to assume legislative intent that is nowhere evident in the legislative history.

The legislature's differentiation between an IME and a mere record review is logical. An insured has an interest in having a voice in which doctor will perform an IME because an in-person examination is a necessary part of an IME. An insured may be uncomfortable being examined by a doctor the insured knows is regularly retained by insurers and so may be biased against the insured. It is also conceivable that an insured whose medical problem involves, for example, sexual dysfunction may want to be examined by a doctor of the same sex. Such concerns are substantially diminished when no in-person examination occurs. Creating differing requirements for IMEs, which require in-person examinations, and nonintrusive procedures like record reviews balances the competing needs of insureds and insurers.

Plaintiffs express concern that allowing doctors to conduct record reviews free of the restrictions imposed by Haw. Rev. Stat. § 431:10C-308.5(b) will encourage insurers to eschew in-person examinations, leading to less well-informed coverage decisions. Again, Plaintiffs are seeking to reach a laudable goal without any evidence that the legislature shared that goal.

The legislature did not require an insurer to have any particular level of information before making a coverage determination. As Plaintiffs conceded at the hearing, an insurer may deny benefits for medical treatment without a doctor's review of any kind. *See Weigel v. Liberty Mutual Fire Ins. Co.*, No. ATX-2002-134-P (D.C.C.A. Dec. 21, 2004). Such a decision may be based on a nurse's opinion, or on a review by an insurance administrator with no medical training. An IME certainly provides the insurer with more information on which to base an insurance decision, but the legislature nowhere required an IME or even a record review. If an insurer elects to deny coverage based on a procedure less complete than an IME, the insurer's record on any challenge to its denial may be more vulnerable than it would have been with an IME. An appeal of an insurer's denial of benefits may then be successful, but that is a risk the legislature left the insurer free to take. Nothing in the legislative history indicates otherwise.

c. Liberty Mutual's Letter to Dr. Lau Does Not Affect This Court's Analysis of Legislative Intent.

Plaintiffs urge the court to consider Liberty Mutual's earlier statement, in its letter to Dr. Lau, that IME fee restrictions applied to his mere record review. Plaintiffs say that Liberty Mutual itself thereby exhibited a belief that a mere record review, without more, was an IME under the statute. The court is unpersuaded.

If the court were construing an ambiguous contract, the parties' understandings of the contract they negotiated, drafted, and signed would be telling. But the court is here construing a statute and implementing legislative intent. 2 The parties' understandings do not reveal what the legislature intended.

> 2 More persuasive to courts than the parties' understandings are interpretations by administrative agencies that apply the provisions in issue. Under Hawaii law, courts must "accord persuasive weight to administrative construction and follow the same, unless the construction is palpably erroneous." *Morgan v. Planning Dpt., County of Kauai*, 104 Haw. 173, 180, 86 P.3d 982, 989 (2004). Citing this authority, Liberty Mutual urges the court to rule in accordance with *Weigel v. Liberty Mutual Fire Ins. Co.*, No. ATX-2002-134-P. *Weigel*, however, speaks to a subject not in issue here. In *Weigel*, the insurance company employed a doctor to "perform the duties typically undertaken by adjusters and bill reviewers." The Insurance Commissioner held that the doctor's actions did not constitute an decision, however, did not address whether a "record review," which is often (but not necessarily) performed by a doctor, was an IME.

d. The Need to Follow the Clear Statutory Language and the Legislative Intent Outweighs the Benefits of Conforming Trial Court Decisions.

Finally, Plaintiffs describe with horror the possibility that this court's divergence from Judge Ayabe's decision will create two tracks for insurance coverage disputes. Plaintiffs predict that out-of-state insurers may rush to federal court, while Hawaii insurers will litigate in state court, with different results. While consistent trial court decisions would indeed be salutary, this court's primary goal is to implement the clear statutory language and the unequivocal legislative intent. That is what the Hawaii Supreme Court directs.

This court notes further that, even if this court ruled in accordance with Judge Ayabe, insurers and insureds would not be guaranteed consistent results. Other state trial judges might disagree with Judge Ayabe, and other federal district judges might disagree with the decision in the present case. Thus, even within the state or federal system, parties could have inconsistent results. That is inherent in every trial court system; no trial judge binds any other trial judge. The effect of agreement or disagreement between a single federal district judge and a single state trial judge should therefore not be exaggerated.

V. *CONCLUSION.*

Liberty Mutual's motions for judgment on the pleadings as to certain claims and partial summary judgment are granted. Plaintiffs' counter-motion is denied.

This order leaves for future adjudication portions of Engle's breach of contract claim, and the bad faith claim insofar as it relates to those remaining portions of the contract claim.

IT IS SO ORDERED.

DATED: Honolulu, Hawaii, July 11, 2005.

SUSAN OKI MOLLWAY

UNITED STATES DISTRICT JUDGE

CONCLUSION

This book has been a collection of twenty opinions from the U.S. Federal Courts that include the word "daschund" or "dachshund". It is hoped that reading these cases presents a somewhat interesting snapshot of the meaning of the phrase and character of the animal in cultural and legal thought. The legal record presents a sort of mirror for cultural ideas and in these cases we see dachshund appearing both literally and figuratively as a character in American law.

Index

ABOUT THE EDITOR

Joshua Warren is an artist, educator, scientist, practicing attorney, and doctoral student with an interest in politics, language and creativity.

This book is part of a study on character creatures in
the U.S. Federal Courts entittled
"Law of the Horse"

Cocker Spaniel in the Federal Courts
Dachshund in the Federal Courts
Red Herring in the Supreme Court
Mad Scientist in the Federal Courts
Ninja in the Federal Courts
Werewolf in the Federal Courts
Zombie in the Federal Courts

Other artwork by Joshua Warren can be found at:
warrbo.com